Global Economies for

Investors

Tony Pow

Contents

- Highlight: My economic theories 6
- Yardsticks for the economy 9
- Highlight: The myths about China 10

Introduction 16

Section I: Misconceptions 21
    1   Why empires fell 21
    2   Is India's demographics better? 23
    3   Hong Kong's Dreams or Nightmare 25
    4   Xinjiang 29

Section II: Common global challenges 31
    1   My Coconut Theory 31
    2   Our major problems 37
    3   The evils of printing money 38
    4   Low interest rates 39
    5   Inflation and deflation 40
    6   Education by example 44
         No homework? 45
    7   Effective health care delivery 49
    8   A prolonged recession 53
    9   GDP and global trades 55
    10   China's poverty alleviation 56
    11   Aging global population 57
    12   Capitalism & democracy 61
    13   Political systems and the economy 64
    14   Immigration 68
    15   Trade agreements 69

Impact of the trade war 70

Section III: The USA 72
- 1 Actions to fix our problems 72
- 2 The worthless job plan 76
- 3 H-1B visa 80
- 4 Too delicious to fall 82
- 5 Generous welfare 83
-   Am I racist? 84
- 6 How to solve trade imbalance 86
- 7 Potential impact of our trade war with China 89
- 8 Modify our election system 93
- 9 The Republican Convention 97
- 10 How to solve our economic problems 98
- 11 Implementation 101
- 12 Solve our deficit problem 102
- 13 The first sip of coffee 103
- 14 Our 4T budget 104
- 15 Natural disasters 106
- 16 Bad business practices 108
- 17 Victims of our own success 111
- 18 National debt and USD 112
- 19 Evidences of our fall 113
- 20 Why I am so optimistic about the U.S. 114

Section IV: China 115
- 1 Brief comparison: China vs. US 116
- 2 Worthy notes on China 117
- 3 China and communism 119
- 4 China's politics and recent leaders 121
- 5 A simplified history of China 122

6	China, the human rights lover?	124
7	Currency manipulation	126
8	Rare earth elements	128
9	Environment	130
10	Intelligence Property, the key to a developed country	133
11	Chinese justice system	136
12	From "Made in China" to "Designed in China"	138
	How far behind is China	139
13	Feeding 18% of world population with 7% farmland	140
14	The rise of China	141
15	Shenzhen	146
16	Necessity is the mother of invention	148
17	One belt, one road	152
18	TPP and RCEP	156
19	Can China say No to us?	157
20	Defending China on pollution	165
21	China's advances in 2020-2021	166
22	China is not war hungry	168

Section V: Other countries 170

1	Japan	170
2	EU's mess	172
3	Africa	176

Section VI: Trade war with China 179

1	Trade war between US and China	179
2	Causes of the trade war	181
3	The root causes of a trade war	182
4	Potential impact of our trade war with China	184
5	From "Made in China" to "Designed in China"	187
6	Decoupling	189

7	The hawks and the doves		193
8	Trade war to a military war		195
9	The end of mankind?		197
10	Winners in a trade war with China		202
11	Losers in a trade war with China		203
12	What and who will replace Chinese products?		204
	Will India replace China?		205

Section VII: 2020 disasters 207
    1   Pandemic 207
    2   Disasters in 2020 and 2021? 212

My wishes 214
    1   My wish on what U.S. would do 215
    2   My wish on what China would do 220
    3   My final thoughts 223

General thoughts 233

Epilogue 240

Appendix 1 – All my books 242
    Best stocks to buy for 2022 243
    Sector Rotation: 21 Strategies 243
    Shorting Stocks and ETFs 245

Appendix 2 – Art of Investing 246
    Your choice for your next book 249

Appendix 3 - Our window to the investing world 249

Appendix 4 - ETFs / Mutual Funds 250

Appendix 5 – Better links to articles / YouTube 256

Highlight: My economic theories

I read this article predicting the "End of the economic cycle".
https://seekingalpha.com/article/4253126-weighing-week-ahead-near-end-economic-cycle?v=1554645177&comments=show

Why most market predictions by economists are wrong

It is interesting. The market cycle usually is 6 months ahead of the economic cycle. Based on this, the 'end' argument does not hold true. However, as of 4/09/2019, the market fundamentals are bad. I would move more to CDs after the settling of the trade war with China. To be warned, all markets are different.

I have about 10 hints for a potential market crash. The most deciding factor for me is the SMA, Simple Moving Average. When it turns negative, it is time to exit the market. The number of days in SMA depends on your risk tolerance. It is described in my book "Profit from coming market crash". SMA does not pinpoint the market peaks / bottoms as it depends on past data.

Most economists are wrong in predicting the market. The former Fed chairman said the economy was great and after a few months in 2008 the market crashed. There are many other factors such as politics and geopolitics. To illustrate, if there is a major war in the Middle East, the market would tank no matter how good the economy is.

The good job report is good for the economy as it would reduce the chance of a recession. However, if it is too good, the Fed would raise interest rates to cool down the over-heated economy and hence it would reduce corporate profits. Historically the market usually responds unfavorably to extreme low unemployment reports.

The job report on April, 2019 is fine for both the economy and the stock market. However, mathematically incorrect, it is close to a practical zero unemployment.

Grouping world's economies
The world's leading economies are US/EU (with Canada and Australia) and the challengers are Japan, S. Korea and China in the last two decades.

The first group's success is due to technology starting in the Industrial Revolution in Britain. The U.S. joined the group after WW2 when Europe was destroyed.

Eliminating resource-rich countries and small countries, we have about 25 countries leading the global economies. There are no strict rules on how to define a leading country. Most use GDP. I use GDP per capita adjusted for purchase power. U.S.'s GNP is higher than GDP as she owns a lot of foreign investments. China may not be counted as one by GDP per capita alone. However, China is the #2 economy due to its huge population and will be within the coming decade I expect.

The first group is declining slowly and is being replaced by the second group. It will take decades to be totally replaced judging from the decline of Spain and Italy which is described next.

In 1850s, Spain and Italy were the richest countries with the 'loots' from South American and other colonies. When the country is rich, the citizens want to enjoy life by asking for higher salaries, more vacation days, better social welfare, more protection for the workers and the environment. Hence, they lack the incentive to work harder and their products are less competitive. Are the U.S. and the EU countries repeating history?

The other factor is population size. Populations in most of the mentioned countries are shrinking. Aging population makes the problem worse. You need more educated and productive citizens. They solve part of the problem by immigration. EU is learning the hard way from many incidents caused by terrorists from immigration. The U.S. needs to immigrate top scientists to make us more competitive and the workers who are taking farm jobs and jobs not wanted by the social welfare recipients.

Most of these countries are borrowing heavily – a common trick by politicians in buying votes. It solves the current problems and buys some votes, but it will be a big burden for next generations. Watch out when the national debt is about twice the GDP. Japan has the lost decades. We and many EU countries have not learned from Japan. China has the same problem now. In addition, China's population has been surprisingly reduced even with the new two-child policy.

Most countries not included in the two groups will remain poor for decades to come. Many countries in Africa and S. America have high fertility rates. They may consume all the limited resources.

Most countries in the second group of the advanced economies are influenced by Confucius who teaches them to serve man and their family (actually the emperor to be precise). Confucius teaches them to be frugal (saving money for investing) and better educated for innovation.

It could be the climate too. Folks in the north have to work hard to prepare and save food for the winter. In warm climates, folks are lazier as described in my Coconut Theory. It does not explain why Australians are wealthy.

Another factor is life style. Many countries not included in the two group enjoy their life style by not chasing material stuff. They are happy by singing and dancing without fancy smartphones. Lack of consumption of fancy products would not make them an advanced economy. Good or bad? You decide. That's one reason Mao's era was backward as they're not chasing satisfaction from these consumers' products.

Globalization

During Reagan's era, globalization was preached and practiced. You do not want to grow sugar cane in Alaska. With the reduced cost of transportation and cheap labor in many countries, globalization has more benefits than drawbacks.

Many of our global companies have been making profits and GM may be saved from the second bankruptcy with the profits from China. We can find many U.S. fast food chains, U.S. movies and music and retail stores all over the world even in China.

The drawbacks are numerous. One major one is our huge trade deficit with China as she becomes the manufacturing capital of the world. As a result, we have been losing a lot of factory jobs. The major drawbacks in China are both the air and water pollution. The other drawbacks are the lack of selection of products as price always favors over value for most consumers.

Both countries are addressing the problems. China will be more aligned with EU if she is being punished by us. China will buy more jets from Airbus than Boeing.

Yardsticks for the economy

This YouTube video has a good summarize on the yardsticks of the economy to summary the current economy in August, 2020.
https://www.youtube.com/watch?v=icUArG-7tXY

The following summarizes them in one page and most are self-explanatory. You can find more details from Wikipedia and/or Investopedia.

Baltic Dry Index. It indicates international trading.
ISM Manufacturing. It is especially useful in U.S. factory activities.
Initial Jobless Claims.
Unemployment. It is similar to above. We started with 4% and then climbed to about 15% after the breakout of the pandemic.
Housing Starts. In 2020, the low interest rate is a plus to the housing starts, but the unemployment is a big minus.
Consumer Confidence. It is similar to the above.
Federal fund rate. It is the low rate charged between member banks. It affects the general interest rate. Today's low interest rate affects consumers, investors and corporations.

GDP.
Most are related to the following: Trade war with China, the pandemic of 2020 and the unlimited supply of money. Dow Transport used to be a good indicator, but the internet takes out some of its predictable power.

The following have a slight chance to occur. The conflict with China could lead to a military war with China and the collapse of the USD as a reserve currency. I recommend having 5% to 15% investing in gold (GLD and other gold ETFs) and gold miners (such as the ETF RING). Some suggest buying gold coins to reduce the effect of government interference and the risk of paying back the investors in gold. Talk to your financial advisor before you take any actions.

Highlight: The myths about China

"China as a sleeping lion whose roar would one day shake the world." - Napoleon.

Yes, China is roaring in this decade and the roar is getting louder and louder.

The most successful story in the last two decades

When the USA played the China card against Russia, it took away the [embargo](). [Deng Xiaoping]() started an economic zone to build infrastructure (electricity, roads, etc.) in a fishing village in South China and the rest is history. It is my [Coconut Theory]() that when hard working folks have a chance to sell their 'coconuts', they will prosper. Lifting millions from starving to death is no small task. To me, Deng and Nixon should receive a Nobel Prize. However, since China has dominated the world, except for the last three centuries, it is no surprise to me.

The Myths about China

Sam Walton was a patriot. He preferred to make less money by not selling Chinese goods. His estimates were wrong about the profits from the Chinese products. When he died, the company turned into stores for Chinese products, making his heirs one of the two richest families and many of his investors millionaires.

Investors should not follow the following myths that have been spread by the TV networks and even professors. All the below are wrong, or not partially wrong, and I will dispute them one by one.

- A TV network advocates "Made in USA" in a series.
- A professor from a prestigious university believed India would replace China as their population is younger.
- A professor from one of our top universities believed colonization was good using Hong Kong as an example.
- China is evil and they are communists.
- They're stealing our jobs, technologies and movies.
- All Chinese products are inferior products.

Globalization

China is one country in the chain of the global economy which promotes free trade. Buy the product from the country that produces the best product at the least cost. Globalization works and debunks the myths.

- China is moving up the product-value ladder. Some manufactured products, such as garments, will be moved to countries such as Vietnam and Burma with wages lower than China. This TV series "Made in USA" makes you feel good and hence makes it easy for them to sell their advertising.

  In reality, manufacturing in many products will not come back to the USA due to our high wages, regulations, taxes and robots. In a sentence, we're hurt by our own success that leads to a higher living standard, protecting our workers, stricter environmental controls... We need to give up these industries that we cannot possibly compete in and concentrate our efforts on high-value industries and industries we can compete in.

- Product quality is controlled by outsourcers. Do you find product quality problems in Apple's products while most of them are manufactured in China?
- When you have a new technical product, you may want to assemble it in South China, where most other components such as cables and batteries are available.
- In many cases we are copying China's mobile technology which China depends on. China has been in the frontier of several industries.
- From 2013 to September, 2016, China has had only one failed rocket launch. It is the cheapest and most reliable launch platform. We cannot use it due to a national security argument. However, it provides a good incentive for the space station and China is building one themselves. By 2025, China could be the only nation on earth that has a space station. Europeans are learning Chinese.
- China has never wanted to be number one. From the Opium Wars 30 years or so ago, China had been bullied by foreigners helping Brits pushing opium to China. China built the Great Wall to keep the invaders away. They could have colonized many countries in the 1400s, but they did not.

- China is not stealing our jobs, but globalization does. Most companies can outsource all functions of the company to other countries where they can find the best workers that cost less.
- China is polluting the world. Aside from the pollution from factories producing products for export, energy consumption per capita is far less than ours. China is #1 or #2 in implementing most green energy technologies. Unfortunately, China is blessed with coal, but not blessed with the less-polluting gas and oil.
- China is stealing our movies and intellectual properties. It is the same for most developing countries. China will enforce intellectual properties before it can move up to the next phase of a developed country. Our companies have to protect our secrets. Even the US had been in that stage briefly. Charles Dickens was so angry that he did not want to visit the US.
- China is closer to a developed country now. Its previous 10% growth is not sustainable but it has been impressive. China will stay in the 5% range for a while.
- Yes, China does have many problems that most countries are facing such as pollution, regulations, corruption...

We can shut ourselves out from all foreign trades, but it will harm us more than help us. We have to enjoy a $50 toaster. All the chicken feet, a delicacy for the Chinese, will be dumped into the ocean. Our high-tech companies, farmers, and the movie industry will suffer.

Communism and China
China is only communist in the second "C" of CCP, China Communist Party. The Chinese are more capitalist than us. If you do not work, you do not eat. This simple rule motivates its citizens to work hard. The safety net is improving, but it is a long way from our social security system; our system may be too generous as it has encouraged too many free loaders and cheaters (also at the corporation level). It explains why they have a high savings rate. Most companies in China do not have unions, inconveniences of labor laws and sometimes companies even receive help from corrupt officials. After a taste of capitalism, China will never return to communism, which encourages folks to be lazy.

Human rights and Tibet
When you compare present day China to the China of 30 years ago, 20 years or even 10 years ago, human rights have grown by leaps and bounds. To me, food and shelter come first before human freedom.

Human freedom should be allowed gradually and it requires educated citizens that China has but not in the rural areas. Allowing freedom to grow too fast would cause chaos (my thought and this is debatable).

Before the 'liberation' of Tibet, only monks could get an education. The one-child policy does not apply to Tibetans and other minorities. Their culture is maintained throughout from the experiences of my two visits within the last 10 years.

Hong Kong

Present and past, Hong Kong's wealth depends on its proximity to China, contrary to the colonialism theory a professor had stated. I had bet on the iShares MSCI Hong Kong ETF (NYSEARCA: EWH) (an ETF for Hong Kong) at the start of the Umbrella Protest. My order had not been executed due to my low price. The reason that the stock market did not drop further could be the plan allowing citizens in China and Hong Kong to buy stocks from the opposite exchanges. It will materialize soon after they finalize the tax and regulation details. Hence, the Chinese have more investment choices instead of investing in real estates.

India

Indians compare themselves with Chinese, but Chinese usually compare themselves with the USA. India will not catch up with China in this decade. It is more corrupt than China, more protective than China, and has more social inequality than China. The Tier I cities in India cannot even compete with the Tier II cities in China when you compare the infrastructure, high rises, subways, airports, etc.

The growing population of India eats up all the limited resources of the country. As a Chinese saying goes, you get rich by making fewer babies and building more roads.

China's advantages

- Huge internal market. The scale of economies is quite obvious.
- An educated and hard-working workforce.
- Relatively low wages for qualified engineers and researchers. The wage of an average US engineer is about the total wages of four

- Chinese engineers from my rough estimates. It is giving some technology companies problems, such as Cisco.
- Government incentives and subsidies.
- Most big projects and major purchases by foreign countries have a clause of technology transfer. If we do not oblige, they buy them from your competitor.
- There were some bitter tough lessons in the past 300 years starting from the Opium Wars to WW2.
- A one-party political system has not been a bad thing. By the time China connects most, if not all, the Tier I cities with high-speed trains, our two parties are still arguing on how to introduce it to our country.

I'm not naïve to believe that China does not have their problems. For starters, they need to control the air pollution, the water pollution and food quality sometimes at the expense of jobs. They need to have more regulations to protect their citizens.

The success of China is good for the world

After the last earthquake struck China, Chinese and the overseas Chinese helped to rebuild the disaster region without asking other nations for help. If China were as poor as before, you may have 20% of the world population begging for money.

When you need a drug to cure a terminal disease, do you care whether it is from the USA or from China? It is too expensive to develop a new drug in the USA.

China has rescued many US companies such as GM from bankruptcy. So is Volvo. China will buy many bankrupt US companies if we allow them to. Some bankrupt US companies do not have much salvage value, but we argue not to sell them to China based on national security.

Vietnam is copying China's model and it is at least 15 years behind. Eventually, many factory jobs will be replaced by robots and countries such as Vietnam with labor costing even far lower than China. It already has attracted many industries such as textile that cannot afford the rising wages in China. The latest riot against foreign factories (mostly from Taiwan) is more political and was not against the Chinese. The Chinese there have been more integrated with the Vietnamese than most other SE Asian countries.

Resource-rich countries such as Brazil and Australia benefit from the demand in China. They will return to normal trade levels when the global economy improves. Macau and Hong Kong have been benefiting from Chinese tourists. With the suppression of corruption, the gambling industry in Macau will suffer. Due to the recent Umbrella Protest, Hong Kong will suffer from fewer Chinese tourists.

China has become number one in tourist spending in France. It is similar to many other countries. Most companies producing luxury products benefit. The myth of an average Chinese citizen making less than $5,000 is debunked by these tourists. First, the median salary is not $5,000 and the size of the middle class is huge. Most countries benefit from the rise of China today, except Japan, which has an islet dispute with China. The Philippines, backed up by the USA, has a similar problem with China. I hope they will resolve the problem diplomatically by sharing resources.

Soon we will compete with China on higher-value products as we're competing with Western Europe now. There are many recent examples that worry me more. A Chinese company captures 70% of the market of the consumer drone that was invented by our military. Chinese military drones cost about one quarter (or half by some estimates) of ours and they have little restrictions to whom they sell them to. The Chinese have a monster machine to build bridges. They have more high-speed rail than all other countries combined. These are just a few of many examples. When the average Chinese student spends at least two more hours studying than ours per day, they will achieve more in life and catch up fast.

Afterthoughts
Being born in Hong Kong, I am naturally biased. I try to present these articles with facts. China has a lot of problems and they are common to most developing countries.

The following data are obtained from Barron's article dated on Nov. 17. 2014.

	Vietnam	Cambodia	Laos	Thailand	Myanmar
GDP Growth	5%	7%	8%	3%	8%
Export Growth	12%	13%	17%	0%	16%
Population	93 M	16 M	7 M	68 M	56 M
Monthly MFG Wage	$250	$130	$140	$370	$110
ETF	VNM			THD	

Introduction

Many economic concepts particularly on Asia have been misunderstood even by the professors in our top colleges.

When we invest in foreign countries, we need to evaluate their economies. This book has many articles covering most economic topics for investors. I also compare our economy to China's, Japan and India.

I discovered the major reason of a secular market is due to wars or lack of wars. My Coconut Theory explains why we're declining and China is rising. Contrary to popular belief, India will not catch up with China in the coming decade and its demographics actually harms India by eating up the limited resources. This book described all the challenges and opportunities to today's investors and how to profit from them.

Both U.S. and China are suffering from the trade war and now the pandemic. China has faced SARS and poverty before, so the spirit of the nation is still high compared to us. By cutting our military expenses, we should fix many of our problems at home.

Sometimes the news reported by the media needs to be further evaluated. The recent example is Bolivia's uprising. It has to be aided by our government to limit China's access to lithium. Have the media told us the truth?

You may not agree with most of my opinions. Do challenge them. We need more thinkers than followers. Human nature is agreeing with the ideas to support their original thinking, and that's why we do not want to listen to the other side of the story.

There are pro-Chinese views and also views by Chinese bashers. I hope my book is in the middle. With the daily bombarding by our pro-U.S. media, I hope to present a balance view.

I was born in Hong Kong and U.S. is my adopted country. My yellow face 'betrayed' me, but I am proud to be a Chinese American. I am naturally biased. Hence, do not be offended if I go too far to defend China. This trade war and any conflict with China hurt me. Currently, China suffers far worse than us. So far, I have donated all my book profits to charities.

My personal welfare is tied with U.S. I have no affiliation with Chinese government and I have not received any compensation from China. This book is dedicated to all the essential workers especially the medical staffs.

Many opinions in this book are from many sources. Most sources from the established U.S. and EU media such as BBC, DW and Economist are less biased. I find CGTN, an English-speaking, Chinese TV network is informative and not too propaganda. So is RT network from YouTube. It seems CGTN stays away more from the U.S. politics than RT. Both are financed (at least partially) by the Chinese government and the Russian government respectively. I also selected and translated from Cantonese on many YouTube videos such as Mr. Gold B Gor and Mr. Albert Ip. They do represent a lot of knowledge from Hong Kong that may not be available to Western audience.

There are so many gray areas today that no one can claim s/he is always right. I have nothing against U.S. From the research of this book, I did find out several incidents that harm our image, reputation and our future. I am neutral in politics. I comment against current government as I want them to serve us better.

How this book is organized

This book has 8 sections covering most areas in today's global economies from my personal experience. The last two sections describe the current events: Trade War and Disaster in 2020.

Most graphs and tables are in landscape orientation (recommended for small screens) for both paperback and e-readers. Some graphs may not be displayed adequately on a small screen of an e-reader. E-readers may be available in the current version of Windows, so you can read e-books on the larger screen of your PC. For better orientation, just flip the e-readers 90 degrees. Some reader lets you select a table or a graph to display it to fit the screen.

A link is usually included for the most screens. Copy it to your browser to display the graphs on your PC if desirable. Instructions on how to produce some graphs are provided as you should try them out. One example is how to produce a chart on detecting market crashes.

The **font size** (Ctrl Minus for browser implementation of e-readers) and line spacing of most e-book formats can be adjusted. The unknown, special character is the "smiling face" that the current Kindle does not convert correctly as of this writing.

There are clickable links to web articles. Most of them are from my own web sites and public web sites such as Wikipedia. Some public links may not be available in the future as they are not under my control and my book offerings may change.

These links extend the usefulness of this book by making available specific topics that may not be interesting to every reader. It also provides articles (most are not written by me) for more in-depth analyzes.

Fidelity Video provides video clips to explain some basic terms and it may require Fidelity customers to sign on in order to view them. Check the trial offer from Fidelity. YouTube offers similar video lessons.

The current version provides most of the links the paperback readers can enter into your browser. Get the same information by entering a search in Wikipedia such as Dogs of Dow.

Investopedia is another source beside Wikipedia.
http://www.investopedia.com/

'Afterthoughts' includes my additional comments and ideas of minor importance.

There are fillers with tips, refreshing pictures (taken by me) and jokes (most original) to fill up the empty space of the printed book. Fillers, links and afterthoughts may disrupt the flow of reading this book. However, no readers so far ask me to take them out even in the digitized version of this book. Many page breaks have been eliminated to improve the flow of the book.

For convenience, this book uses SPY, an Exchange Traded Fund (ETF) simulating the S&P 500, as the benchmark for the market.

Annualized returns (Return * 365 / (Days in between)) are used where appropriate for more meaningful comparison. To illustrate this, I have a 10% return in 6 months, a 10% in a year and a 10% in 2 years. It is more meaningful to use annualized returns of 20%, 10% and 5% respectively in this example.

Usually I do not include dividends, so you can add an estimated 1.5% to the annualized return. In addition, compounding is usually not used for easier calculations, so the actual return should be a little different.

About the author

I graduated from Cal. State University at San Jose in Industrial Engineering and University of Mass. in Amherst with a MS in Industrial Engineering. I have retired from a job in IT. I have been an investor for over 30 years. Email ID: pow_tony@yahoo.com.

Dedication
To all retail investors and future retail investors including my grandchildren.

Acknowledgement

Thanks to:
Wikipedia and Investopedia for the many helpful links to enrich this book. Yahoo!Finance and Finviz.com for the tools and charts used in this book.

Important notices

© 2014-2022 Tony Pow. Email ID: pow_tony@yahoo.com
- 1st   01/2014
- 2nd   04/2014
- 3.0   02/2020.
- 3.6   02/2022.

No part of this book can be reproduced in any form without the written approval of the author with the following exception. It is fine to produce up to two pages with mentioning of the source.

Disclaimer

Do not gamble money that you cannot afford to lose. Past performance is a guideline and does not guarantee future performance.

All information is believed to be accurate, but there it is not guaranteed. All the strategies described have no guarantee that they will make money and they may lose money. Do not trade without doing due diligence and be warned that most data would be obsolete. All my articles and the associated data are for informational purposes only. I'm not a professional investment counselor or a tax professional. Seek one before you make any investment decision.

The above mentioned also applies for all other advice such as on accounting, taxes, health and any topic mentioned in this book. I am not a professional in any of these fields. Same for all the links contained in this book. Some articles may offend some one or some organization unintentionally. If I did, I'm sorry about that. I am politically and religiously neutral. I try my best effort to ensure the accuracy of my articles. Data also from different sources was believed to be accurate. However, there is no guarantee that they are accurate and suitable for the current market conditions and /or your individual situations.

Section I: Misconceptions

1   Why empires fell

Many empires and Chinese dynasties rose and fell.
During my high school days, I found the following easy way to answer why a Chinese dynasty fell instead of spending days studying the long, 'boring' history of China. The dynasty became corrupted, treated their citizens badly and led to uprising and finally toppled the dynasty. In addition, foreigners from the north invaded China and formed the Yuan Dynasty and the last dynasty; Mao made the two foreigner tribes part of Chinese minorities and hence turned their invasions into civil wars.

We can learn why these empires fell and how they are related to today's U.S. There are some similarities. If I want to extend this chapter into a book, I should include many empires such as the Ottoman Empire and get my Ph.D. as a 'boring' research paper. Actually one can spend $50 for a 'Ph.D.' certificate from an on-line website.

	Roman Empire (27 BC – 476)	U.S.A.
1	Invasion	No[1]
2	Military Spending	Yes
3	Over-expansion	Yes[2]
4	Economic problems	Yes
5	Government corruption	Average
6	Political instability	No
7	Social injustice	Average

[1] No one invaded us except from terrorists, but we invaded others from Vietnam to today's Iraq and Afghanistan.
[2] No colonies but in foreign military sites and being a big brother and global policeman.

	British Empire (1851 – 1951[1])	U.S.A.
1	WW1	No WW3 yet
2	Rise of Germany	Rise of China
3	Colonies uprisings	No
4	Rise of USD as a reserve currency.	Chinese Yuan to some extent.
5	Loss of several wars.	Vietnam & Afghanistan.[2].

| 6 | Huge military expenses | Yes |
| 7 | Social injustice (among colonists). | Yes (among minorities). |

[1] 1997 if you consider the return of Hong Kong is the end year of the empire.
[2] Korean War is a tie to me.

We have similar factors of the falls of these two empires. The major difference between these two and ours is our mighty military. It also enforces the status of the USD as a reserve currency. However, our revenues cannot cover our huge military expenses and social spending. We need wars to support our defense industry selling fighter jets, tanks, bombs, missiles, etc.

The USD was at one time supported by our reserve gold, but not anymore. We ask the world to trade all oil with USD (also known as the Petrodollars) and we enforce it to some extent by our mighty military force. The currency in trading energy (oil and gas) by China with Russia and some other countries is using Yuan. Economically the British Empire fell when the pound as a reserve currency was replaced by the USD.

The collapse of the U.S.S.R. (a modern empire similar to the U.S.A. in recent history) was partially due to price erosion of oil and natural resources in addition to the huge expenses in the war in Afghanistan.

The primary reason for the fall of most empires is **spending too much especially on the military;** in some cases the empire spent too much or too little on infrastructure. The second primary reason is poor governance such as ignoring education / research, ignoring competitors and increasing wealth gap. Sounds familiar? For my selfish reasons, I do not want the U.S. to fall.

Links
Fall of Roman Empire.
https://en.wikipedia.org/wiki/Fall_of_the_Western_Roman_Empire
Fall of British Empire.
https://www.historyextra.com/period/modern/the-decline-and-fall-of-the-british-empire/
The next superpowers
https://www.youtube.com/watch?v=9dgpuzawqn8

2   Is India's demographics better?

It is not as described in the Chapter in Aging Global Population.

Comparing China with India

In the 50s, India was ahead of China. For the last 30 years, China is decades ahead of India and over the next 30 years India will still be behind China.

Most favorable articles on India are written by Indians with their dumb nationalism (Saxena is a notable exception) and very few have been written by Chinese who prefer to compare China to the U.S. The Tier I cities in India cannot compete with the Tier III cities in China in subway, airport, train, high rises, electricity, corruption enforcement, intelligent property enforcement, protectionism, quality, and etc. The last four must be a surprise to the Westerners who have not been to both countries, but they are true. The list is endless.

Indians are happier, and it could be due to less internal competition and global competition with trade barriers and the religion beliefs. It is also the prime reason of poor product quality.

Most Indians here want to stay in the U.S. without waiting for the improvement in their native country while Chinese have a lot of 'sea turtles' who return to work back in China, meaning "swimming back to the mother land". India is grossly mal governed.

India's advantages are English speaking, more established democratic system, better capitalist systems (such as banking). China is improving in all these areas.

Why there are so little FDI (foreign direct investment) to India compared to China? You have to ask how long it takes to open a business in India and how many bribes you have to pay.

I do not see a lot of Chinese settling down in India, but Indians are the second among all Asian countries settling down in Hong Kong after the housekeepers from Philippine.

Count how many high rises in Hong Kong and how many in the largest city in India. Count how many top 100 computers from each country, literacy rate (compare apples to apples such as the number of years of education that is compulsory; 9 in China) and many other measures you can think of (Source: Ted Talk).

From my contact, Indians and Chinese in the U.S. have the same intellectual level. Actually Indians are doing better here due to their better mastering of English and better educated (due to H1-B visa requirements). Many Chinese settled here due to political prosecution in the 50s and slave labors before then. The problem with India is poor governance, similar to Mao's reign in China.

India cannot catch up with China in the next ten years. It is better for the world that India would catch up with the rest of the world and it is my wish they do. However, the reality looks too bleak for India. You need to understand the problems of your country before you can fix them.

Afterthoughts
Click for Ted talk.
http://www.ted.com/talks/yasheng_huang.html
Click for more on this topic.
http://blog.hiddenharmonies.org/2011/12/india-vs-china-weve-got-facebook-whatve-you-got
Click here for a good blog written by Shobhan Saxena.
http://blogs.timesofindia.indiatimes.com/Main-Street/entry/why-india-will-remain-a-nation-of-losers
Click here for a good article written by a PhD. with good data.
http://seekingalpha.com/article/836451-china-and-india-is-either-a-good-bet?v=1346412463&source=tracking_notify

Religion could hinder the economic development as demonstrated by the holy cows roaming in major cities in India and many Muslim countries (not against any religion and man should not live by bread alone). The only folks can fix their problems are Indians themselves. An explosive population, corruption and poor governance are three major areas to start. Copy China's economic zone concept is a great idea.

3   Hong Kong's Dreams or Nightmare

Did Hong Kong benefit from colonial government according to the article below?

If the next link is deleted. Replace it with the following link.
http://abluteau.wordpress.com/2009/09/06/city-of-dreams/

Click here for the comment and the article I wrote.
(http://blog.foolsmountain.com/2009/09/07/city-of-dreams-or-nightmare/)

I wrote this article commenting against this full article from Boston Globe. Click the link to the Boston Globe article if it is still available. This syndicated article was in most Sunday papers. This article was written by a 'renowned' professor from a top university who did not understand how Hong Kong became so wealthy. In addition, I find it utterly insulting on his trumpeting the benefits of colonialism with Hong Kong as an example.

Furthermore, the colonial model will not work in black ghettos as mentioned in the article. We have many miserable failures in the U.S. by throwing money by not properly understanding the problem. At one point, Hong Kong's GNP per capita passed its master, the Great Britain. There must be other considerations besides the colonial governance as there is no such precedent that the slave is richer than the master. Sounds logical?

I describe in my humble opinion why it works in Hong Kong but not in some U.S. ghettos or some African countries. My points are:

- Proximity to China.

Before the U.S. allowed the importation of mainland Chinese products, a shirt labeled "Made in Hong Kong" was actually, essentially and entirely made in China. Hong Kong was the back door to the U.S. Markets and received some easy profits for doing so.

- Confucianism.

Asians have strong family value and pay attention to education from the child's early life. Most all black / Hispanic families in America lack that strong trait. There are too many single parents, teenager mothers and fathers in prison (tough to be a role model). Our generous welfare makes it worse and harder for them to break the vicious cycle.

We teach children here to make easy money instead of hard work.

- Before 2002, Taiwanese needed to go to Hong Kong before they could fly to China when Taiwanese corporations invested a lot in China.

- The laborers were desperate and abundant, and most were refugees from South China. They knew there would be no food to eat if they did not work hard. There was no welfare in Hong Kong at that time.

- HK children studied hard. Most of the U.S. college graduates cannot pass Hong Kong's Grade 6 certificate examination at least in math. Sad but true. When we're wealthy, our children are naturally permissive. Hong Kong kids and even kids in Mainland will be when their countries are as rich as the U.S.

- Most Chinese in Hong Kong work smart and efficiently. Hong Kongers know the Chinese practices as well as the West, so they utilize the best of each side for their own benefits.

- The deep harbor is ideal for ships to export their products to foreign countries.

- Lifting trade embargo from China.

When the U.S. recognized China and legalized the trade with China after 1978, Hong Kong's factory towns became ghost towns. However, very efficiently and very fast they moved the factories to South China's special economic zone (SEZ) after 1992 and became factory managers / owners, investors, consultants and technicians. Today, Hong Kongers still manage a lot of factories in S. China.

- To their credit, the British did provide Hong Kong with a stable government and legal system, so foreign investment and tourism flourished. A special agency (ICAC) with utmost power, fixed the wide-spread corruption. China, take notice.

Seeking independence for Hong Kong?

It will never happen. Possible 300 years ago, not now and not in the near future. This is the bottom line for China and Overseas Chinese. China has not used its military might yet. I hate to see another Tiananmen Square incident. These trouble makers most likely will migrate to US or Norway. The citizens of Hong Kong found out the harms to the economy in the previous protests and will not vote for these trouble makers in the next elections.

Some want to be kings and queens in the wildest and impossible dreams. These are the stupid chess pieces manipulated by the chess master who has nothing to lose right now. It is similar to Puerto Rico that obviously independence has no advantages for the citizens except for the potential kings and queens.

I doubt the US would subsidize these future 'kings and queens' as US seems it cannot say "No" to China for this issue at least and we have been busy in the two wars draining our resources. When we do not have a robust economy to back up our military, we will be the true 'paper tiger'.

Afterthoughts

- Another example of my Coconut Theory.

    It is a cultural difference for different races. It could be the background or the environment, so we cannot say just race.

    Most Chinese refugees in Hong Kong do not have a coconut tree, so they have to work hard and think smart in order to survive. After many years, they could be smarter and work harder than the environment that forced them to adapt.

- Srenscense says:

Agree with TonyP4 who probably knows more about economics and history than Stanford professor Paul R.

Hong Kong succeeded mostly because of its location as a great harbor to a strategic part of the world, Asia, investment by émigré Shanghai businesspeople, and cheap labor by desperate, hardworking refugees. The British provided only basic governance and laissez-faire as they collected their profits. They did provide opium which impaired many in that generation which to their credit (in all fairness), Mao and the Communist did eradicate and reformed.

- Ironically I, being born in Hong Kong, benefited from the British rule. I did not have to suffer from China's dark periods in 50s and 60s. However, without the Opium Wars, China's history would turn out to be very different and I bet to be far better.

- With the growing wealth, Hong Kong is adapting to changes as follows:

    - It becomes a metropolitan city. There are more foreigners mainly from Britain, the USA, the EU, India and Philippine. It used to be a Chinese city and there was no race discrimination but class discrimination.
    - There are more foreign reporters in Hong Kong than before.

    - With the growing population from China and foreign countries, real estate is always the number 1 industry and the number of high-rise apartments could be #1 in the world. Many apartment units with about 600 square feet are sold for about half a million USD.
    - Most do not know much about HSBC. It is the largest bank in term of asset in the world.

        Although its headquarter is in London, it is a Hong Kong bank. I believe the original headquarter was in Hong Kong and they moved it to London before China's takeover. It could be formed by some Shanghai folks (the savviest business folks in the late 40s in China) escaping from communists. HSBC spells as Hong Kong Shanghai Banking Corp.

It is the main bank in HK and it prints money for the HK government. Most of the initial assets were from Chinese escaping from China and the overseas Chinese especially the SE Asia where many Chinese become rich after years of hard works and these countries are politically unstable (at least at one time). The Chinese control the local economy but not politics. Many SE Asian countries such as Indonesia did not (may be same today) let Chinese to move their assets out of the country. There are ways and they move the money to Hong Kong for safety. I call it 'travel money' until I find a better term. Their only purpose is a safe place to park their money.

To split the bank to avoid some of the restriction shows how the restriction limits banking operations. It is no difference in splitting a division that loses money, or has high liability...

- A joke.
A manufacturer of luxury hand bags found a defective hole in a new product line. They shipped them to Hong Kong, and sold them at double the price with a label 'Limited Edition'. They were all sold out in minutes.

Links
Boston Globe:
http://www.boston.com/bostonglobe/ideas/articles/2009/09/06/city_of_dreams_a_radical_plan_for_helping_poor_countries/?comments=all

4 Xinjiang

When we sanction products from Xinjiang, we would make many Xinjiang folks, particularly the Muslims out-of-jobs and lower their living standard.

Since most of the masks from China are made with cotton from Xinjiang, will they be sanctioned too? So are the rare earth elements.

China has tightened the control of the dissidents there after the riots a few years ago. Since then, Xinjiang has returned to normal and tourists have returned. The following are the arguments that there is no genocide in Xinjiang, especially comparing how we treat our native Indians.

- If there is one today, our satellites can spot them easily. We cannot depend on some dissidents with their own agenda. We have our share of dissidents in our country.
- So are some U.S. politicians with their own agenda. They care about getting more votes. Demonizing Chinese gets their biggest bang for their efforts. It gives rise to the racial discrimination against the Chinese here.
- Xinjiang's population has been increasing rapidly. Partly it is due to China's investments in exploring the resources and the "One Belt, One Road" projects.
- The capital of Xinjiang has a brand-new subway system recently, which rivals the best in the U.S. Why does China invest so much money in an area they want to genocide?
- China's high-speed rail extends to Xinjiang. It will never be economical, but it should improve the living standard of the Xinjiang citizens. It is similar to the extension of the train system to Tibet.
- China's minorities did not have the one-child policy as the majority (the Hans) had.
- The majority of cotton is harvested by machines, not by forced labor.
- Local language and culture are maintained in Xinjiang. I enjoyed many cultural shows in the western China. Many famous beauties are from Xinjiang.
- The religion in Xinjiang has never been oppressed to my knowledge.
- China's minorities have given more priority to higher education than the Hans.
- The alleviation program is not too extensive in Xinjiang due to a higher living standard.

Section II: Common global challenges

1 My Coconut Theory

Coconut Theory

In a tropical island, every one sleeps under a coconut tree assigned to him. He wakes up only when a coconut falls on his head once in a while. He eats the coconut and goes back to sleep. He is lazy due to the nice weather (no need to find shelter) and the nice resource (the coconut tree). He is happy and rich by his own standard. However, he is lazy, fat, and stupid due to the lack of any need to work, exercise, and think out of his 'perfect' environment.

The worst that happens to the natives is borrowing coconuts from other natives with the coconut tree as collateral or cutting down the coconut tree to make a canoe without plans to replenish coconuts in the future.

This is a simple theory. It can be used to explain how and why many countries are rich, poor, and continue to be so. Let's check how this theory stacks up with countries.

It also explains why people migrate to places with lots of coconuts. It is demonstrated by the Chinese during war time to South East Asia and the Irish moving to the US during the potato famine.

U.S.A.

The U.S. is one of the richest countries due to its development, highly educated citizens, hard-working immigrants and the huge natural resources per capita (i.e., having a lot of coconuts in my theory). The U.S. is declining as we spend more time enjoying our wealth (borrowing coconuts so he can eat more) rather than creating more wealth (i.e., not planting new coconut trees in my theory).

The wealth is equivalent to the bountiful of coconut trees that were available originally and the many that were planted by our ancestors. There were fewer natives to consume the total number of coconuts, so there was a surplus of coconuts grown, eventually to be given away (as welfare and entitlements). Many of our citizens have no incentive to plant more coconut trees (work) when they have unlimited coconuts to them (generous welfare).

Because of WW2, most coconut trees in the world were destroyed while ours were isolated from the war. We were rich enough to ship our better coconuts to the rest of the world.

God gave us plenty of natural resources, good soil and climatic wealth (coconuts hidden under the land) and hopefully we continue to be wealthy. Unfortunately, we're now consumers (of coconuts) instead of producers (planting new coconut trees).

Why is the U.S. falling? We cut down a lot of coconut trees and made spears. We used the spears to threaten our neighbors to give us coconuts. In some cases, we borrowed coconuts from other countries.

Norway
Norway is the richest to its population group (3 million) while Brunei is richest in its own population group. Norway is rich due to its rich resources and its intelligently governed wealth. I hate to compare any country to Norway as most likely we are comparing Apples to Melons.

From its long coastline Norway has rich off-shore oil fields and abundant fish exports which is second in the world-- only 6% of its export, after China but far, far #1 per capita wise. Because of the world's oil addiction and food dependence secures its income flow.

Peru has a long coast line, but it is not wealthy. My theory does not apply fully here, as there are always exceptions. It could be Norway's educated citizens, close location to its trade partners and buying assets around the world (planting more coconut trees). The dividend payments allow Norway to prosper for decades. They have about 600 billion sovereign funds to be shared by 3 million citizens. Simple math!

Norway will be rich for centuries to come as they plant coconut trees all over the world.

Iceland
Some smart guys suggested cutting down all the coconut trees (their financial asset) made canoes (more global banks) so they can earn a rich

life by fishing (lending). The world blindly loans them with coconuts. When fishing (no global market esp. after 2008) failed, their land was lost with no coconuts and no coconut trees left. Do not bet all the coconuts in one venture and always have an exit strategy.

Singapore and SE Asia

Singapore is rich due to its important location for the sea route for trade and commerce, as well as being the cultural intersection between the east and the west and its industrious citizens (most are Chinese). When the hard-working folks land on a land of coconuts (i.e., resources), they naturally become rich.

The Mekong River is a good resource providing fishing, irrigation, transportation, and fertile land in the delta for SE Asia. Hence, SE Asia should be rich, and at the same time should attract hard-working immigrants from India and China to enhance their wealth. However, the river is being polluted by industries and the future is cloudy.

Japan

Japan has few natural resources. Its only resource is the educated and hard-working citizens. With a decreasing population and the policy not welcoming immigrants, Japan will face problems.

Haiti

Haiti used to have enough coconuts for its small population. French imported African slaves to the sugar cane plantation and changed the allocation of natural resources per capita. Coupled with frequent natural disasters and bad governance, Haiti becomes the poorest country in the world.

Haiti and many countries have their coconut trees destroyed by hurricanes from time to time. That's why they're always poor. So are some states in the US that suffer from periodic flooding and hurricanes.

UAE

When the west helped UAE to explore its oil resources (the hidden coconuts under the sand) about 50 years ago, UAE became one of the richest countries. She expands in different areas and it could be over-expanded. When the oil dries up in 100 or so years and/or the shale energy competes better, they could be in big trouble. [Update: the problem appears as of 1/2015.]

Russia
Russia is a country full of resources (coconuts). Its citizens become lazy having a good time under the 'coconut' tree. Chinese are just the opposite. That's why the Russians hire the hard-working Chinese to farm on the border while they enjoy life with plenty of Vodka.

The primary reason why the USSR fell was the temporary low prices of their resources oil and timber (coconuts). Trying to be #1 was another reason by spending more resources (coconuts) than they had..

China

China has roughly 20% of the world population, but it has far less than 20% of the world resources (coconuts). For example, it has only 6% of the world land area. The situation was worsened in the last 300 years during the Opium Wars, and then semi colonization by the eight countries (led by Brits, the opium pushers). It bankrupted China by their colonial masters. It caused massive migration to escape from the land without coconuts. It was followed by WW2, war lord era and then the bad governance. Their bitter lessons ensure this generation and the next generation to work hard and be smart. When they do not have 'coconut trees' (the colonial masters cut most of them down), you have to work hard or die.

China ranks #2 in the economy. It is only important to its trading partners. Its own citizens care about their living standard which is about the middle in the rank of all countries.

Greece
Greece has its natural resources: tourism (coconut). Euro gives them unlimited borrowing. Olympics boosted their dumb ego. The result is bankruptcy.

Caribbean islands
Literally a lot of their coconuts are destroyed from the hurricanes every year. It makes them poor even they have a lot of coconuts (ample

sunshine and beaches for tourists). Many set up tax shelters for rich folks and corporations. It is similar to earthquake prone countries.

Hong Kong & Singapore

Both have good governance learned from Britain and are supported by hard-working Chinese. Hong Kong is rich due to its proximity to China and Singapore due to the sea port location between the East and the West. Coconuts are in many forms.

Ancient civilizations too

Greece, Iran, India, China and Italy are among the oldest civilizations. Most do not do well in today's economy and many of their citizens have immigrated to other countries. My theory suggests that they have exhausted their coconuts (farm land and metals) throughout the long history. Hence, they have to migrate to lands with more coconuts. To illustrate this, there is a huge discrepancy in natural resources (oil, metal and farm land) between China and the U.S., which has a relatively short history.

Corporations too

Microsoft was a tougher company with more innovations fifteen years ago than today. However, they are enjoying easy profitability of upgrades of Windows and Office (coconuts planted by their ancestors). For a long time, she only has one successful new product, the Xbox. Her managers are counting their bonuses instead of taking risk. The Coconut Theory works again.

Rich families too
It is very rare to have rich families that last over three generations. The first generation grows the wealth (planting coconuts), the second generation enjoys the wealth, and the third or fourth generation usually becomes poor due to the easy life.

Conclusion

So far, no one tells me that this theory has been 'discovered' by others. Shamelessly I claim it is mine. To me, it is just common sense.

Afterthoughts

- I did not have a coconut tree (i.e., financial aid or money from my dad), and that is why I worked two jobs in my first summer while attending college here. The first one was a bus boy job from 5 pm to 10 pm. The other one was cleaning slot machines from 4 am to noon for 5 and usually 7 days a week. Lack of coconut makes you desire to work hard or you vanish. With an average IQ, I can make it by working hard in a land of coconuts.

    My children have too many coconuts and they live in a more lavish life style than the old man. They ask me why I work that hard during my retirement or why I still go to Burger King with a coupon even they do not treat me like a king.

- According to my friend Norman, the problem with a small place filled with coconuts is someone would likely to colonize you and steal your coconuts as happened to Norway during WWII. Similar to China about 250 years ago. Once a while, need to cut down one among many coconut trees to make spears to protect the rest of the coconuts.

2   Our major problems

As of 2015, we're running out of tools to stimulate the market. The zero interest rates has lost its effectiveness especially when most countries are using the same tool. We cannot pass our debts to the next generations forever.

We need to cut down expenses by:

- Ending our participation in the wars in Middle East.
- Not turning the illegals into legal.
- Reducing our generous welfare.
- Encouraging able folks to work.
- Encouraging constructions over consumptions.

Filler:

$80 sneakers

Amazingly, some kids from welfare families show off their $80 sneakers that I cannot afford (or not too stupid) to buy. It is same as going to see a doctor for a minor cold.

Tufts is giving scholarships to children of illegals. How many want to disguise as illegals (no proofs are needed to be illegal)?

No one saves. When you save too much (like myself), you lose all the goodies from the government such as free health care. With more than 40% not working, we're a nation of free loaders.

Actually the rich can afford to buy good stuffs more as the stock market is great. It widens the wealth gap and causes disputes. The problem is 1% cannot support the rest even if they spend like no tomorrow as the rest of our citizens are doing.

What's wrong with this country (compared to 50s and 60s)?

3 The evils of printing money

I just explained to my grandchild that money does not fall from the sky or grow on trees. Every time we print money, it does the following:

1. An invisible tax is added especially to the rich as their purchasing power will be decreased via inflation.
2. Your children and grandchildren will pay for the new loans.
3. Selling a piece of our asset to foreigners.
4. Our products are less globally competitive as we have to add more taxes to pay for the loans. It is more competitive initially as our currency has been depreciated, but this will not last long.
5. The retirees would suffer due to inflation and low interest rate that usually follows.
6. Give more reasons for the rich to give up citizenship and move to another country. Besides via inheritance and/or marriage, most become rich by being hard working, smart and/or opportunistic.
7. The USD being a reserve currency is shaken.

The only winners are the lobbyists and politicians, who bought votes with the money from your pocket.

It will help the stock market in the short-term, but it is very damaging for the long-term economy. In 2020, our national debt suddenly jumped to almost 25T in May, 2020. With the easy money and the fixed amount of assets such as stocks and gold, the values of these assets would rise. That's also the primary reason why the recovery of our economy is taking forever. Printing money to the maximum is not a solution but a problem. Today most countries are printing money excessively.

Afterthoughts
- We have inflation (such as most products in the super market) and deflation (such as housing expenses) since 2008.

- As of 6/2012, we have 16 trillion of debt and it is substantially less depending on whether you include the entitlements. Besides the poor environment, unpromising economy, our children and grandchildren inherit our huge debts. So far, it is about $55,000 debt for each baby born today. However, many foreigners want their babies born here, so everything is relative.

4   Low interest rates

As of 2021, we have the lowest interest rate for a long while. The Fed usually lowers the interest rate to stimulate the economy and the stock market during a recession. It is not the case in 2021, as the economy is recovering after the pandemic, and the stock market is record-high already. With low interest rate, it is a great time to buy a house (so are big-ticket items such as a car), when the houses prices are depressed and / or low borrow money.

It is half true in 2021 when the house prices are record-high. It is all due to politics. Our government wants to buy votes by giving cash to her citizens via printing money excessively. This should need to inflation (buying gold as a hedge). The disadvantage is raising our national debt and the status of USD as a reserve currency is shaken. These are adverse long-term effect that the government only cares about reelection.

Statistically, the stock market is up when the Fed increases the interest rate. Before 2008, the interest rate was low and the market crashed. Afterwards, the interest rates had been raised and the stock market was up. It is opposite to the logic that the company has to pay more to borrow. The explanation is the Fed feels the prospect of the economy is good. Low interest rates have many impacts on our investment:

- Usually, they're better for the stock market as corporations can borrow at cheaper rates and hence improve the bottom line. In theory but not today, it should be great for the housing market and retailers.
- Corporations can borrow money at favorable rates to buy back their own stocks or acquire other companies to boost their own stock prices. So are investors using margin. Usually, the fundamentals have not changed but the management would get a boost to their options and stocks they own. However, prolonged period of low interest rates would damage the economy. Japan is one example.
- Folks including retirees, who depend on fix incomes, will suffer.
- Dividend stocks will prosper as the new bonds with low rates are less attractive. The long-term bonds become attractive.
- Eventually the current long-term bonds will suffer big time when interest rate moves up as the higher-interest bonds are more valuable.
- As of 2021, the yield of 10-year Treasury bill is about 1.6%, the lowest in my recent memory. It is better to keep cash now than CDs.
- The tariffs we added to Chinese products pass back to the consumers. With the increase in price of iron ore, China has raised prices on steel and cut down export.
- The pandemic reduces our manufacturing output.
- When the CPI exceeds 2% (as of 2021, it is 3%), the Fed should increase the interest rate. At that time, the market and the employment would be hurt.

5   Inflation and deflation

The historical annual average is about 3% inflation. CPI is not a good gauge any more after energy and food have been excluded.

Inflation is:

- An invisible tax especially to the rich.

- A strategy to lessen the loan burden. To illustrate, your loan of $1 can buy a loaf of bread now, and you will pay back the $1 plus negligible interest that can buy only half a loaf of bread due to inflation.

- An invisible salary cut.

- An invisible cut to your entitlements/welfare. Social security is supposed to be adjusted to CPI, which can be manipulated by the government by not using food and energy to reduce social security payment increases.

- An invisible cut to your investment incomes (dividends and appreciation).

Deflation is no angel

Deflation is far worse than inflation to the economy. When the company produces a product and finds out they have to sell it for less due to deflation, then their profit would be cut and they might need to lay off employees.

Deflation would destroy all financial institutions. It makes all their collaterals on all loans less valuable and the borrowers may give up their collaterals as they're worth less.

Inflation and deflation at the same time

As of 2014, we have both inflation and deflation at the same time for several years now.

We have inflation in most of our basic necessities: food, gasoline and heat (especially important for the NE) with the exception of rent due to the depressed house prices. Electronic stuff and PCs are deflated considering how much we can buy today vs. last year. Cars have been slightly deflated when figuring in the extra features. They are due to technological advances.

As of 2016, our energy cost has been deflated due to OPEC's dumping in order to finance their current projects in this poor global economy.

Outlook

The government should ensure inflation and deflation are within an acceptable range (3% to me). It has printed a lot of money and lowered interest rates to stimulate the economy. At the same time inflation has been accelerated in many sectors. When the economy does not improve, the government has run out of tools to improve our depressed economy.

However, beside time the shale energy may cure all problems. When the economy improves, the inflation and the interest rates would most likely increase. Oil price depends on supply and demand. The poor economy will decrease the supply and hence the oil price would be depressed.

Afterthoughts

- The dollar has lost more than 90% of its value since the FED was created due to inflation. However, it only affects you if you save your cash under the pillow. Our capitalism system punishes those who do not invest and take risks. If you invest in long-term CDs, you're doing barely OK. If you buy any stock such as Edison's new venture or a piece of real estate in your town in 1913, most likely it beats inflation by a good margin and Uncle Sam would be glad to share your fortune via capital gain taxes when you sell them.

- From my personal experiences.
  The Big Mac Value Meal cost about $1 in 1970 and now (2020) it costs $7, 7 times in 45 years.

An average house in my hometown in 1980 cost $45,000, and now it costs $450,000, 10 times in about 30 years.

Houses in most cases are better deals. Besides paying the tax-deductible property tax and interest, we can live in them.

The $10,000 under my pillow in 1980 has no gain today, but it gives me a headache every time I sleep on it. LOL.

- In 2013, a bag of 10.5-ounce Lays potato chips is $4.25, and the next day it was downsized it to 9.5 ounces. All the items in the grocery store are just like that. The millionaires have no complaint as their stocks (as of 6/2013) have been up since 2008.

- Strong USD is bad for the stock market as our products would be more expensive in foreign countries.

- For those who have jobs, you have deflation when your same income can buy you more of your basic supplies / services than last year with the exception of food and gasoline as in 2013.

Most investments are beating the inflation from the last several years. The wealth gap has been widened between the middle class and the rich. Five years ago, the gas price was less than $2 and now it is over $3 [Update: $2 as of 1/2015 and same in 2020]. We still have high unemployment and high under-employment. Most recent college graduates cannot find jobs or jobs in their choices. It happens all over the world.

- Inflation is controlled by the government via the rate of money being printed and / or easing credit. When we have more money chasing the same quantity of products / services, we have to pay more for them or we call it inflation. In the shorter term, it may be distorted by other events such as the deteriorating housing prices. With excessive printing, I see hyperinflation in the coming years.

- Inflation is rising.

Labor

We have to divide it into two categories: labor that can't be outsourced and labor that can be.

Labor outsourced to China (your iPhone for example) and India is still relatively cheap.

Labor in the US like flipping burgers, fixing your plumbing problems, or your telephone services will be increased in cost. If they are not, they will be manipulated by the government via welfare (we pay for them via our taxes) or the unions. A worker at Burger King cannot survive without government subsidy or family largesse.

Commodities

All commodities including farmland will increase in value due to:
- Supply and demand - the net growth of population is rising but it is offset by the poor economy.
- Excessive printing of money. You will be able to buy half a loaf of bread with the dollar that used to buy you the full loaf.

Better stocks to hedge inflation

- Stocks that can raise prices without facing loss of sales such as Apple.
- Stocks that have to borrow a lot to run their businesses, such as Facebook that can reduce new developments.

However, both Apple and Facebook are fully valued in Feb., 2022.

Links
Buffett: https://www.youtube.com/watch?v=1Hxy2NBD7J8

Filler: My official definition of Fed in my joke book.
The Fed acts more like a mistress to the president than an agency. The two are not officially related. But, they're on the same bed most of the day.

6 Education by example

A good economy has to be supported by an educated workforce. We still have the best higher education system in both quantity and quality. Our [pre-college education](#) is failing with a high percent of dropouts.

When you find out your store under charged you by $1, do you go back to pay them back?

I do not for two reasons:

1. The store has cheated me before intentionally or unintentionally, so it breaks even.

2. We also need to teach our children to conserve energy. ☺

Despite the above reasons, I'll go back to set up an example for my children. The primary problem with our education system is education should start at home. No matter how much money you throw into the system, it will not work if the students do not want to learn. With so many single-parent and teenage-mother families, I do not see a bright future.

It happens all the time that you have a convict and a doctor in the same class as indicated by this [video](#). It proves my point again that education should start at home.

(http://www.YouTube.com/watch?v=Xu1Q0E7oGQU)

Some of our discrimination and biases are passed to our children unknowingly. That will hurt them eventually. Be careful what we talk / act in front of our children.

Education by example is the most powerful and most effective, but unfortunately it is the most neglected. It is about time for the politicians resolve our root problems NOT by throwing our money (not their money) recklessly at the problem. Everyone with a first-grade education can write a check and we do not pay our leaders to write checks.

We need to limit the generous welfare for teenage mothers and preach family value to stop the vicious cycle.

No homework?

I am furious that my grandchildren do not have homework. It is not only my town, but it is for the most of the nation.

If it is used to lower the education gap between poor and rich, it is the STUPIDEST argument I ever heard.

We have to compete with Europe and Far East students. They routinely study at least two more hours already. If you believe the student without the extra two hours study would accomplish the same in life, you believe in miracle.

The extra hours will be used most likely in watching TV and/or playing video games. Some Chinese 10-year-olds are programming video games and assembling PCs.

Yes, some students do not need to homework. Personally I know one or two in one hundred. They're the exception, not the norm. My granddaughter is one of them too. In kindergarten she can read and answers correctly on how many minutes left to pick up my other grandchild giving her the current time. She was bored in doing the compulsory homework.

I do not know whose stupid idea is this. It would drive us far behind from the top rank (Singapore, S. Korea, Taiwan, Hong Kong and some EU countries). I would fire that decision maker right away.

Afterthoughts

This short article attracted a lot of feedbacks.

- My elementary class in Hong Kong of 45 students produced one world-known chef, one movie director, one MIT Ph.D., one pharmacist, one doctor... I am the under achiever or the black sheep of my class. Our teachers were not from Hong Kong University (the best there). The incentive to learn is simple: If you do not study hard, you will be a nobody. No one will bail you out. Our average class size is 45, so do not use class size as another excuse.

- We need to select college trainings in the fields that the society or the corporations need. It is a luxury to take a major you're interested in but is not demanded by the society. I did not have that luxury. However, even though I could not speak English well, I managed to start a professional job as a programmer while some college graduates with perfect English Xeroxed manuals for me.

- The problem of many high school students is the loss of respect to their teachers. You cannot learn from someone you do not respect. I feel bad for the teachers in many urban cities as your lives could be at risk every day and many lose their initial enthusiasm to teach after they face their cruel reality.

  My friend Norman added and it never happens in the city I grew up: My wife taught reform school in Richmond and was threatened several times. Once the girls in her food service class grabbed her and held a pair of scissors to her throat.

- The U.S. college education is a big export. It does not seem to be counted in our GDP and it should be. In addition to the highly-qualified professors, we have the best research (both on equipment, procedures and systems).

  The landscape has been changed. Though most professors are still born here for more than one generation, a lot of students are foreigners and the children of the first generation of immigrants. Our high school systems are not graduating qualified students in the same scale as the last generation and foreign countries especially Asians are catching up and some are even passing us.

- Some Chinese students here are tutored by their parents on science and mathematics every night and a lot of students in China go to tutor schools after regular school. If we do not have the dedication and support to our children, we cannot catch up with them.

- 'Leave no one behind', 'Race to the top', 'No homework '... are just ideals and bear no fruits in the real world except for the big-mouth politicians.

  After our best effort to educate the problem kids, should we still leave them to disturb the rest of the class?

  China's one-child policy gives rise to better education of the next generation. The child is raised by two parents and four grandparents. It is all good as long the child is not spoiled.

- One guy who was among the top in the unified examination for high schools in Hong Kong drove a bus to make a statement. We need these geniuses to create more jobs such as discovering a new drug to save many lives, not driving a bus.

- One child plays video game for two hours extra and one studies two hours extra every day. Do you believe they will achieve the same in life provided the last names of them are not Kennedy?

  One Chinese high school has an average class size of 70 and has equipment below our standard. The difference is the students study at least three hours after dinner. It is in Tier III city and it is just a typical school.

- Why Mass. is rich? It is due to the large number of high-tech companies including those involved in bio tech formed by former researchers of higher-learning institutions such as MIT and Harvard. It proves my point that we need about .5% of geniuses to provide jobs for the mass.

- Robots will be harmful to the employment of the unskilled workers. In next five years after 2015, we can see the more replacement by the robots.

  Five years ago, robots could not do much. Now, they can do something useful from vacuum cleaners to bionic limbs. In ten years, they can do almost everything like a human being except one task (i.e. reproduce but they can assemble robots).

Robots are still expensive for many jobs today. To illustrate, Apple can assemble thousands of workers to manufacture a new product in China. They cannot have that large number of robots and program them in a short time.

- Non-correlation of education and the economy.
Brazil's booming economy (due to high natural resources including oil) can benefit more with better education and harder working citizens. The education is lacking in Brazil. It gives rise to corruption and widens the wealth gap.

Brazil is one of the major countries participating in today's globalization. When China slows down, Brazil will feel the pain too.

Philippines has the opposite problem. It has a lot of college graduates working at factories. The economy does not support enough professionals. The poor economy is due to lack of natural resources, long-term corruption, poor governance, etc.

Hong Kongers hire nurses and teachers from Philippines to be their household servants. It appears to be inequality, but actually it reduces inequality by providing them the best jobs they can find.

Links

- Click here for Asian education model.
http://tonyp4idea.blogspot.com/2012/10/asian-model-for-education.html
- Stuffs that college do not teach.
http://tonyp4idea.blogspot.com/2012/11/stuffs-school-does-not-teach.html

Another example.
http://www.huffingtonpost.com/2015/01/30/rescue-leftover-cuisine_n_6563516.html

Filler: Inflation meter

When the beggar asked me for a spare dollar, I felt the inflation pinch. That's the real inflation meter. Forget what the government tells you.

7   Effective health care delivery

Obamacare has an impact on businesses. Large businesses will gain an edge over small businesses unless there will be subsidy and that will add to our deficit. Small businesses will suffer with several side effects:

- They will need to work around the requirements of forced health care insurance by limiting the number of hours for an employee and the number of employees.

- Most of the new ventures are seeded from money from their home equity loans. With falling home prices, they will have less new businesses. The banks already have more restrictions in loaning money since 2007.

Most proposals on health care delivery do not care about how to cut down costs (we pay more than most developed countries), and how to make it fair and practical. We need to know how to pay for it first, how much, and the consequences to businesses and employment. My proposal and comments are as follows:

1. Basic treatments for all.
   Better coverage is paid by an individual. We should encourage folks to work hard and then there is no more free lunch. It is abnormal for the poor to have free health care while the middle class does not enjoy the same. The poor in many states receive free health care. I hesitate to visit a doctor as I have to pay even after the insurance.

2. Fair regulation for nursing home.
   Those with low income and/or those without a house most likely can receive free nursing home care, free drugs and a free doctor visit in most states. Those on the borderline qualify for the free nursing home care by giving their houses to their children, hiding their income and/or just quit working. They are lazy but not stupid.

   The government should spend an agreed percentage of the GDP on public health care. We can use the average percent from developed countries or let the voters decide. We cannot ignore other spending such as education or keep the budget unbalanced which is not responsible.

When we over spend on any entitlement, there needs to be a corresponding hike in taxes. High taxes reduce the United States' global competitiveness and lead to more unemployment.

3. Prevention: Voluntary and non-voluntary (via taxes) on smoking, fast food, soda, etc. It is fair for the citizens to take care of their own health. You can select to live recklessly in an unhealthy life style, but the rest of us should not be burdened with your bad habits. In his book The China Study, Dr. Campbell recommends a whole food, plant-based diet that would reduce a lot of diseases.

   When we ban smoking totally, many hospitals ought to free up many resources. In addition, the second-hand smoke kills too. Why should the rest die from your bad behavior? The children of parents with drug problems have a higher chance of birth defects and problems than the average person.

4. Limit lawsuit awards on malpractice.
   Our health care cost is being jacked up partly due to the legal expenses.

   Most do not realize these lawsuit awards will pass back to each of us. It is also the reason why the doctor would hesitate to care for us when we fall and lie in the street or why our clinical charges are so high. Lawyers and insurers get their share.

5. State-of-the-art treatments are less effective than prevention such as a low-dosage aspirin for all those over 50 years of age and the routine shots for babies / children. Aspirin is the miracle drug that is hated by all drug companies due to the low profit margin.

6. Outsourcing the expensive treatments in foreign countries and drug development / clinical tests.
   Our costs are outrageously high. Try some Caribbean countries, Thailand or Shanghai for example. The money we save pays for a free vacation, not mentioning the free massage every day for the entire trip in Thailand. Many Caribbean countries offer some dentistry services at half the cost. This is a temporary solution until we solve our high-cost problem.

7. Cut down the expensive drug marketing (such as giving money / goodies to doctors).

Personally I know of doctors receiving free golf trips to some of the most expensive golf courses for the entire family. They also got unlimited lobsters at medical conventions in Boston. Should doctors receive the 'lecture fees' giving phony lectures, or sales pitches in return for recommending the drugs, or prescribing them to their patients? Guess who ends up paying for all these goodies eventually?

8. Stop the illegal aliens and foreigners from using our medical systems for free. Their employers or the patients should pay for their expenses. It is nice to help the rest of the world, but we do not have money to do that right now.

The emergency room is the most expensive delivery method and its usage has been abused by many.

9. Before we send soldiers abroad or explore space (both have some merits but the average citizen does not benefit from these ventures), should we solve our problems at home first such as health care? Let's get our priorities straight.
10. The average last two years of one's life would be the most expensive health care cost. Many do not want to live through pains and sufferings. Should we let them pass away in peace if they want to?
11. Stem cell research has proven to be promising.
We should not let our politicians dictate the policy for religious reasons. The desperate will go to foreign countries to receive the riskiest treatments anyway. Why let them know their risk and do the treatments here in a better environment?
12. Stop all the insurance and Medicare fraud. If you spend $10,000 on inspectors and get back $1 million, it is a great investment. Whistle blowing is the most efficient way to prosecute violators. Each successful, publicized prosecution warns thousands of potential violators. Stop hospital monopoly.
13. Why some stores such as Walmart and CVS charge the prescriptions less than some insurance companies? My friend's friend got a bill of $350 (facility and handling charges) for the vaccine for the pandemic of 2020, while some got it free. Before you buy prescriptions, particularly the generic, check out both prices first. Free enterprise at work?

14. Importing foreign doctors and nurses here is the worst thing we can do to a poor country. These foreign medical professionals are seeking a better economic life for themselves to come here, but they forget their original purposes in seeking these noble professions. Why do we send aid to these poor countries and steal their medical professional resources?
15. Need to learn from other countries such as Europe's low cost of their health care system and China's effective health care system, which includes one unique health ID for all citizens and how they control this pandemic.

Afterthoughts
Finally, we have a national health care system. Give it a chance to succeed. I have to give credit to Obama in starting Obamacare in a recession. It may have many holes as most big systems have. Fix the holes instead of rejecting the entire system with all our investments just because of the politician you do not agree with. Roughly we spend double the average of a developed country on health care per capita but our health care system is rated as average.

Filler: Happy Mother's Day Poem

The following is my translation from poet Yu's work in Chinese. I changed some words as some could not be translated effectively.

-------- Two Cries -----------
I cried at two unforgettable times in my life.

The first time when I came to this world.
The second time when you left this world.

The first time I did not know but from your mouth.
The second time you did not know but from my heart.

Between these two crises, we had endless laughs.
For the last 30 years, we had joyful laughs that had been repeated, repeated...

You treasured every laugh.
I cherish every laugh for the rest of my life.

8   A prolonged recession

As of 2014, we're in the 6th year of this recession even the market recovers fully. It is the longest from my memory. We tried too many short-term solutions such as massively printing money and rescuing big companies that should have failed. They work for the short term especially for the stock market, but it does not work in the long term. The temporary fixes are definitely not beneficial for the economy and its capitalist system. Politicians want to buy votes and voters do not want to bite the bullet. In addition, our economy is globally connected. What happens in foreign countries including EU and China would affects us.

Sometimes no solution is the best solution and let nature take care of itself. No companies are too big to fall. We cannot spend recklessly to solve our problems, and that is the main reason to get us into this recession on the first place.

When we let big banks or corporations fail, the job unemployment would rise and their buildings will be empty. It is a temporary problem. Companies with better management will take over, start hiring and fill the buildings. It is called capitalism and it lets the fittest to survive. The lessons will be told but we never learn.

Our money has been used unproductively on unemployment and welfare. I'm glad we did not bail out Lehman Brothers. Otherwise, their former clients all over the world would ask them to pay back for misinterpreting the safety of their derivatives with some of them bundled as 'mini bonds'. Many of the banks selling these derivatives would be liable since Lehman Brothers had gone.

As of 2014, the investors are doing fine in the market as it is close to the 2007 level. It is still a depression when you lose your job and/or your house.

I'm looking and longing for a prolonged bull market when the two wars will finally and completely end. The U.S. is still full of natural resources especially per capita wise. Everyone who wants to work should have a job. The environmentalists should allow the oil companies to drill unless the concerns are real. The politicians should have a longer vision beyond four years and we cannot pass our debts to the next generations forever.

Afterthoughts

- From Eric: I think you are completely on the spot on with this point. The system needs to cleanse itself once and for all, and current policies are only prolonging the agony at this point. I was OK with QE1, as a chaotic unraveling could not have been allowed, but I still wonder if we wouldn't be much further along in putting the crisis behind us if QE2 was left on the shelf back in 2010. Sure the adjustment process is painful, but so are many things in life that must inevitably be endured before things can get better.

- From Wheels: Recession for 4 years...hmmm...sounds like a depression to me...And we all know the reason why nature will never be allowed to take care of itself: because it's not politically tenable. No politician can stand up and speak to the dumb masses that we're in trouble.

On the investing front, can someone please tell me how it is possible to get real valuations for the market with all the juice that global central banks have put in? Trying to invest with "fundamentals" in mind is making my brain hurt, because there is no such thing as fundamentals with all this intervention. And, 2008 is still staring us in the face, and scares me. And I think I'm a pretty average Joe investor out there.

Filler:

Politics. It is very seldom we have the third term won by the same political party; based on this I predict Republican will win. Republican is pro-business but statistically the market does not fare well under the Republican leadership. Will it be true this time? Only time can tell.

9   GDP and global trades

GDP normally means GDP growth after inflation.

Inflation is important. If the inflation is 10%, the GDP of 10 without including inflation is actually GDP of 0.

If the GDP is calculated in the U.S. currency, the currency conversion rate is important.

The average GDP for developing countries is about 5.5% and that for developed countries like the U.S. is about 3%.

China was about 6.2% in 2018. It is not a fully developed country. It used to be around 10 digits for many years after joining WTO in 2001. It is down from 2017's 6.9%. I predict it will be down below 6% if the trade war with the U.S. continues.

WTO rules have not been enforced fully on China esp. on subsidies and exporting their excessive capacity (product dumping for some). Most countries subsidized in some of their industries. Product dumping will in theory benefit the importing countries. We make sure that they will not raise prices after the local competitors have been driven out of business. Microsoft did dump their Office products one time. In addition, Microsoft and Apple copied many ideas from PARC.

China's GDP depends on the GDPs reported from the provinces. Most likely most provinces over-reported their GDPs.

Absolute GDP takes a back seat to GDP growth. The Debt / Absolute GDP ratio is important. Absolute GDP per capita is important when a living standard is concerned.

China is #1 in global trade. China owns less farm land and many natural resources such as oil per capita. China can use her trading position for political gains. During the current trade war with the U.S., Australia who is siding with the U.S. would lose a lot of Australia imports to China.

10   China's poverty alleviation

If you do not agree with most accomplishments by China, you have to whole-heartedly agree with the accomplishment of China's poverty alleviation program. About 90% of Chinese agree, and it is the highest for all China's policies.

Compared to the West, China has come a long way in helping the poor, but it is still not up to the standard of the West. China still needs to do a lot in the coming years.

The U.S. and most countries in the West have good safety nets. The poor enjoy a lot of freebies, such as subsidized housing, food stamps (in the U.S.), free or low-cost medical care and the miscellaneous benefits. Our welfare system is so good that it discourages folks from looking for jobs. I believe our poor are sometimes better off than the middle class in many developing countries including China. However, we have more beggars, homeless, addicts and drunks than China. We have more pessimists than China. Chinese citizens think their leaders have been doing better jobs than 10, 20, 30 or 40 years ago.

I have to admit China's program is way too late. However, the days of "no work, no food" disappeared decades ago, and today almost no Chinese starve to death. China's wealth gap has been reduced. The easy part has been done efficiently and effectively. The remaining part is tougher. It has to relocate more rural habitants who live in mountain areas or the areas that do not allow them to make a decent living. Some elders and disabled do not want to relocate.

The above are my personal opinions. For figures and updated info, "Google China poverty alleviation" or click the following.

Wikipedia: Targeted Poverty Alleviation - Wikipedia

YouTube: 1   2 Homeless
https://www.youtube.com/watch?v=eDKMecq9iFw
https://www.youtube.com/watch?v=6YsB5HG6KYA
https://www.youtube.com/watch?v=0WvEcHh0kQU&t=227s

11 Aging global population

The aging of the global population is due to the proliferation of baby boomers after WW2.

- India will suffer from the population explosion despite the abundance of younger citizens.

    They will eat up all the limited food and consume most of its limited natural resources. They will run out of water in 100 years which is also controlled by China as more water will be directed to the north of Tibet. There are too many problems that cannot be resolved easily. There is no bright future for India. I wish I were wrong as a poor India would affect the rest of the world.

    http://en.wikipedia.org/wiki/South-North_Water_Diversion_Project

    They classify themselves literate if they can write their name in any language compared to 1,500 Chinese characters for China. Chinese have nine years of compulsory education. These statistics are just being manipulated.

    Source: Ted Talk.
    http://www.ted.com/talks/yasheng_huang.html

    The brain drain is alarming as the most privileged / educated do not want to wait for India's infrastructure, its economy and its governance to be fixed.

    I hope rich countries like the U.S. will not take too many doctors / nurses from poor countries such as India as we're doing now. This is the worst disservice to a poor country. We deprive thousands from medical care for each doctor we import. Why do we send our doctors to help the poor while we take their doctors? It just does not make sense. There should be more foreign aid allocated to medical training to poor countries.

    Just compare the subway system and the number of high-rises in India to any Tier 3 city in China. The top Indian city just built its subway recently in 2011 while Hong Kong has developed into a modern metropolitan with a modern and extensive subway system many years ago. As of 2012, more than half of India's population live on less than $2.50 a day (the UN definition of poverty is $2.50 / day).

India has to understand its problems first before they can fix them. It has to fight inefficiency, corruption (partly due to inefficiency) and protectionism (to improve quality and encourage foreign investment). Copying China's model is a good idea. China's model is to create specific economic zones close to a port with the essential infrastructure for that area. You need to build infrastructure like highways, electricity... for that area first. It should target its products first to the foreign market and then include the home market.

The 2011 Indian Kolkata airport has limited road access while the 1980 Hong Kong airport is supported by extensive suspension bridges. Without the road access support, any airport would not be world-class as demonstrated by all major airports in the world. Documentaries on both projects are available from Netflix.

Some told me it could be old, wealthy families control India's economy and they do not want changes. I argue the opposite is true. Expensive projects usually allow the corrupt rich and the local governments to steal money from public projects.

- China still has plenty of cheap labor.
  Cheap labor will be minor but education will be important as they need to move up to the next level of industrialization with higher-value products. China is already there in many areas.

  China has its own problems, and plenty of them, but demographics are not the major one. Gender imbalance, pollution and corruption are many among others.

  Click this link http://bit.ly/ybAnoW to compare India and China.

- Russia and Brazil still thrive on commodities and oil as long as the global economy grows.

Russians fit my Coconut Theory. They become lazier (and more intoxicated with Vodka☺) as the economy continually grows from its wealth of natural resources including oil. As long as the global economy is humming, there are demands for these resources, and vice versa.

- Africa and some S. American countries.
  The explosive population will bring miseries to their worlds. There will be more wars for food and life expectancies are already lowered. The citizens will migrate legally and illegally to richer countries like the U.S. for a better living. If the farming technology to produce more food with less farmland did not improve drastically over the last 50 years, the world's supply of food now would not meet the demand. As 2012 closes, there are higher food prices due to the floods and droughts all over the world. It will continually be rougher for the poor countries that cannot afford to pay for it especially when China and India have more cash from their exports.

- The U.S.
  In 2023, the U.S. may look like Japan is today as most developed countries whose populations shrunk to below zero growth. However, the U.S.'s black and Hispanics have a higher fertility rate and the U.S. has more immigrants than all other countries combined. The U.S. will have its different problems / advantages as below.

  The U.S. welcomes immigrants (as opposed to Japan). Most qualified Indians are welcome and so are Chinese (who come for economic reasons, to escape from pollution, or because of corruption prosecutions).

  In the U.S., today's minorities will become the majority. If you look at their high school dropout rate, social welfare recipient percent, prisoner percent, etc., we do not have a bright future. There will be more political leaders from these groups as we usually vote for politicians that belong to the same race as ours. These are facts and it might be offensive to you if you're a minority.

  When we do not have jobs for everyone, a large population is a big burden. We have recent college graduates begging for any job for years, lines for unemployment and welfare offices are getting busier.

Why we encourage illegal aliens to come here for jobs and welfare is beyond my comprehension.

The brightest future for us is agriculture and its demand from many countries grows by leaps and bounds. The other is American culture, like movies and music since English is, and will be, the most popular language. The recent discoveries in shale gas and oil are very promising. It could lead us to be a major energy exporter in the next 50 years. Military weapons are a big seller that I do not think it is good for the rest of the world.

Starting in 2012, the baby boomers are retiring (those who were born after WW2). Hence, we will have about 20 years of increased entitlements such as Social Security considering the average life expectancy of about 82 years. Now we should have a boom in health care delivery.

- Japan.
  Japan does not have a lot of natural resources, and the educated citizen is their most important resource. Japan will suffer the most due to the aging population. However, most of us will still drive a car from a Japanese company, play video games on Wii or PlayStation... Its competitors (now Korea and later China) will share their market. Japan will continue its lost decades to another decade. Japan seems to be turning around in 2013 but it could be just "the dead cat bounces". Only time can tell. Depreciating its currency further stimulates its export at least in the short term.

Conclusion
Investors should look at the sectors that will be benefited from the aging population for the next 20 years. They are health care delivery, medical equipment, drugs, elderly housing and all sectors that cater to this growing age group.

Links
Water re-directed.
http://en.wikipedia.org/wiki/South-North_Water_Diversion_Project

Ted Talk.
http://www.ted.com/talks/yasheng_huang.html

12 Capitalism & democracy

When we use communism to describe China's political system, it is not 100% correct. Communism started about 60 years ago, but Deng modified it to be socialism with Chinese characteristics. Now, it is highly capitalistic.

Capitalist-Socialist is a better term to describe China's political system. However, China is also ruled by a single party with about a handful of rulers who determine the next leader every decade. It is a consensus rule by a few within the context of party authoritarianism.

Communism shares food and other stuff evenly. So, communism encourages laziness and China today is capitalist where its citizens starve if they do not work.

Socialism is in between capitalism and communism. Democracy could lead to socialism, which in turn could lead to self-destruction as demonstrated by Greece today.

What do we call the U.S.? Socialist-Democracy? We have generous welfare and free speech. Some may call it a welfare state.

Western Democracy may not work for countries with low education. It could and have led to corruption as indicated in many Asian countries, past and present.

To use healthcare as a yardstick, China practices capitalism. If you do not pay, you die literally in the lobby of a hospital. Canada is socialist. Everyone has some basic form of healthcare. Many U.S. states offer free medical care to the poor and even the illegals, so the U.S. is communist or a welfare state.

Afterthoughts

- We cannot weigh the same vote for an educated citizen and a bum. We should have an IQ meter in the voting booth. Your vote is multiplied with your IQ. In the U.S., your tax return from last year will be handy too as we should not allow representation without taxation. Quite extreme even for me but just a thought. ☺

- As Uncle Deng said, "If the cat catches the mouse, I do not care whether it is black or white". I see a lot of holes in the current Chinese system. However, China has lifted millions from poverty (i.e. starving to death) and just for that it is a good system in my book.

  Deng should get a Nobel Prize for that. It is better than Obama's for doing nothing and even before spending recklessly. Well, the current Nobel Prize committee has become a political clown who only gives prizes to folks against China. Hope Mr. Nobel would rise up and give them a hard spank on their stupid heads.

- The authoritarian system has some advantages like bulldozing all the houses to give rise to a highway or a high-speed train rail. As long as it is not my house, it is OK.

- The problem of the current system in China.
  The central government sets up good policies. However, the local governments' top priority is how to sip money for themselves. The central government should take action on corruption by the local government and ensure they follow the rules and policies.

- We spend too much time in planning, arguing (especially the silly objections between two opposite parties), lawsuits, financing in a large public project such as the High-Speed Rail (HSR). By the time we start the actual work, the project plan is obsolete and the landscape has been changed.

  BTW, High Speed Rail (HSR) is not cost effective for the U.S. even though it works in China. As in Business 101, you need to calculate benefit over cost (i.e. rate of return of the project). You should select the most cost-effective projects first and HSR is not one of them except for political reasons. We're not as densely populated as China. Airlines will compete better than HSR when the driving distance is more than four hours. In addition, how many workers want to work in that kind of conditions in laying rails instead of collecting welfare?

  As most if not all big projects in the U.S. (actually same in most countries) are painted in a very rosy picture initially and then end up in cost overrun and diminished returns. The Big Dig project in Boston is one of them and it was full of holes before it was started. We did not have so many problems on similar projects decades ago even though we have updated technologies and know-hows today. This project has been late, cost-overrun and unsafe. It is easy to give all concessions and expensive dinners to everyone as the money is not his. Ronnie did not get the presidency because of this project even though he did not have any control.

- The cornerstone of our capitalistic system is "Supply and Demand". If you can find a better job, take it. If you cannot find a better worker, you have to pay more.

That's why we have starving artists as the society does not need their work and that's why we pay accountants and programmers a lot of money relatively. If the rich do not invest (taking risk for the potential profit), there will be no jobs. It is also the catalyst (better wages) to ask folks to study what the society wants instead of what they want. I did not have the luxury of studying the field I really wanted.

Do not blame others but yourselves. Do not treat the rich as parasites. Do not blame China as a 50 cent per hour could be heaven for them. Again it is Supply and Demand.

My classmate wondered why the West wanted to take away his only job as a child labor. He needed that job to buy bread. There are always two sides of a story. Do not force others to follow your ideals. If you do, we have wars.

Links

Next Leaders:
http://en.wikipedia.org/wiki/Elections_in_the_People%27s_Republic_of_China#Indirect_elections

13 Political systems and the economy

Our economy is largely controlled by our corrupt and lethargic political system. All political systems have their strengths and weaknesses.

Use China as an example. In principle, Communism solves the class problem and reduces the wealth gap. However, it makes folks lazy and managers bureaucratic as extra effort is not rewarded. The workers do not work diligently as there is just ordinary compensation, as the union labor in the U.S. That's why today's China is not run by communists but capitalists.

The differences in political systems

The Maoist[1] Communist China allowed folks to have a job just to fulfill the people's needs. Today, the unions make the United States non-competitive in high labor industries, such as clothing and textiles; whereas innovative industries or non-transferrable services thrive here. The unions can only work when the labor market cannot be outsourced such as climbing up the telephone pole.

Socialism is a form of an economic system characterized by social ownership of the means of production and cooperative management of the economy, and a political philosophy advocating such a system. "Social ownership" may refer to cooperative enterprises, common ownership, state ownership, or citizen ownership of equity. For a rich country such as Norway, it works marvelously. For a poorer country such as Greece, it would be a disaster in the making and today that disaster turns into a reality.

In modern usage, the word "communism" is still often used to refer to the policies of self-declared socialist governments comprising one-party states which were single legal political party systems operating under centrally planned economies and a state ownership of the means of production, with the state, in turn, claiming that it represented the interests of the working classes.

By the beginning of the 21st century, states controlled by communist parties under a single-party system included the People's Republic of China, Cuba, Laos, Vietnam, and North Korea. Communist parties, or their descendants, remain politically important in a number of other countries[2].

Capitalism[3], an economic system, is based on private ownership of the means of production and the creation of goods or services. I cannot classify China in one term. The best I can come to is Capitalism / Dictatorship as it is ruled by a handful of top party leaders. The U.S.A. is Democratic / Capitalist / Socialist. We have freedom, big corporations and generous welfare.

The high ratios of debt over GNP in most PIIGS (Portugal, Ireland, Iceland, Greece and Spain) make them uncompetitive. Those governments need to pay high interest rates on that debt, and hence in theory, a heavy taxation burden. Because those taxes make your production exports expensive and uncompetitive in the global market where many countries do not have this debt problem.

Does democracy or capitalism lead to socialism?

It seems that the U.S. is following the same path as Greece to self-destruction. But this is mostly due to its irresponsible credit-based consumption and generous welfare.

Changing of political system in China

The last 30-year success in China is due to:

- The U.S. played the China card against Russia and lifted the trade embargo against China.

- Deng's reform utilizes designated specific areas as low taxation, special economic zone. It has been done before but never at this scale. It is not possible to modernize the factories and infrastructure to ship the products in a year in the entire country. But, it is possible to limit it to a small area, especially the one that has a sea port. The first one in South China also takes advantage of the know-how from Hong Kong people and their financial investment.

    The political system is as good as how it is administered. Another example is how democratic India is poorly governed and remains poor. Democracy is always ideal. I believe democracy needs an educated and wealthier population to be effective. The vote from an uneducated peasant cannot count the same weight as a sophisticated, educated city dweller.

Do you remember Peter's Principle? When a successful manager is promoted to another position that he has no experience nor qualified for, he usually performs badly in his new position. Mao is the most representative of this principle as he was unable to transition from a great revolutionary leader to a governing one. To be fair, he is well respected by most Chinese in the Mainland and he contributed a lot to China in his revolutionary days.

As the late Chinese leader Deng Xiao Ping said, we need some (entrepreneurs and professional managers) to make money and the 1% capitalists are the ones for China and for the U.S. too. We need them to invest more so they can hire more workers.

Footnote.

[1] Definitions of Maoism vary. Within the Chinese context, Maoism can refer to Mao's belief in the mobilization of the masses, particularly in large-scale political movements; it can also refer to the egalitarianism that was seen during Mao's era as opposed to the free-market ideology of Deng Xiaoping; some scholars additionally define personality cults and political sloganeering as "Maoist" practices. Contemporary Maoists in China criticize the social inequalities created by a capitalist and 'revisionist' Communist party.

[2] The People's Republic of China has reassessed many aspects of the Maoist legacy; it, along with Laos, Vietnam, and, to a lesser degree Cuba, has reduced state control of the economy in order to stimulate growth. Chinese economic reforms started in 1978 under the leadership of Deng Xiaoping; since then, China has managed to bring down the poverty rate from 53% in the Mao era to just 6% in 2001. The People's Republic of China runs Special Economic Zones dedicated to market-oriented enterprise, free from central government control. Several other

communist states have also attempted to implement market-based reforms, including Vietnam.

[3] Capitalism is based on private ownership of the means of production and the creation of goods or services for profit.

Afterthoughts

- From Elliott. Lee Kuan Yew, the former Prime Minister of Singapore said that Western "democracy" would not work in a developing country because of many different ethnic/religious groups. An "iron hand" government is needed to keep people who hate one another from killing one another (like Saddam in Iraq or Tito in Yugoslavia). The other problem for a rapidly growing country using democracy is "stasis". You can't get enough people to do anything, like building a railroad or expressway through private land.
- The Chinese Communist Party creates jobs to reduce this social unrest. The "tofu" projects are those bridges and roads which collapse in the first year or two of completion due to this negligence, incompetency and corruption.
- With its substantial foreign reserves, China is in a healthier position relative to most other countries.
- Many analyses I read on China using western mindsets and free market systems are wrong and they may be right when China reaches the same state as the West.

Links
Trade embargo:
http://www.washingtonpost.com/wp-srv/inatl/longterm/flash/june/china71.htm
Special Economic Zone:
http://en.wikipedia.org/wiki/Special_Economic_Zone

#Filler: Nothing perfect
If we have no wars and no pandemic for the last 2,000 years, the population would explode.

If we have no sinners, heaven would be full.

14   Immigration

Most immigrants come here for economic reasons like the famine in Ireland, wars and food shortage in China especially during Mao's era. The majority of Hong Kong's population was formed by illegal refugees from mainland China.

With a comparatively booming economy, huge natural resources per capita and small population per square mile, the US is heaven. We need cheap labor and more top professionals/scientists.

The other reasons are political oppression, freedom, better opportunities, etc. My reason was the lack of good colleges in my homeland Hong Kong at the time.

Today many rich Chinese want to migrate to the US for better opportunities for their children. The US had missed the opportunities to attract them when Hong Kong was taken over in 1997. The current investment requirement is a good vehicle to attract wealthy Chinese. It is better than the economic refugees who burden our welfare system. Some Chinese are escaping from potential prosecution of the crimes in corruption - there are better countries for this purpose.

In the last century or two, Chinese came here to build the railroad and/or mine gold. Some were cheated to come to work in the slavery conditions. The tougher parts of the railway connecting the two coasts of US and Canada were done by them and their efforts were not recognized. I have not seen a single picture with a yellow face in any milestone of the railway. In the old days, Chinese migrated to Southeast Asia. Their hard work pays off for themselves and the adopted countries.

It is an easy choice for Indians as no one in the right mind wants to wait for India to fix their basic infrastructure. So are the Mexicans.

In simple words, they migrate for better living conditions and opportunities. Most do not want leaving the places they grow up and the friends and families if they have a choice.

The adopted countries should benefit from immigration if handled correctly by filling jobs their citizens do not want or are not qualified.

Rich immigrants also bring money to invest in the local economy. However, some immigrants become permanent welfare recipients, criminals and/or even terrorists. Japan does not welcome immigrants and they do not have terrorist attacks from immigrants.

Wealthy Chinese drive up the price of the housing market in Vancouver and other cities that welcome them. It is good for the current house owners. It is bad to those who start out as they cannot possibly afford the appreciated houses.

After the [Tiananmen Square protests of 1989](#) incident, Chinese students were allowed to [stay](#). China lost many top students, and the U.S. gained a lot. How many students returned back to China with the skills they learned in the U.S. is another story. It is another example in my Coconut Theory: Folks without coconuts move to places with coconuts.

Recently, many Chinese scientists were accused of treason or joining the China plan. I support 100% to prosecute treasons. However, due to the flip flop of our policy on China, some accusers may not have enough time to change their cooperation plan with China. The American Chinese need a united and powerful organization such as the ones for the black to protect their human rights if they are violated.

15   Trade agreements

As opposed to the name, trade agreements are used to exclude specific countries (those who do not sign the agreements) for trades. It means no free trade, which allows the consumer to buy the best product at the least cost regardless of where the product is from. Free trade works as long as all the participating countries play the game fairly such as no product dumping. Product dumping usually drives the industry of the receiving country bankrupts the competitors and then raises prices.

It is enforced by tariffs. About 250 years ago, the Brits wanted China to open trade. It was enforced by battleships and advanced weapons. When they had nothing to trade, they found opium in India. A nation pushed opium to another nation. Millions of Chinese died and China was bankrupted for paying the 'damages'.

Today, it can also be enforced by alliance and investment.

North American Free Trade Agreement (NAFTA) provides jobs for Mexicans at our expense. Trump declared victory of not moving a Carrier's plant to Mexico. However, it is the tip of an iceberg. Why should Ford or Toyota not build a plant in Mexico when there is no tariff penalty?

In China, the price differences between a locally manufactured product and an imported product is huge, especially for luxurious products. That's why you see long lines of Chinese tourists buying brand name products in Paris and Rome. Due to the safety of some Chinese food products, Hong Kong experienced selling out of baby milk products bought by Chinese mainlanders.

It is similar to the British tourists buying Polo products or the Canadians crossing the boundary to buy consumer products. They are reduced when the USD appreciates against the foreign currencies. Recently, the strong USD reduced our exports and the overseas profits converted back to USD.

Filler: Tips

- You need to know both value investing and the basic technical analysis to be successful in today's market.
- Buy in fears and sell in greed instead of the other way round.
- An inflated sector will return to the average value.
- Be conservative and diversified. The turtles are always the winners in the long run.

Impact of the trade war

Chinese foreign students

Coupled with the pandemic, U.S. banning of students to specific areas of study and nationalism of Chinese students, there are fewer students from China. The U.S. universities lose financially and will miss the contribution in research by the Chinese students.

Most Chinese students pay full tuition. Many wealthy Chinese who drive fancy cars and pay in full; ask any car dealers in the college area to confirm yourself.

Most Chinese students settle and contribute to the U.S. after they graduate. Examples abound. The recent one is Eric Yuan, the Founder and CEO of Zoom. His company contributes a lot to the U.S. business. Very few are spies sent by China. Some such as Harry Shum (a chief scientist at Microsoft) go back to China due to the demonizing of the Chinese by Trump. Many Chinese scientists are leaving due to not being able to secure security clearance. Hence it creates a small brain drain in the U.S. and China gains a lot. The statistics of Chinese who were born in the U.S. and spied for China is the same as the rest of the U.S. citizens.

Fewer Chinese tourists

They represent the big spenders of all tourists; in 2018 Chinese tourists spent $277 B while the second place U.S. tourists spent $144 B. The expenses of the trips could be paid off by the goods they bought in the U.S. due to the heavy import taxes.

Cultures meet
Chinese understand our culture more than the other way from the net import of students, tourists and movies / music. Many citizens in the central states never leave the country.

Links

Contributions of Chinese Americans

https://contributingacrossamerica.economist.com/

Section III: The USA

1   Actions to fix our problems

1. We consume more than we produce. Cut down on consumption, applied to both citizens and government. Our false prosperity depends too much on consumer spending. It has created all imbalances including a Federal deficit and trade deficit.

    Raising the interest rates would reduce consumer loans and investment loans at the expense of the stock market, building industry and big-ticket sales. We have to bite the bullet before it is too late.

2. We borrow more than we save. U.S. citizens save about 2% while Chinese save about 15%. Save more and do not max out your credit cards. We cannot postpone our debts to the next generations. Once-the-richest country borrows from the once-poorest country to support our spending.

3. We are not as competitive as we were in the 50s and 60s. Do not give out money generously to foreign countries. It made sense in the old days, but not anymore while the EU, Japan, Israel and many have about the same wealth as us. When the government spends more in paying dividends on our gigantic national debts, we have less money to invest in infrastructure, education... that are important to boost our competitive edge.

4. The expenses of endless wars should go to investment for our future such as infrastructure.

    We no longer depend on oil from the Middle East, so we do not need to use military force to protect our oil route.

    Does Vietnam being a communist country today threaten us?

    We need to concentrate on cyber security. The lack of it would collapse our financial systems and expose our secrets / technologies.

5. The world is more competitive (esp. China) and it looks like it is getting worse. We can negotiate better with our trade partners. The trade war is not the solution but taking out trade barriers on our products are. We have to understand why we are not competitive. However, doing too much and too fast could lead to a global recession.

6. We need to give up some sectors such as those that are labor-intensive and/or environmentally harmful, and evaluate the benefits and losses.

7. We need to motivate our able welfare recipients to work to take up the jobs currently performed by illegal aliens. Our generous welfare system encourages folks not to work. If they work, they would lose all the subsidies. They are lazy but not stupid.

8. We need MORE (not less) H-1B visas to attract top scientists, engineers... in order to remain competitive. However, only let immediate children come. Many of their parents come here and collect welfare to further burden our entitlement system.

    We also need international collaboration, relax restrictions on science-based research such as those in stem cells and promote starting new enterprises. Government should fund basic research. That's why we were leading the world in science and technology. China would eclipse us in a matter of years if we do not think long term and take corrective actions now!

9. We need to balance the budgets, cut down entitlements, rebuild our school system, fund research, fund infrastructure (including security to protect our IP), etc. Make our broken health care delivery efficient.

10. We need to be doers instead of talkers. While we talked about the high-speed rail (HSR) in California (that may not be useful here), China has over 60% of the global HSR. To start with, get the two parties to work together more. They disagree frequently with each other if the idea has not come from their own party.

11. Our children cannot compete with the Chinese, Japanese and Koreans. They spend too much time just enjoying life. If you believe

they will achieve the same in life, you believe in fairy tales. Education starts at home. When we have too many single parent families and teenage mothers, where is our future? We need to protect our youth from shootings, strong drugs and violence.

We need to bring back discipline and strong work ethics. The school must be a place to learn. Have we learned from too many shootings? We have to love our children more than our guns.

We need to fund research and education. The Chinese are catching up due to acquiring our technology (not a lot to steal now), recruiting (such as the Thousand Talents program) research and recruiting. Quantum communication was initiated due to the finding out our NSA stealing their secrets (nice for a change). Most of China's researchers in this field did research overseas.

12. The military should be supported by a strong economy but not in our case. If we were a company, we would have bankrupted with debts and entitlements. We have to put our priority and effort in improving our economy and be competitive.

13. We need to look at the long term. Investing in infrastructure today cannot buy votes as the payback is too long.

14. We need to control the excessive claims of the lawsuits. The juror naturally agreed with fining MacDonald's for spilling hot coffee on the customer. They did not know it would pass the claim back to the consumers. It also discourages citizens from starting new businesses.

15. The country should be united. I do not like everything Trump is doing. However, some of his actions are good and he has the guts to challenge problems such as trade war that his predecessors avoided. I was with the folks in Views. However, when their views are ALWAYS opposite to Trump no matter what he does, the Views loses credibility to me.

16. We need to have a fair political system without interference by special-interest groups. Gun control should be done in a realistic way. How can the police enforce peace at the risk of being shot?

Stop blaming others, especially China, for our problems that the politicians fail to fix. I blame the corporations for giving up our jobs and secrets to many countries including China in order to access their huge market and save on labor costs.

Realistically, most of the proposals above cannot be executed by politicians. They are more long- term solutions that the politicians are not interested in. The voters want to have the maximum benefits with the least taxes. We are a nation of freeloaders unfortunately.

We are still leading the world in many sectors. We still have top-notch universities and profitable multinational corporations. Do not live in denial that we are not declining. Check out any top-notch college or any big high-tech corporation, you can find many foreign faces compared to 30 years ago. Most are new immigrants and their children.

It is hard for the leader of the global world to be humble. Our arrogance prevents us from collaborating with the rest of the world. If we can learn from our competitors and/or enemies, we could reverse the trend of our decline.

We may be following the footsteps of the great British Empire. Our technology revolution since WW2 may collapse like the British Industrial Revolution. Our reserve currency could follow the British pound in losing its status. Hopefully we will make corrections to reverse the trend. If the trend does not reverse, hopefully it is not in our lifetime.

2 The worthless job plan

Most government's job plans have the basic problem: Spend, spend and spend without worrying about where the money comes from. It does create some jobs but at a huge expense. The problems are:

- Pass our loan burden to our children and grandchildren.

- Will have high inflation (not now due to the deflated prices of houses). However, judging from the price of gold and most items in the super market in 2015, we already have inflation. Inflation is an invisible tax to use especially the rich.

- Will raise our debt ceiling and hence it will harm the economy in the long run. The extra money to service our debts could be used in improving productivity and infrastructure.

- Do not spend wisely.
  To illustrate, education starts at home, not at school. With high drop out of poor students (unfortunately more from minorities today), we do have a grim future. Instead, we should limit the number of single parent families. This is one example among many. (http://nces.ed.gov/fastfacts/display.asp?id=16)

- Creating more government jobs is not a good way to boost employment. We should calculate the actual cost of each job created. We can learn from Greece before it is too late. Now Greece has to cut half of the government employees and half of their salaries when the country is heading to go bankrupt.

- The farmers will be the chief beneficiary when the trade war settles with China and the Chinese consumers will benefit too. A win-win situation. As of 2020, it seems the trade war with China will never end.

- The most our government can save is ending the current two wars. Check out how many billions of dollars we could save a month without the two wars. We really need to fix our economy and unemployment first. We cannot afford the two wars and any future war. Even with the mightiest army on earth, we're really a paper tiger if we cannot fix our internal problems such as employment. It is similar when Mao told his starving citizens that they're #1 on earth; they could cover the eyes and minds with dumb nationalism but not the growling stomach.

We have given too much to foreign countries. Helping the desperate poor is fine, but not buying influence in foreign lands to corrupt officials.

- All of us ought to bite the bullet by increasing taxes across the board and decreasing welfare / entitlements. They are not popular to voters, but they will be the most simple and effective solution to a complicated problem. However, we need to implement them gradually, so it will not prolong the recession.

Obama is a good communicator, but he should have acted far earlier to solve our economy problem that was created by the previous president. It is obvious that Obama is buying votes for the 2012 election to satisfy everyone. It could be the same for any president. They all play with the rules of the game. We need to change the rules and make their objectives for longer term.

We elect our leaders, so we have to be blamed too. The major flaw in our political system is the election every four years. Our leaders plan for four years and not for the longer term. We've more poor citizens than the rich citizens, but each has one vote. After they've been elected, they have to pay back to the special interest groups who have funded their campaigns. That's why our democratic system could lead to corruption, American style.

Unemployment report

Investors do not want too good an employment report. If it is too good, the Fed would raise the interest rates to cool down an over-heated economy and that would hurt the corporate profits.

We do not want to be too bad neither. Otherwise, a recession could materialize.

Mathematically incorrect, today's 3.8% unemployment is 0% unemployment. The unemployed take advantage of the generous welfare.

Adjusted for inflation and as of 4/2019, we do not have the same median salary before the 2018 financial crisis.

A lot of information on jobs can be found in this BLS web site.
https://www.bls.gov/oes/current/oes_nat.htm

Afterthoughts
- Unemployment should be a temporary safety net. When the unemployment benefits are extended, the incentive to look for jobs is also decreased. Many have given up looking for jobs after trying their best. The better yardsticks are comparing the following two with values of previous month: 1. Participation rate and 2. Median salary. 3. The changes of the above two.

- Why should you work if it means you would lose all the generous benefits such as the free health care, food stamps and housing subsidies?

- We really have more than the official 8% unemployment if we count how many of our own friends/relatives are still employed or under employed. 5% is the employment rate for the U.S. for 'full employment'.

- Many are under-employed and they're not counted as unemployed; as of 3/2015 we have the lowest participation rate. To illustrate, an ex-manager flips hamburgers at McDonald's making a fraction of his previous salary.

- As of 5/2013, Obamacare will decrease jobs in small businesses. The owners do not want to hire full-time employees as they do not know how Obamacare will impact their businesses. Most likely it will require them to conform to the new laws that require businesses that hire over a specified number (say 50) of employees to pay a good portion of the health insurance premium for full-time employees (could be defined as working more than 30 hours per week).

- IPOs for local companies usually mean more jobs. When we see a lot of IPOs in the U.S., we can predict the employment is recovering.
- Globalization changes all the traditional, conventional wisdom. Most large companies are global companies. Corporations find the best workers anywhere in the world at the least cost. Typically the US, EU and Japan design the high-value products and their products are assembled in foreign lands where they can find cheaper, better and more flexible labor.

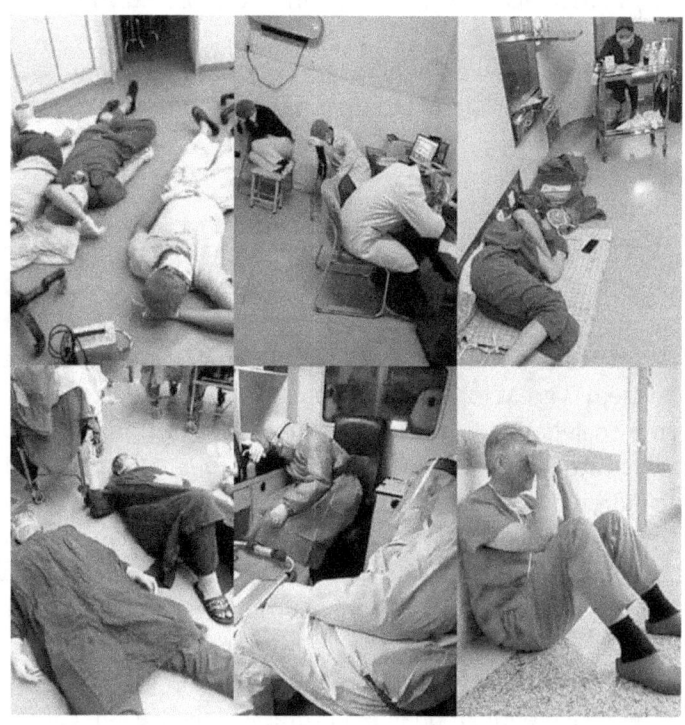

Not taken by me.
They are more important than ALL entertainers and athletes.

3 H-1B visa

On my bus commute to downtown, I noticed a lot of Indians and some Chinese besides myself. Many of them are on H-1B visas and work in banks, insurance companies and brokerage firms downtown. Some have applied or will apply for the green cards. Their living standards of many Indians have been improved greatly here and no one is naive enough to wait for India to fix their infrastructure and offer similar job opportunities for the equivalent salaries.

If you're a technical manager, which one would you want to hire:

1. An H-1B visa worker who will work hard for peanuts, but it is gold to them when comparing to their native country,

or

2. One who has no incentive to work hard except trying to get your job eventually.

We should encourage our children to get into science and math. Our system is great for creative geniuses like Steve Jobs, Gates, etc. However, the society needs more folks with the right training to corporations. To illustrate, most well-paid, high-tech jobs are held by foreigners and children of foreigners who study programming, engineering, science and math. These professionals are not geniuses, but they have the right training to enhance and / or market the products / services from the visions of the geniuses. From my rough estimate, we probably need one genius for every ten thousands of these professionals.

If we have enough qualified professionals, we can cut down H-1B visas; however the government has to give incentives to hire local professionals to offset the lower wages from most potential H-1B holders. Today and in the near future, we can't cut down these visas otherwise our high-tech industry will not be competitive. Most H-1B recipients eventually get their green cards, and move their parents to the U.S. burdening our welfare and entitlement systems. The employers do not care as this is not their problem. The alternative is setting up research / development centers in foreign countries such as India and China at the risk of our proprietary secrets being stolen.

Afterthoughts

- In 2014, there are 3 million (4 million for some reports) jobs last year in the US are unfilled due to lack of skills while we have many college graduates who cannot find a job. We have a serious problem of skills not matched.

  There are about 2 million unfilled positions desperately needed by programming including the cloud computing. Our high-tech industry is expanding their training programs in order to fill these 'skills gap' positions.

  There is why the Congress is slapping permanent visas to those foreign students who graduated in the US universities with the right training in science and computer science and advocate larger number of H-1B visas.

  Vocational colleges and apprenticeship should be encouraged. The high school graduates should match their careers to jobs that are plentiful. A college degree without a job potential is a waste of money and time, not to mention the heavy loan that will take years to repay. My plumber makes very good money with less than a year of training.

Filler

When we legalize the illegals, do you think they are stupid enough to work instead of collecting welfare legally? Who are doing to do the jobs that no able welfare recipients want?

4 Too delicious to fall

Unions are supposed to protect the working class from being exploited. Today unions reduce our competitive edge by setting up higher compensation. Globalization weakens the power of the union by moving some of our jobs to other countries such as China and Mexico. We have to define two classes of jobs: jobs that can be outsourced and jobs that cannot be. Some unions are more effective in the latter category such as climbing up telephone poles. Few mayors in big cities are elected without the approval of the local police union, and hence some unions are politically powerful.

Hostess's fall is a bad day for capitalism, at least our style of capitalism. There is too much blame to go around:

- First, the management (and some hedge fund managers) did not update their products to meet the trend of the market.

- Unions are out-of-touch. If your patient is dying, you do not want to shake him hard. You need to have plan B when you're bluffing.

  They're the parasites and they will die too when their host (hostess in our case) is dead. The dream of owning the company will remain to be a dream that they never want to wake up from. They tried to violate the basic business rule of supply and demand, but failed miserably.

- The workers are really dumb to let their master manipulate them until they lose out big time. Do you think you can protest and win in this kind of economy and the shaky state of the company?

- The politicians will not bail them out especially it is long past the election. This time they cannot buy votes by blaming China, as these jobs can't be outsourced (unless you want to buy your Wonder bread shipped from China). Hence, even if it were before the election, the government will not bail you out on the ground of 'too delicious to fall'.

It is a lose-lose-lose (management-unions-workers) situation and only stupid folks will get into this situation.

5 Generous welfare

Last Saturday, a television commenter suggested legalizing illegal aliens and moving them to Detroit; it has worked well before in several other American cities.

I totally disagree with that notion. Instead we should ask the able poor to work and take less welfare benefits to encourage businesses to move in and provide jobs.

In addition, the city has to concentrate on education to provide an educated work force. It does not take a genius on how to lure back businesses by protecting the businesses first. If I open a business at the constant threat of being burned down or being looted, I do not open a business there.

We also have to train the unemployed for jobs that are *needed* by the society. Investing in education is productive, while giving out generous welfare is not. It is a balancing act by the city administrators.

Unions and generous welfare will work in the short-term for a specific group of the society. In the long run, they will have opposite effects as demonstrated in Detroit.

One cannot survive by making the minimum wage in the USA. They will be subsidized with welfare and you know we all have to pay for these benefits eventually. We need to encourage folks to work by reducing the generous social welfare that should go to the real needy and/or serve as a temporary safety net.

In Mass., the system takes away free health care when the income is above a specific level. Hence, it does not encourage the poor to work.

There are too many frauds in our welfare system. We should take care of our citizens first before we take in more immigrants who compete for the limited jobs available.

In addition, when they are legalized, do you think they are stupid enough to work when receiving welfare is a better deal? The newly legalized will help their immediate families to immigrate and further burden our welfare system.

Today, some new immigrants ask for the closest welfare office on the first day they arrive, or where is the closest hospital to give birth to a USA citizen baby free of charge. Taiwan has a book titled "How to Retire Rich in the USA with No Money and No Effort" from my memory. The objective is seeking an easy life without work in the land of generous welfare; the rest of the world calls us suckers!

Many Vietnamese refugees cheat on welfare. I do not blame them considering the miseries they went thru. Most of them were government employees (servants and soldiers) and Chinese merchants. Most are educated, hard-working folks with tough experiences. In just one short generation, you do not find too many of them collecting welfare and most become respectable and productive citizens.

Am I racist?

When I talked about the problems of the black, I would be likely called racist. If they do not know about the problems, how can they fix them? Hence, most likely the problems have to be fixed by the black. Despite all this, I still have to say they have to start in family education. With multi-generations of teen age mothers and high percent of male in prison, the future does not look good.

If you have a museum for white, you will be called racist. But, one for black is OK. It is fine for black making racist jokes, but not for white on black.

The editor of China Airline magazine had to apologize to the Indians and Africans for telling her readers not to visit some parts of London due to high crime. It is true that many mentioned minorities reside there. It would be quite innocent as they've not deal with minorities that much.

Undoubtedly, the white had done something wrong by enslaving the black. But, that is more than a century ago. Today, does racism limit one from success if life? The opposite is true such as college admission and job promotion.

Besides some bad apples, police are doing great job at the risk of their lives. We have to admit and fix our racial discrimination. Peaceful protests are fine but not looting.

Do you call me racist or white lover?

Afterthoughts

- The welfare department and the immigration department do not share information. I wonder why the welfare officer does not check whether the applicant is legal or not. We have an illegal alien in Boston who sued the employer successfully for not paying minimum wages.

- A 25-year-old with 9 children received more than 100,000 per year without working. It is the best get-rich scheme and a best-kept secret. Social security contributes about $8,850 per month for each recipient in the family.
  http://tonyp4idea.blogspot.com/2012/11/making-over-100000-without-working.html

  I did not write this article. It was distributed to me. I hope it is an exception.

- I debated whether this article should be included in a book on investing. Generous welfare benefits dampen our capitalist economy.

- Another subject of debate is whether education improves employment as many college graduates have been unemployed or under-employed for years. A city with well-educated citizens usually has lower crime rates, which is a prime consideration for businesses.

  Judging from bailing out big businesses that are too big to fall, the government seems to be pro-business (it is welfare for the rich). It is good for political campaigns to lay off fewer employees, but it is not good for the economy in the long run.

- Some suggest to raising the minimum wage to $15. Sounds like communism to me.

- Sam sent me this article comparing work and welfare.
  http://blogs.wsj.com/economics/2013/08/19/work-or-welfare-what-pays-more/?mod=trending_now_3

The authors found that in 11 states, "welfare pays more than the average pretax first-year wage for a teacher. In 39 states, it pays more than the starting wage for a secretary. And, in the three most generous states a person on welfare can take home more money than an entry-level computer programmer."

- The USA citizens can be divided into 3 groups according to taxes they're paying:

1. About 40% not paying Federal tax. When this group grows, we will go bankrupt. Representation without taxation is worse than taxation without representation.

2. Middle class (55%). We're being squeezed by the other two groups.

3. The rich 5%. They pay most of the taxes. However, in the last two years, they're fleeing to other places that have low tax treatments. The geese that lay the golden eggs are flying away. Without them, the middle class are squeezed even harder until we're forced to move to the first group and bankrupt the country.

6 How to solve trade imbalance

The U.S.'s wage of $20 per hour cannot compete with the $2 per hour (no matter it is from China, India or Vietnam).

You cannot live with the $2 per hour wage in the U.S. It is easier and better to live on welfare with food stamp, housing subsidies, free health care (in some states) and many other freebies, when your income is low or $0. Our generous welfare encourages our citizens to be lazy and some cheat on the declaration of their incomes. The disability claims excluding veterans from the wars increase substantially in the last decade even our work environment is far safer. It also encourages our citizens not to save.

The solutions are (some are satires):

- Abandon industries that use low-wage labor and / or outsource manufacturing jobs like what Apple is doing.

There is no quality problem with Apple's products that are outsourced to China, so it really depends on the company who outsources and how the product quality checks are conducted. Apple is making good money, paying taxes, hiring top earners and at the same time providing great and affordable products to the world. As of 2012, Apple is the most valuable company in the U.S at least for a brief period.

- Take out the embargo of military products to China at least on the products that China can obtain from other sources such as Russia and some European countries. Currently, it does not serve the purpose of preventing China from becoming a military power and we're losing the sales.

  Why should we be afraid of China when our military might be far, far away from any country on earth? We can sell China missiles with no fear. Just program the missiles to return to the sender when the GPS detects it is heading to our direction. My genius idea just saves us billions of dollars☺.

- Beg China and other countries to loan us more money with states as collateral (by now no one is stupid enough to use the USD and loan us without collaterals) starting with all non-Democratic states first (according to Obama) and Washington, D.C. will be the last to sell. Just a joke☺. As in a capitalist system, if you cannot service you loans, you have to give up your collaterals.

- Selling Alaska back to Russia (with Sarah) for oil is a no brainer. It is just like killing two birds with one stone.

  Selling Hawaii is just genius like selling something we do not own. Most properties in Hawaii are owned by Japanese already.

  If we sold NYC to China, we would make a huge, huge capital gain. It is even more sweet if you recall we bought (cheated is a better word) a good piece of NYC from some native Indians for trinkets. The Indians / Eskimos were Chinese crossing the frozen strait due to losing their direction after too many hot drinks. I have my genes to prove my theory. So, it is the same as selling to the original owner for a huge gain without paying any taxes.

In reality, we sold Manhattan to a casino operator. Wall Street is the biggest legal casino. The only difference is all the hotels are outside the casino. Sell Silicon Valley to China and the rest of California to Mexico (similar to selling Florida to Cuba if they can pay for it).

The only place you cannot get rid of is Washington D.C. No buyer can live with the lazy government servants and politicians fighting each other every day to see who is on top.

It is the similar to the bankers foreclosing your house when you cannot service your mortgage. I hope it will remain as a joke forever.

- Close all trades with all foreign countries but we have to enjoy the $50 toaster that is produced by the U.S. workers! The U.S. is one of the few nations that can close out all foreign trades and survive. However, the movie and music industries will suffer and decline. Boeing will have to park their shiny planes in the desert to collect sand. We will have so much grain in storage that eventually we will have more rats than people.

- Without the rare earths from China, our Apple products will cost double and our missiles will cost us far more. However, it would be good for the world as folks will use their Apple products longer and fewer missiles will be produced.

The chicken feet would be better thrown into ocean instead of shipping them to China for cash.

Technical metrics in market peak, bottom & correction

	SMA-50	SMA-200	SMA-350	SMA50/SMA200	RSI (14)
Market					
Peak		5%	9%	101%	65%
Bottom		-32%	-31%	78%	25%
Correction					

Peak	4%	6%	11%	102%	65%
Bottom	-5%	-6%	-7%	97%	26%
Stock					
Peak					70%
Bottom					30%

Joke

Measure the success in one's life

Contrary to popular belief, your success in life is not measured by how many friends or how many stocks you have. It is measured by: When we die, we're
smart with all toys;
dumb with all toys not upgraded (Disclosure: I've stocks on Apple);
stupid with all money not converted to toys;
genius with all toys being shared with the poor (Gates and Buffett).

7 Potential impact of our trade war with China

As of 7/15/2018, Trump may ask for a forest and settle for a tree. Hopefully it would end the trade war. This article describes what China would react to the full-fledged trade war. Even if there is no trade war, China would prepare herself better for the future.

- China will not meet the demands of the US and cannot counter react effectively.

  The gap of trade deficit is huge. Part of the trade deficit is due to including the component costs (such as the iPhone), not counting the service deficit (Chinese tourism and Chinese attending colleges here) and profits of our companies in China. China's estimate of trade deficit is 60% less than ours.

- China would fall into a recession. I guess it would be brief and mild. Her GDP growth would fall to 5% which is still good for most developed countries.

China's economy depends on her export to the US. It will turn to other partners such as the participants in the "One Belt, One Road" projects, outsource the manufacturing to other countries that have little tariff impact and concentrate more on her huge internal market.

- It would be a blow to China's scheme in cutting internal debt, which has been high and risky.

- China will speed up research and investment on core technologies such as manufacturing of chips. The middle class will suffer except those who involve in core technologies.

- From the ZTE experience, China should weigh more on US supply on core technologies such as chips than tariffs.

Once China masters these technologies in 10 or so years, China can really stand up and say no to us. Today we have about 65% of our science Ph.D. graduates are foreigners with a good percent from China.

China recently ban Micron's memory chip. The world's second fastest computer (after three times number one) is made of CPU chips by China after US banning US CPU chips to China. The world may under estimate China's potential in core technologies. In addition, it is not impossible to buy many components from other suppliers.

- China will continue to attract Chinese who have technical skills to return to the motherland. China will also attract top scientists from all over the world. It is easier than before when research funds in US have been reduced.

- China would have closer partnership with many countries such as Canada while we would be more isolated.

- China will withdraw or at least will not buy more of our Treasuries. It would raise our interest rates and it would have adverse effect on our stock market. The Fed would be forced to buy more.

- China will devalue the yuan. When it has been down by 10% recently, the tariffs would be not as effective as before. It would make her products cheaper and tourists will flood to China. The payback of the loans in USD will be beneficial to China.

- Profits from many corporations will suffer such as Boeing, GM, Ford and companies that supply chips and/or components to China. The stock owners of these stocks will suffer.

- India and many countries will benefit from the trade war. To illustrate, India will be more competitive in farm commodities replacing US export to China due to tariffs.

- US will gain some jobs, but not as much as expected. Many even predicted we will have net job loss. Some jobs will be replaced by robots and some will be lost due to the trade war. Most manufacturing jobs cannot compete with low-wage countries such as Mexico.

- Some of our products depending on imported commodities will cost more to make and hence less competitive. More corporations will move their manufacturing to other countries to minimize the effect of tariffs. Tesla announced opening a plant in China. A motor bike company is moving their production line to S.E. country to benefit for tariff-free among these countries and less tariffs for steel and aluminum. Many other companies will follow.

- Some Chinese imports will be replaced by other low-wage countries. In this case, we gain nothing but our consumers will pay more. It happened before when we banned Chinese tires that were replaced by lower-quality tires at higher costs from other countries.

- Even with the tariffs, some Chinese imports are still competitive to US and/or other low-wage countries. Hence the tariff is a kind of tax added to our consumers.

- China has not used her most powerful chip: rare earth elements. If we ban core technologies such as memory chip to import to China, China will take this ultimate weapon.

- The farmers especially the soybean farmers will voice their discontent against Trump. Trump would not last for another term with the opposition from farmers, Hispanic voters and Obamacare recipients.

- China is waiting for the next political leader replacing Trump and s/he may have different view that is more favorable to China.

Trade war is a loss-loss scenario. In the long run, it would be good for China but bad for the US. In the short run, the reverse would be true.

Even without a trade war, the damages have been done. China will focus on long-term solutions such as core technologies. China will reduce the holding (about $1 trillion) US treasury bonds. The yuan has started to depreciate. We become more isolated from our best partners Mexico, Canada and EU.

I hope the trade war will not materialize and we settle down with cutting at least half of the deficit. But, from whose estimate?

8 Modify our election system

Our voting system works but it has problems that need to be addressed as follows:

1. Reduce campaign money.
   When politicians spend a substantial amount of time fundraising, they have not concentrated their efforts on important issues such as the economy. Gun control was not even mentioned in the last election despite we have constant shootouts. We need to set a limit in the amount of the campaign money they can raise and they can spend. Hence, the presidency is not won by how rich you are and / or your party is, but how you can resolve our problems.

2. Over-promising for votes.
   The last election was so close and the outcome could have been altered by the inclusion of Hispanic votes. The changing of the legal residency status could create many legal welfare recipients to further burden our bankrupting country. If the welfare is so generous, why should they work when they are legalized?

3. Special interest groups.
   The politicians optimize their policy to favor the special interest groups who finance the campaigns. Entitlement recipients belong to another group. They ought to be paid according to how much they have contributed. The social security system was designed for life expectancy less than 70.

   I would include the big businesses in the special interest groups. Via their connections, they had been bailed out many times. In short, it is a conflict of interest.

4. We need to set up a ballot to indicate what percentage of our tax money will go to a specific budget, such as offense, education, etc. Spending too much on one budget would hurt other budgets. I would like to spend less than 2% on offense.

5. Representation without taxation is worse than taxation without representation.

The votes of those who do not pay any Federal taxes, the mentally challenged or those with low IQs, the uneducated, and the criminals should be counted as at most half votes. The votes of all veterans should be counted at least one and a half as they sacrifice their lives for the country. A kind of controversial at first glance!

We have about 50% illiterates in Detroit. The politicians have to satisfy these voters in order to get their votes. It is not hard to predict the collapse of the city. Taxing the rich and giving more to the poor seems to be good deeds similar to Robin Hood. However, businesses cannot function over there and they have options to leave. It is another example that uncontrolled socialism could lead to self-destruction.

The voters are not always right. We had selected Trump, which had no previous experience in politics. He is a businessman. I have to agree with him to move jobs back home, which is a tough job.

6. I suggest the second term of the presidency should be 6 years instead of 4. This is the term that the presidents usually do well for the country to build up his or her legacy without caring about votes for him or her. Today, most second-term presidents have only 1 ½ years to do so.

The following are related to governance but should be discussed during the election.

7. Need to balance the budget. It should be a constitutional law. We cannot pass our debts to the next generation forever. Most states require balancing their budget, why not the Federal government?

8. Need a long debate in the Congress before we can start another war. Most major wars from the Vietnam War to the current two Middle East wars cause most of our financial problems. We are not wealthy enough to be the world's policeman, and fighting for ideology and freedom for other countries. Being #1 or a big brother is not important when our economy is bankrupt and most of our graduates cannot find jobs.

9. Need to encourage the able poor to work and be educated to break the cycle of poverty. There are too many holes and misinterpretation in Clinton's law to force welfare recipients to work.

   (http://en.wikipedia.org/wiki/Personal_Responsibility_and_Work_Opportunity_Act)

10. Need to control government expenses by a smaller and more efficient government and cut frauds such as Medicaid and disability entitlements SSDL. Increasing government employees and assigning them small workloads is reckless consumption.

    To illustrate this, building a road to improve transportation is productive, but defending other countries is consumption (unless the benefits justify).

Afterthoughts

- Why did we shut down the government due to the debt ceiling? Run the government like what businesses do. Calculate the rate of return in the following two options.

    1. Benefit in shutting down the government.
       Or
    2. Benefit in not shutting down the government.

    Select the option that gives us better benefit.

    The majority of government employees have tiny workloads (most got their jobs in DC due to what party they belong to). Furlough (layoff could be better just like most businesses do) half of them and it would maintain the same service if they work in the private sector. A win-win decision.

    Closing all the free museums (say in DC) will cost a lot of pain to tourists and future tourism. Actually it costs more than 10 times of the saved wages in shutting down. Only the stupidest managers make this kind of easy decision.

However, our government makes decisions based on politics: Want to show who is the boss and put the blame on the other party. They are all wasting our time, money and energy. We need to have a smaller and efficient government.

When the problem is resolved (by approving funding or moving the debt ceiling even higher), both sides will declare victory shamelessly on how smart they 'fixed' the problem to insult your intelligence.

- Usually we vote for the candidates we associate with without considering the ideas and the qualifications of the candidates. That is evidenced from the reactions of the O.J. Simpson's verdict from the students of a black college and the students of a white college. This is bad for the country.

#Filler: Ghosts

I have proven there are no ghosts. If there were, the Chinese ghost and the American ghost should act and look the same.

9   The Republican Convention

Why do we need to know Mitt (or any candidate from any political party) is officially nominated or he will accept the nomination in a convention? Who has turned it down in our history? If this is the main purpose of the convention, it is a TOTAL waste of money and time that can be used to deal with our real problems such as how to cut down spending. Isn't it ironic or demonstrating how the big government wastes our money or how big businesses buy influence?

If you really do not know whom will be nominated (I'm shamelessly insulting your intelligence and assuming you have been living in a cave for the last year), just watch the news on TV and save millions.

The convention must be sponsored by airlines, hotels, restaurants and Florida or big businesses / special groups wanting influences. The hidden sponsors are the prostitutes and the drug companies who provide Viagra and condones. They are the winners in this convention, not the handsome Mitt and his lovely wife. All the conventioneers using other folks' money to wine and dine are the free loaders and parasites. Sorry to offend all the politicians and their running dogs.

I like to attend any convention if someone is stupid or rich enough to pay for this unearned but lavish vacation – I'll vote whatever you want me to. Sign me up for any convention, Republican or Democratic, now or in the future. I hope it will be in Hawaii or somewhere without any hurricane and with great and expensive food. You will pay for it eventually one way or another.

I must have some mental problems if I talk to an empty chair with a ghost rocking on it. When you guys laugh at the chair, you might have a more serious mental problem than I. Even with no one sitting on it, the chair still rocks. It symbolizes the do-nothing government could be the best government as it rocks! My point is we need a small, frugal and effective government. The best government is invisible but it provides all the basic services at the least cost!

10 How to solve our economic problems

The United States is still rich and powerful, so the economy should be easier to fix. However, we all have to bite the bullet. Bailing out everyone only buys votes for the politicians and will not help the economy in the longer term. The economy affects everyone and it should not be a political game. Here are some of my thoughts.

- When GE does not pay any tax to the U.S. but to some foreign countries, we've a problem. So are many U.S. companies which should be headquartered in the U.S. instead of in some foreign countries. We've not done enough to lure them back and give them incentive to stay. At least we need to force them to pay taxes on the profits they made in the U.S.

    It is similar to the cruise ship companies. They pay minimal taxes even most are the 'real' headquartered in the USA and most of their customers are USA citizens.

- The rich should pay their fair share of taxes. If we force them to pay more than their share, they will move elsewhere. This is the straw that breaks the camel's back or killing the goose that lays the golden eggs. The top 10% rich folks paid 70% of all Federal tax collected in 2010, up from 55% in 1986.

    More than 40% of the total population did not pay Federal income tax and they received most welfare benefits and entitlements. Our socialist system would bankrupt when it does not have any to give.

- Relax the environmental enforcement on drilling and start the construction of the pipe lines such as the one from Canada. We may have more than enough trapped natural gas for the next 50 years. Now, oil countries are dumping oil to fight off our shale energy. Should we have a new tariff to protect our industry?

- The complicated regulations, religious concerns and the high legal expenses force some drug companies move the research elsewhere. If nothing is being done, I predict Asia will be the center to produce more new drugs in the next decade and we will lose the competitive edge.

- We need to limit the unemployment obligations and the burden of Obamacare to small businesses.

- We should give companies the rich incentives to take risk to start business and new ventures here, or they will invest elsewhere. Investment creates jobs.

- Practice free trade, not protectionism but ensure all partners are playing fairly. All the trade agreements are used to exclude some countries such as TPP against China.

- Protectionism with tariffs will save some jobs initially but will weaken our competitive edge in the long run. Buy the best product from the country that produces it at the least cost. We have to give up some jobs from lower-wage countries. A $20 wage will never compete with a $2 wage. These products from foreign countries would increase our living standard.

- We have to reduce our national debt. Obama saved our market by excessive printing / borrowing. Our children and grandchildren who do not have a voice have to pay for them. Our competitive edge will be reduced for serving our debts instead of investing in infra structure for example.

- There are many ways to balance the budget.

    We need to cut the entitlements. We need to encourage the able poor to work instead of receiving welfare. Why should they work if work means cutting the housing subsidies, food stamp and free health care (in many states including Mass.)?

    We cannot tax the rich to the max. I belong to the middle class and I cannot give up my citizenship, my social security and Medicare that I contributed during my work life. However, the rich can and they even come back to live here as a foreign citizen. It has happened to many high-tax countries and we never learn.

There are many U.S. jobs that are being done by illegal aliens. Check out who pick your lettuce, or empties your waste basket in your office. The poor should take up these jobs instead of fixing up their motor bikes, or watching TV all day long. When we legalize the illegals, will these new residents collect welfare instead of working?

Hiring more employees for government jobs is the most inefficient way to boost employment, as our government is too big already. We can cut down half of them without degrading the services as most are working half of the time already.

We cannot afford the two wars; one war costs us $2 billion a week. Many well-known projects overseas cost about $2 billion each. Why we need a carrier powered by two nuclear generators is beyond my comprehension when we have more weapons to destroy the entire world by pressing a button. Should we solve our problems first such as Detroit before we send soldiers abroad and/or help foreign countries?

All the measures should be executed gradually to avoid the so-called fiscal cliff and related problems in different terms. I'm in IT and now about investing. I do not know much about social science and economy, but they're just common sense.

#Filler: 12 noon is not 12 pm

The Chinese restaurant I went to says they open at 12 am. Are they wrong or the world is wrong?

The next hour from 11 am is 12 am, NOT 12 pm. The one who set it up did it totally wrong and no one complains until now. If I were born earlier, I would have corrected it. If I were born here, I would be the president and every one would have a job by now.

The same if I stayed with the Fed (I actually worked for them briefly and I still had the key to the executive rest room to prove it), we would not have this financial mess today.

Or, if I played for the Celtics (I need two more feet), they would not have a losing season.

11   Implementation

As of 2015, this recession is the longest in my memory. Usually we have recessions that last for two to four years and then we recover. Some recent college graduates have been out-of-work for over four years and many work on jobs that they do not have to go to college for.

It could be due to the failed stimulations, printing too much money and the bailouts that did not fix the root problem. If we did not do the above, there is a better chance for a faster recovery than a deeper recession. Hopefully 2016 will be the year we finally recover, but only time can tell.

We need to let big businesses fall. No one is too big to fall. Let nature take care of itself. If you cheat and / or do not perform, you need to be out of business. It is Business 101 and the fundamental of our capitalist system. Why it is so hard to understand? Why do we need to bail out companies that should fail? Why the greedy CEOs have not gone to jail? Why they were rewarded with bonuses from our bailout money to bring down the companies?

Our problems are easier to fix than they appear to be. I can think of many easy solutions, so the politicians who are hundreds of times smarter than I (or at least make hundreds of times my salary) must have many solutions already.

Identifying the problems and finding solutions are the easy part. However, the implementation is hard, as the agenda of all politicians is simple: Get reelected. They have to satisfy the special interest groups who finance their campaigns and the voters who do not want to bite the bullet. When we have more voters benefitting from welfare and entitlements than the tax payers, we're going to be a welfare state. In addition, big businesses control our government via special interest groups; I call it corruption, American style. When one party takes over the other party after the election, most politicians and their helpers get jobs from the companies that they gave favors to.

12 Solve our deficit problem

We should have a 10% corporate tax, a 3% VAT and extra 2% for luxury goods.

Advantages:
- All the corporate golden geese will not flock back.
- Our dividends will not be taxed twice.
- Corporations will plow back the money for investment and hence ignite employment.
- VAT discourages unnecessary consumption and spending. The 2% surcharge for the rich is fair and simple. The above numbers are arbitrary. We need to set up a budget and require the government to enforce it. If we have excess, we can cut down the income tax that would encourage working.

You may say we do not have money to run the government. It is simpler than expected.
- A small and efficient government.
  If you're one of the lazy government employees surfing the net and waiting for the 4 pm stampede (after the two-hour lunch followed by your nice afternoon lap), you know exactly what I'm talking.
- Why the government employees can retire at almost full pension at the early age (comparing to corporate employees) is just beyond my comprehension.
- Stop being the world police. We've more problems to solve at home.
- Cut down the generous welfare and ask the able to get off the couch. Watching TV all day long for the rest of your life is boring and not good for your health. Remember when we run out of money to give you, the host and the parasite will die together
- Prosecute the welfare and disability cheaters.
- Prevent illegals to come in by prosecuting employers. If there are no jobs, they will not come. We do not need all those fences and patrols.

13 The first sip of coffee

Our politicians are 100 times smarter than I, 100,000 times richer than I, handsomer than I (debatable for most esp. Trump)..., why they always made the wrong decisions? Simple answer. Their agenda is buying votes and mine is for the good of our country. Here are the easy fixes.

* Corporate headquarter exodus. Lower their taxes first.

* Health care problem. Lower the medical expenses first.

* Building border walls like the Great Wall of China. Punish the employers who hire the illegals first.

* Social welfare. Do not punish folks for working and give more welfare to workers than those able welfare recipients. It is similar on how to dissolve multi generation of teen-age mothers.

* Fight terrorism. Understand why they want to be one (patriot for them). Think like one on how to give us maximum pain with the least resources.

* Improve the economy so everyone has a job. Our 'offense' budget is more than the next four countries combined. Unless for our own benefits, do not send soldiers overseas. Today's weapons are missiles and cyber security, so how many soldiers we need?

* If we learn the prediction from the Bible or the endless religious wars, we would not be involved in the Middle East conflict.

Just write down this list at the first sip of coffee. It could be an endless list.

14 Our 4T budget

Our budget for 2020 is 4.7T (1T = 1,000 B). Do we have tax income to cover 4T? As of March 6, 2020 and according to the government budget website, we do not.

Budget projections for FY 2020	As of 3/6/2020
Outlays	$4.7 Trillion
Revenues	$3.6 Trillion
Deficit	$1.1 Trillion
Debt held by the public (end of FY)	$17.8 Trillion

I bet the numbers have not been updated. As of today (4/4/2020), it would be even worse considering the extra $2 T to fight the Coronavirus, the fast-rising unemployment and the reduced tax revenues from businesses and the capital gains in the stock market.

We need to balance the budget to start with. It is irresponsible to borrow money and ask our children and their children to pay for our debts.

With the huge national debts, the status of the reserve currency of our USD is shaken. We know what happened to the United Kingdom when the pound was replaced by our USD as a reserve currency.

Obama saved the stock market, but doubled our deficit in his terms. He satisfied his voters by giving them what they needed. Are we the voters to be blamed? The deficit is important in the long run as we would lose our competitive edge when we have to service the hefty debts. We need to invest in infrastructures, but not in wars.

I propose the following:

1. Add the following in the Constitution. If the president cannot balance the budget, s/he cannot run for the second term.

2. In mid-year, make adjustments to the spending according to the budget / tax income.

Steps to balance the budget:

1. Reduce our burden as a world policeman.
2. Cut down on welfare to ABLE recipients.
3. Cut down on corporate welfare.
4. Prosecute violators such as price gauging by drug companies and disability frauds.

If the U.S. were a corporation, we have bankrupted already.

Link: National debt: https://www.youtube.com/watch?v=1POexHDKoS8

15   Natural disasters

As of 2018, there are two new threats to our economy: trade war with China and natural disaster. China will be discussed in detail in this book and this article is on natural disasters. Momentum investors, take notes and actions.

Hong Kong has no death for the biggest typhoon. Philippines has far more deaths. Indonesia has more than one thousand (could be far higher) deaths. It explains some 'facts':

- The richer the city, the better the preparation.
- Natural disasters are getting more fatal and frequent. Global warming?
- My Coconut Theory. That's why some countries are always poor due to the poor locations that allow disasters to destroy their coconuts.

More on natural disasters
We have less fatalities due to better preparation such as better house construction to withstand typhoons and earthquakes and better predictions. But only in richer cities.

For example, there are few if any wooden houses with no foundations compared to the 50s and 60s in Hong Kong. It would cause many deaths in the last typhoon if they still exit.

For the last two years the world has record-high natural disasters - a statistics that cannot be fake news. Some policy is terrible. Why the government continues to give money to the same destroyed house in the beach front that happens once every 3 years?

The impacts of constant flooding and constant droughts cannot be avoided but can be reduced if we devote more of our resources here than fighting endless wars. The recent disaster in Florida makes Hog Kong's worst typhoon a child's play.

Global warming
The recent natural disasters may be caused by global warming. The warmer water and warmer air pass the energy to storms. The melting of the poles give rise to sea levels.

Better to believe it and take actions than ignoring global warming.

There are many we can do.

1. Reduce carbon gas. Live in a smaller house to save energy to heat and cool the house. Wear more clothes instead of turning up the heat Use public transportation and/or drive energy efficient cars.
2. Protect the environment. We need to repair rather than buy new stuffs such as iPhone and cars.
3. Build sea wall.
4. Control flooding.
5. Do not build houses next to the ocean unless they're safe.

Fillers
Tibet today
Watched a travel show on Tibet. Tibet's living standard has been at least doubled after the train. It has made everything cheaper to import to Tibet and has attracted a lot of tourists. I bet the 'liberation' is good for Tibet. They do not have one-child policy and children can go to school.

Wheel of Fortune
My late mom was a big fan of the show even she did not know English. It is the biggest compliment to the show.

Charity donations
In lieu of flowers, I donated. Why they asked me for the phone number? Use 1234 for the last 4 digits if it is a requited field to enter.
Chow Yun Fat, the star in Crouching Tiger and Hidden Dragon, donated most of his money to charities and leads a frugal life style. Great Mr. Chow (not Mr. Fat).

I should not mock at Buffett's income taxes as he had donated most to charities too. His foundation uses money more wisely and effectively than the government. Two thumbs up!

16   Bad business practices

I have so many bad experiences recently. I bet their competitors do the same, so I do not want to show the names of the offending companies if I have an option.

- My car problem.
  I could not take the key from my ignition switch all the time. It is a new car from one of the two major Japanese car manufacturers. They honestly acknowledged it was a common problem for my model. After several unsuccessful fixes and giving me goodies such as free oil change, I called the service manager and yelled at him it was THEIR problem not mine.

  Finally, it was fixed with a solenoid costing about $5. What a waste of time, theirs and mine. This customer will not be happy and they still have to spend the $5 plus the oil change and all the free apples I can pocket. I still have not received my customer satisfaction survey.

- I received a letter from my one of my funds asking me to respond so it will not be treated as an abandoned property. The checks of the dividends and the capital gains must have been cashed by a ghost. I responded by closing the account. My daughter closed her brokerage account. She had 14 cents. After more than 10 years, she still received monthly statements!

- I was lured to another cable company for their generous offer. I asked my current cable company to match the same deal and they refused. I switched. Since then and 5 years later, I still received their junk mails offering better offers I cannot 'refuse'. Cut down many trees in the process.

- My Sunday paper raised the price to $5. It is a dying industry as I got all my news from TV and the web. I quickly cancelled my subscription. Since then, they have left many messages and sent me junk mails almost once a week. If they did not raise the price, I would have stayed with them. Try to squeeze the last milk from a dying cow.

- I had a reader telling me to improve my writing style. I asked him whether he followed the book's techniques to accumulate cash before the correction in August, 2015. He did not and he was supposed to be a keen business man. Wrong objective for buying a book on investing!

- My 'favorite' charity called me 8 times for donations. I will not donate via them again. I hate to be disturbed during dinner. So are all the phone calls from politician calling for votes and I do not vote for any of them.

- My printer needs replacement of inks at least once every 3 months even I seldom use it. I will never buy anything from that company.

- The 'new and improved' upright washers are problem-prone. My old ones never need repair for over 10 years. So are Yahoo!'s new 'improved' systems. So is Microsoft's Solitaire – why the 'improved' system takes many times longer to load as they expect players also own Xbox. They all lose contact with their own products/customers or their stupid management tells them to do so.

- I want to know how all the three market indexes, oil and gold are doing at least once a day. One major financial web site now 'hides' this information in order to show their programmer can do a fancy job without caring what the customer wants. For me, just switch to another web site.

- I almost missed my connecting flight to Boston in Toronto. First, why I have to clear custom in a foreign country? Second, why the old process took minutes and this one takes almost an hour. The designer must have to change the system so s/he can hire more employees or just had too many drinks during lunch.

- One luxury hand bag company takes out the logo on their bags which is why their customers pay premium. One company name is hard to spell and remember by their potential major customer Chinese.

- Volkswagen, Wells-Fargo and Samsung are recent examples. They all want to be number 1 and end up last. The first two can fool us sometimes, but eventually their misbehaviors will come back to harm them. Samsung should have tested their phone longer. Most companies want to rush their products to the market in order to compete without all the testing; what happens to beta test and alpha test that are taught in colleges.

- Usually I stay away from retail stocks including the rising Amazon. I expected Coach and some luxurious retailers would have a tough time. Partly due to the falling Chinese economy. Partly due to not understand their own market. Chinese buy a lot of these stuffs. If you do not believe me, go to these stores in NYC, Paris…, you can see them buying a lot to avoid paying tariff and help them to boost their social standing.
  When they take out the logo, they make their products not sellable to Chinese as many Chinese (esp. those to be impressed) do not know English well.

- Costco was sued. If you look at the marketing departments of most big companies, you can see many good-looking young kids. Most do not have common sense and lack of experience. At least hire a good one to manage them and in this case it is logical to be sued.

- Boeing's management made a wrong decision by not building a new plane from scratch 10 years ago. They wanted to squeeze more profits from a plane designed for 1969 or so. The current engine is too heavy and too big for the body. The software system tries to compensate the problem but it is not bullet proof. At least they should have included the extra safety sensors as part of the basic package.

- Why 'smart' companies including Staples and Home Depot failed in China? They do not understand the local culture to start. Staples sold chairs that are fit for the large Americans but not the smaller Chinese. Most Chinese live in apartments and most hire cheap labor to remodel their houses.

#Filler: Kings of California

Due to its huge size, California should be broken up into two countries. The South and the North are quite different - some laws worked in the South do not work in the North. I will assign Trump to the South to fight the nasty Mexicans and myself to the North to enjoy all the wine and fresh air/water LOL.

17   Victims of our own success

We are the victims of our own success. The workers have to be protected with regulations and higher wages, so is our environment. Citizens spend more time in enjoying life; basically we consume rather than invest. The fixes are not too hard. To start with, we should cut down our military expenses and divert them into infrastructure projects and education. Here are some actual examples.

San Francisco. Even with the highest minimum rate ($15 per hour), it is impossible to rent a small apartment without sharing. As a result, they have a lot of homeless folks and many of them have a job or two. Due to the lack of rest room facilities, the entire city smells.

TSMC. The recent example is why TSMC, a Taiwan chip foundry, would not make financial sense for them to build a factory in U.S., as the Japanese auto companies have been doing for years.

First, it is expensive to build a factory in U.S. due to the labor cost, material cost and the insurance. We waste a lot of money in suing each other, and the non-productive lawyers make out like bandits. Our health care delivery system is one of (if not) the most expensive in the world.

The infrastructure is deteriorating. Check out the problems of the Tesla factory just moved to Texas. Our leaders care about 4-year reelection.

The skilled labor is small. The work morale is low. In addition, they have to deal with unions. In Taiwan or similar countries, you have a strong team of technical support. Even with all the tax incentives, taxes are still high with the rising labor cost.

Education. 50 years ago, we had a lot of scientists and engineers with a lot of achievements. Today, we depend on foreigners. You can find Chinese and Indians in high-tech companies. Many with advanced degrees are foreigners. We encourage students to go to good-income professionals such as lawyers and financiers. When we cut down H-1 visas to these folks, we will not be competitive in these fields. In the other end, we have missed millions of students due to lack of remote facilities and laptops for remote learning during this pandemic.

18 National debt and USD

If you believe we should receive more free money from the government during this pandemic, think again. It is the tool that has been used by our government to buy votes for decades, as well as many foreign governments today.

Our government prints more money to buy our national debts. We have printed 20% of USD in 2020. As of 3/7/2021, the Senate passed the bill to print another 1.9 T (many zeroes after $). Do the individuals making $75,000 need the aid? Obviously it is used to buy future votes. That is why our national debt has been sky rocketed. The poor should be helped for sure. However, the wealth of the rich has been increased substantially due to the rise of the stock market. It also reflects that we have plenty of free cash that are being invested in the stock market. It is a very unhealthy sign that the market rises while the economy is falling.

It is the same as in 2009. However, the economy did pick up and the debts were quite manageable. This time could be very different. Our children and grandchildren have to pay for the debts. When we have to service the debts, we will not be competitive in global markets. It is easy to pass the blame to China.

This is NOT the major problem. The major problem is the confidence of our USD as a reserve currency is shaken. The "supply and demand" rule works again. When we have too many USD circulating, we should have inflation. When one USD can buy only half a loaf of bread and previously we could buy the full loaf, we are in trouble. Foreigners would dump the reserve USD that are used for trading and our treasury bills they own. With today's internet and financial systems, it could happen in a day or even less.

USD is not backed up with gold today. Most likely, there will be new USD issued to replace the old one with one-to-ten, and then even higher. But, it is not helping us. In the 50s, the British pound was replaced by USD as the reserve currency after WW2 and at that time many British colonies became independent.

Today, USD has been challenged. We gave Iran a tough time for not using USD in trading oil. So are Russia and China. I sincerely hope the USD would not be weak or valueless in my lifetime. I can tell inflation has come. When all the foreign central banks dump the USD, the market would drop and the long-term depression would begin. From many internet articles, China's national debt to GDP in 2021 varies from 65% to over 300%. I do not know whom should we trust. However, China government owns most of the land and they invest in infrastructure rather than our financial assets and welfare to all.

Link: Fiat currency: https://www.youtube.com/watch?v=bgPDW0ZpgJU

19   Evidences of our fall

Unfortunately, many of our problems are showing up. We need to fix them now before it is too late. They are:

- Texas freezing. Many do not have electricity and water for a long while. Many have their electric bills over several thousands. It is the evidence of our infrastructure is falling.
- Our ability to control forest fires and other potential disasters is questionable.
- Pandemic. We have one of the top countries with highest deaths from this pandemic. We are supposed have the best health care delivery.
- We have record national debt, and the reserve status of USD is shaken.
- Our wealth gap has been widened in this pandemic. The stock market has been rising (as of 2/2021), while we have serious unemployment.
- We have too many homeless and beggars in any big cities in U.S. I tried to find one beggar in China unsuccessfully; I was told the beggars use QR code. If there are beggars in China, they are professional beggars making good money, or their wives kick them out for drinking too much LOL. Our government and the media lie so badly to brainwash us.
- In 2021, we had higher trade deficit with China than last year. When China fixes their chip problem, we would lose our huge export of chips to China.
- Our alliance with German and some other EU countries is not as close tie as before.
- We have not ended our participation in the wars in Middle East. We use our military force to enforce the concept of Petro Dollar.
- The capital rampage indicates that the country is deeply divided.
- "Black life matters" and racial shooting indicates that our racial discrimination problem still exist.

We just have too many problems our government has to deal with. We can start by cutting the huge military expenses and concentrate our efforts towards our own citizens. Blaming China for all our ills are not the answer to fix the problem.

20 Why I am so optimistic about the U.S.

China may have passed up in GDP with adjustments to buying power, but China is far behind us in GDP per capita, which is more important in living standard.

The ending of the Afghan war have stopped a big hole in burning money. If we do not start another war (wishful thinking), we can divert our resources into our economy, education, infrastructure and many social/politics issues.

We are still number one in many areas. However, do we need to be #1? The cooperation with China would bring us better living standard and a better world. I estimate the world can move to caron neutral 5 years earlier if the two countries share their technologies on green energy. Due to the rising wages in China and our sanctions, many factories have been moved to low-wage countries such as S.E. Asia, Africa and India. Most of these countries are similar to China 30 years ago, when the environment was not the prime reason.

It is not possible to move manufacturing back to the U.S. due to our high living standard. This is the benefits of free trade and the reason why our corporations (so are our citizens) enjoy the rewards in the last decades. We need to help those who have lost their jobs. We are #1 in farming, energy, finance, software… China needs to trade as she lacks many resources.

Our culture, global economic systems and language help us in many ways. For example, China can attract overseas Chinese to return home to advancing the country, while we can attract the best from all over the world. Ironically, it includes the top Chinese scholars and scientists from the best Chinese universities. They enjoy better research/jobs, better education for their children and better environment including food safety and pollution. The number of spies may be insignificant compared to the rest of foreigners here.

Every country has her problems. We have wasted too much energy in politics, particularly the unity of our country. We still have problems in gun control, wealth gap, inflation and the recent pandemic. All are fixable. China has her own that does not affect me, so I skip most in this book. With our resources, we can self-contained with a lower living standard, while China cannot.

Do not let your dumb nationalism cover your eyes. I do not expect that you will agree with everything discussed in this book due to different cultures and viewpoints. Just use your wisdom to decide which one is right or wrong.

Section IV: China

The politicians cannot fix our problems and use China as a convenient scapegoat. Many newspapers / magazines and TV stations (excluding Wall Street Journal, New York Times, Washington Post and 60 Minutes) want to sell their stuffs by giving what you want to hear / see by twisting the facts.

As a Chinese American, I am naturally biased (so are most of you) but I'll not let my dumb nationalism cover my eyes or yours. There are Chinese bashers and U.S. bashers who do not convince us as they're not using facts. They promote distrust and confrontation that I try to avoid.

There are always two sides of any story as illustrated in the next two chapters on human rights. I posted them in many forums and score some points for China. I hope you agree on the facts and let me know what are not true if you find any.

The two chapters followed demonstrate China is more a victim than an aggressor in its recent history. Actually Chinese have not been an aggressor during the entire, long history unless you include Mongolia as part of China. The kingdom has been rich until the last 250 years and that is why they built the Great Wall to keep aggressors away from stealing their wealth.

The recent wars with Vietnam and India are not that recent and are quite brief. China has lost many territories to Russia, India (on the boundary line drawn by Britain who governed India then) and other countries. Tibet is controversial with its long historical relationship with China. Mongolians once ruled China in the Yuan Dynasty and Russia wanted part of it to be independent to set up a buffer zone.

Most of us are biased due to our cultures and the way we are raised. Depending on your background, you should not agree with everything I wrote, but hopefully read the following articles with an open mind. If I step over the line, drop me a line for future updates in the web site http://ebnation.blogspot.com. Fair enough?

These chapters obviously defend China, but I use facts to the best of my knowledge. If I write another book on similar topic, I will write it for

Chinese audience in Chinese and defend America. My purpose is to help the two nations to understand and respect each other and nothing else.

Links

China:	http://en.wikipedia.org/wiki/China
Tibet:	http://en.wikipedia.org/wiki/Tibet
Boundary:	http://en.wikipedia.org/wiki/McMahon_Line
Yuan Dynasty:	http://en.wikipedia.org/wiki/Yuan_Dynasty

The following articles give you an overview of China.

1 Brief comparison: China vs. US

We can understand the two countries better by comparing the basic information such as economy. Most data are estimates from 2017 numbers from CIA and other sources. The world rank may be appended.

	USA	China
Population	326 M (#3)	1.38 B (#1)
GDP (ppp)	$19 T (#2)	$23 T (#1)
Per capita	$57 K (#20)	$15 K (#106)
Military expense	$611B (3.3%)	$216 B (1.9%)
Combat aircraft	3,318 (twice)	1,500
Physicians per 1,000	2.3 (52% more)	1.5
Life expectancy	79	75
Crime level	56 (#30) 3 times more	22 (#83)
Land	3.8 sq. miles	3.7 sq. miles
Arable land	174 million hectares (69% more)	103

USA is #1 in GDP but not GDP (ppp), which stands for Purchase Power Parity. China is improving her economy, hence reducing the gap in GDP per capita. I estimate China's GDP per capita in 2018 is $16,500.

USA is richer in resources and arable land and shared by fewer citizens.

Links: 1

2 Worthy notes on China

Here are some common confusion / pointers for non-Chinese readers:
- For illustration purposes, China's population is 1.3 billion (actually 1.375 B in 2018). However, Chinese would tell you it is 13 billion. Our system is more rational by having a term for every three zeros such as thousand, million, billion and trillion. Chinese has a term for 10,000 and it has merit as 10,000 is a popular unit.
- China is officially named as "People's Republic of China" as the name "Republic of China" has been taken by Taiwan. Chinese like to add "People's" in many other names. Some Chinese think "People's" is better but in reality not necessarily.
- China's currency is Yuan (translated as "dollar"). Renminbi is translated as "People's money". They are exactly the same.
- Chinese use metric system. Chinese have the convention of "Last Name" first such as "Chen John".
- Do not be surprised if a Chinese asks you how much you are making. It is a cultural difference.
- Many Chinese behave badly in public but it has been improving especially with the educated citizens/students residing in the West/U.S.
- Do not talk about the sensitive topics especially in China such as Tiananmen Square incident and the Hong Kong riot. The actors learned it the hard way and so is the NBA guy. When they are blacklisted by China, the organization they represented would lose a lot of incomes from China.
- As of 2019, Google and Facebook are not available in China. Some use a simple trick to get away – not recommended.
- "Four" sounds like "death" in Chinese so it is not a good number. "Giving clock" is meaning "going to a funeral". Hence, do not give your Chinese friends a clock.
- When you want to be successful in running a business in China, you need to know the culture and the language, or hire someone who knows.
- "Three" sounds like "live" in Chinese. "Eight" sounds like "getting rich" so both are good numbers.
- Observe Chinese Feng Shu if you want to sell your house to Chinese.

 # Filler: Understand and accept cultures, traditions... different from ours

It is the first step to alleviate discrimination. I was surprised that my friend reacting her Indian friends eating with fingers and cleaning up with another hand. Chinese are discriminative even among Chinese from different regions in China.

Some Chinese made a lot of money in selling their village land. Most are not educated and behave very poorly in public. Unfortunately, they give a poor image of Chinese when they travel outside China. Some poor behavior is due to the loss of education during the Culture Revolution. However, the younger Chinese have been improving in this area especially those who study aboard.

Huawei
In a report in 2021, Huawei is not even in the top 3 in phone business. They should still be profitable in setting up 5G network and collecting royalties in their 5G patents. Once China fixes this bottleneck, U.S. chip companies will be worried.

#China's problems
There are still a lot of problems to be fixed, and some have been fixed such as poverty alleviation and corruption. Chinese should invest more in the stock market than the real estate that has created ghost buildings. These are their internal problems, and we the outsiders do not understand. We have to fix our own problems before interfering with others' problems such as constant gun shootings, deplorable infrastructure, pandemic, homeless folks and panhandlers.

Filler: Fact or not
The USA never wants to adopt the metric system. It is mainly due to the love of our football game which uses yards. 0.9 meter does not sound right, right? At one time, when two identical missiles were fired between here and Russia, the Russian missile would arrive here earlier due to no extra calculation to convert to metric values. It is not true now as the CPU is super-fast today.

3   China and communism

China is not practicing communism today as communism does not allow her citizens to set up shops. China is group ruled, so it is not ruled by a dictator. It is single party. Chinese has restricted freedom. Chinese can travel and study aboard. Chinese can set up shops.

The current system is a central system and is controlled by a handful of directors such as our board of directors in our corporations. The directors have experiences and the smartest politicians. They do not care about short-term gains but long-term gains for the country. The country is less divided as the decisions are made from the top.

The first advantage is the smooth transition of power and hence better political stability. The second major advantage is not wasting campaign money, which is supplied by special-interest groups such as the NRA. In addition, they do not waste time in arguing with each other as our two-party system does. We had wasted a lot of time in impeaching Trump, even they knew it was not possible. All land is owned by the government and it makes many infrastructure projects such as high-speed rail easier.

If they change CCP to CSP (S for socialism), it would be more appropriate and avoid many naïve criticism. The membership of CCP provides the Chinese many privileges such as admitting to good universities and jobs. Most smart students try to get the membership.

Communism eliminates the wealth gap. The major fault is it does not encourage folks to work hard as everyone is paid the same. It sounds like our unions but in a larger scale.

Today China still cannot be an efficient democratic country as it requires the majority of her citizens to be fairly educated. U.S. is far more educated for decades. However, today we have more free loaders than in past decades. They fight for more freebies and the politicians have to buy votes from this group.

All political systems have their advantages and disadvantages. We waste a lot of time and resources in our two-party system. To illustrate, Trump wants to abolish some of the systems / agreements set up by the previous president such as Obamacare and several international treaties. Trump should fix any holes in the system instead of redoing the entire system. India is another bad example of the democratic system.

There are many disadvantages too. My grandfather was a land owner and he suffered a lot when communism took over. When the central government makes a mistake, the whole country suffers. The sad examples are the Big Famine (1950) and the Cultural Revolution.

I blame the leaders at the time, not the political system. Deng took over and opened up China. China has grown from a third-world country close to a first-rated country in 40 years. The world has never seen this fast growth in this scale. The next 40 years would bring them to be at least with par to the rest of the world and hopefully in a peaceful way.

Today with few exceptions, no Chinese starves to death. A government that can provide the basics such as food, shelter and clothing is a good government no matter what political system she has. The basics are far ahead of freedom. Few starving men really care for freedom. Compared to 40 years ago, freedom in China has grown by leaps and bounds.

All political systems have their strengths and weaknesses. Every country should adopt their governance system to how far the country is developing and her current situations. There are only **two governances: good and bad**.

China has a bad governance in 1950-1960; that is why some Chinese hate communism. However, China has been a good governance since 1970. China has to compare herself today to 10 years ago. China should not compare herself with countries in the west. The closest country to compare is India with similar population and similar financial conditions when they started their countries in 1940s. China is far better than India, a democratic system. Most Chinese compare China with U.S.A., while India compares herself with China.

Links
China's political structure.
https://www.youtube.com/watch?v=kd6_6nKSMmQ

Communism and capitalism
https://www.youtube.com/watch?v=4eUS8trd_yI&list=WL&index=1

4 China's politics and recent leaders

From Wikipedia:

"The **politics of the People's Republic of China** takes place in a framework of a semi-presidential socialist republic run by a single party, the Communist Party of China. State power within the People's Republic of China (PRC) is exercised through the Communist Party, the Central People's Government and their provincial and local representation. The Communist Party of China uses Internal Reference (zh-tw) to manage and monitor internal disagreements among the citizens of People's Republic of China.[1][2] Document Number Nine was circulated among the Chinese Communist Party in 2013 by Xi–Li Administration to tighten control of the ideological sphere in China to ensure the supreme leadership of the Communist Party will not be challenged by Western influences.[3][4][5] The PRC only controls mainland China, Hainan island, Hong Kong, Macau and some South China Sea islands."

To me, China is "Socialism with Chinese characteristics". The government is authoritative. The elected president is controlled and decided by a handful of her communist members. The president is elected every 5 years with two terms maximum (being changed). The following presidents are most influential to China.

The presidency of Xi may have more than 10 years. Xi has been doing great jobs for China and the world too. If it does not break, why fix it?

Uncle Deng opened up China after US played China card against Russia and took out the embargo. He had lifted millions from starving. He deserved a Nobel Peace prize more than many including Obama.

Mao was a great revolutionist but promoted to a poor governor with the disasters of "Big Leap Forward" and "Cultural Revolution". History may not be kind to his legacy.

5 A simplified history of China

China has dominated the world for 16 (some say 15 and some say 17) of the last 20 centuries. It was too tough for me to learn Chinese history in high school. The best way to answer questions in exams is to memorize some important figures and guess all the way. Dynasty rises and falls either due to foreign invasions or revolutions.

China has influenced the world in last 20 years and will continue so in the next decades. As investors, we need to understand China at least with the basic concepts.

It has 5,000 years of civilization. For simplicity, I divide it into 3 periods: 1. Before the first emperor of China, 2 all the dynasties after and 3. Opium Wars and WW2.

I skip Mao's period and China today. There are so many articles on it.

1. Before the first emperor. It would be about 3,000 years. It is amazing how Chinese discovered bronze and how advances are their civilization compared to other civilization such as Egypt and Roman.
2. All the dynasties.
   I would compare the first Emperor to Roman Empire.
   The Yuen were set up by Mongolians and Qing by Manchurians In modern China, Chinese declared them as part of the 50 minorities. In a way, they were not foreigners.

   Tang Dynasty was the most advanced compared to the rest of the world.
3. The two current important recent events Opium Wars and WW2 will be described in the next two chapters

The Chinese history has been well documented. Even over 2,000 years ago, they had a court historian to record the daily important events. First they're carved on bamboos and then on paper. Thanks to the first emperor, the written Chinese language is about the same as today's traditional Chinese. Many terms and names have to be explained due to the changing names for officials, cities, etc.

This article is intended to be my casual introduction of Chinese history with all the links for further study. The next chapters will describe why China declined after the Opium Wars and their problem with Japan. I wrote these articles in my own personal experiences but links are provided on the actual historical events.

Click the link for YouTube on China.

Filler: A nightmare?

I got a call from Buffett asking me to lead their stock research.
I asked him why for a nobody; you may be asking the same question. No kidding.

He told me that he should have read my book Scoring Stocks to buy Apple instead of IBM in May, 2013. It would save his company millions of dollars minus $10 for my book. Not to mention the market timing technique that had worked in the last two major market plunges.

I told him, "OK, I'll beat your mediocre returns of the last 5 years."
He said, "You can do better than that and at least beat SPY. If you do so, no one will be that stupid to leave my fund and pay the hefty capital gain taxes."

I told him, "I cannot beat the market as you are the market especially after your expensive fees. In addition, I do not know how to avoid day traders from riding my wagon in trading. Also most of my big profits were made in small stocks that your fund cannot trade besides owning the company."

I woke up trembling. I'm glad it is only a nightmare.

6 China, the human rights lover?

Agree that you find it contradictory by the title of this article. Hopefully at the end of this article you agree with me more. With an open mind, please read on.

Human rights have priorities: Food, Shelter, Clothing, Job, Freedom... China in the last 30 years have lifted millions from starving to death. From 1950 to 1961, millions starved to death during the big [famine](). Today, very, very few starve to death in China. For this alone Deng deserved a Nobel Peace Prize, but instead Obama got one for doing nothing.

Compared to U.S. and many European countries, China is not up to their standard, which was set up by them. However, comparing China 40 years ago, freedom in China has grown by leaps and bounds.

China does not afford to have the same freedom as the West as it is still not a fully-developed country. To illustrate this, China does not have the resources to have a similar trial on O.J. Simpson. Even he was found guilty, a two-cent bullet is far cheaper than the [$31,000]() USD per year per inmate in the USA.

China has strict laws and punishment, where the West would find China violating the prisoners' human rights. You are only right if you ignore the rights of the victims.

When there are CCTVs everywhere, the West would find China violating the citizens' privacy rights. The potential crime committers would think twice if they realize they could be caught easily and they would have to hide for the rest of the lives. When there is automatic death sentence to rape an under-aged kid, do they still commit this crime such by Epstein in the U.S.?

Social [Credit]() System is another way to cut down riots and protests. For a wealthy country, riots and protests are needed to remind the government on injustice. China will reach this eventually.

Most Chinese do not care about being watched by the government. It could be due to different culture. Most Chinese do not want to fight against the government as their living standard has been improved substantially in the last 30 years. Most Chinese are busy making money. In addition, they cannot possibly fight and win as evidenced by the last time they rioted against the government. China has been enjoying a very stable society for decades.

Most Chinese feel safe in public places such as cinemas and schools. Gun control is a violation of individual rights here. Is constant shooting not a human rights violation?

We want other countries to follow our standard and our culture. It does not always work especially in the poorer countries. If your country does not follow our standard, we and our allies will isolate / embargo your country. China has a non-interference clause and does not force any country to follow their ideals. For example, China does not force any country to join their "One Belt, One Road" projects.

China does not practice communism as communism does not allow individuals to set up stores. The major fault of communism is discouraging her citizens to work hard. All political systems have faults and advantages. Our fault is the constant arguing from the two political parties. During the recent impeachments, the politicians had wasted a lot of time and effort that should be directed to improve our country.

Even rich countries such as U.S., we have a lot of homeless folks and many live from paycheck to paycheck. Both countries are facing the problem of wide wealth gap (a human rights to me). But, China has been working hard via the governance's actions for years. I do not agree moving the poor to the cities to solve this problem.

Racial discrimination exists in both countries. When I was in China, I could tell the cultures of minorities were maintained. There is no 'one-child policy' for minorities in China.

China should put higher priorities in public heath, clean air, clean water and safety regulations. Unfortunately, freedom of speech has been tightened a little recently.

7 Currency manipulation

First, no country including the U.S. has the right to tell other countries to appreciate or depreciate their currency. The era of 'you are either my puppet or my enemy' is long past and our politicians are still living in this past. They blame China for all our ills, since they cannot fix our problems.

Keeping the Yuan low actually helps the U.S.'s consumers and the U.S. in buying wind turbines or high-speed rails from China at lower prices. The U.S. also depreciates its currency to lessen their loan burden from foreign countries. This would not be prudent if the foreigner's currency depreciates at the same time. When our government prints money at the current rate, it is our way to manipulate currency especially the USD is the reserve currency.

Japan did not work well with the appreciation of the Yen in the late-1980s as advised by the USA. Why should China follow this bad advice? China does not want (or cannot) to withdraw the bad loans, as it does not want to kill the goose that lays the golden eggs.

The major products of China (mainly low-cost consumer products) and U.S. (mainly farm products and high-tech products) do not compete with each other. If we do not buy these products from China, most likely we'll buy the same products from Mexico, India, or any other numerous countries with low-labor costs.

China's rise in last 30 years is due to many factors that have nothing to do with currency manipulation:

1. The U.S. took out the trade embargo from China when the U.S. played the China card against Russia.

2. Deng Xiaoping's economic reforms.
   http://en.wikipedia.org/wiki/Deng_Xiaoping#Economic_reforms

3. The bitter lessons Chinese learned from the Opium Wars to WW2. It bankrupted China and led to the last two centuries of humiliation. They understand that if they are not strong economically and militarily, they will suffer from same oppression.

Now, the U.S. may play the India card against China. However, China and the U.S. are not enemies on day one with minor exceptions during the Opium Wars / Boxer Rebellion, Korean War and Vietnam War.

Until China builds up its local market for its growing middle class, I do not see the Yuan appreciating by more than 5% a year but I never say 'never'. The current problem of high inflation in China is partly due to the pegging its currency with the USD. The peg is loose now and the Chinese should accelerate to do so when the local market is more important and has been fully developed.

A strong China is good for the world including the U.S.! As part of the global economy, there are other players, such as research / high tech companies from the West and the U.S., oil from Middle East and Africa, and commodities from Australia, Brazil, etc. Free trade benefits everyone including the consumers in all countries. When one country is weak, all others will be affected.

Our president and his advisers can do a lot of good if they looked longer-term (more than four years). To give generous welfare to buy votes and creating jobs for the lazy government servants are definitely not good for the country. Have we learned from California or Greece? The QE1, QE2, and the coming QEn are depreciating the USD. Are we ignorant and arrogant hypocrites to blame China on exactly the same practice we're doing?

It was an error that the U.S. and other countries asked China to change the value of the Yuan during SE Asia crisis. China is not that dumb to fall in the same trap that made Japan's economy suffer in the last two decades when they followed the U.S.'s advice.

8 Rare earth elements

Note. This article was written in 2011 when many wanted to invest in rare earth mines outside China. As of 2016, this article served as a good warning. From one of my readers:

"it was you that warned folks to get out of Molycorp(MCP), thank you, and today it's bankrupt and shutdown but they're loaded with rare earth elements for which China undercut and killed the market for causing them to BK."

China has the right to reduce the rare earth export to its advantage. It is similar to how OPEC controls its oil exports. China has grown for the benefit of the world trade and economy at the expense of its own environment. China did not consider the cost to repair the damage of its own environment in its reckless growth.

The top layer of earth is hard to replace after it has been mined. The vast amount of water in mining should be recycled and/or controlled. Both damage its environment severely.

Doesn't China have the right to restrict the rare earth elements exportation?

China uses the rare earth as a weapon against the dispute with Japan and/or other countries. Despite the mutually beneficial trade, Japan has been brutal to China particularly during WW2 and has not admitted its wrong doings.

With the restrictions of the importing weapons from the U.S., should China do the same in restricting the rare earth elements that are needed in some U.S. weapons?

Rare earth minerals are available in many parts of the world. They are not mined extensively due to the cost and the irreversible environmental damages. China ought to care for its own environment and charges its minerals as much as the market can bear; it is a free market after all.

All the companies in mining these minerals will enjoy appreciation in the short term as long as they can get permit to open such damaging mines. As of 2011 (this article was written and has been updated since then), it is the riskiest investment by now as we do not know what China's next move is.

Chinese want to use this strategy to improve foreign direct investment and take advantage for its industries that use these rare earths like hybrid cars and turbines. The WTO cannot accuse China in limiting export of these rare earths as there is no such precedent. Sometimes we accuse China of product dumping and now we accuse of China not dumping rare earths. How ironic!

China will and should charge these rare earths at 10% below the closest competitors. If they are more than 10% less, the local governments will step in to protect their industries and/or take actions.

As of 2011, China has at least two years before these foreign mines are ready. [Note: As of 8/2012, some new mines on rare earth minerals are ready to be mined outside China. However, with the global recession, they're not profitable.] By then, China will decide the prices again based on whether they want to capture the rare earth market and/or their products that use these rare earth elements.

To summary, China should limit the rare earth element export and price them as high as the market can bear. **I would avoid betting on rare earth elements by foreign miners as they are too risky and it depends on China's policy.**

Update 11/2015. This article was written several years ago when investors flocked into miners for rare elements outside China. If you've read this article and acted accordingly, you would have saved a lot of money and even more if you shorted these miners as many of them were bankrupted.

9 Environment

Recently there have been a lot of discussions on China's rapid development, industrialization, increased pollution and destruction of environment such as deforestation.

China, as a developing country, can do so much in protecting the environment. Jobs are more important than the environment, but by now it should be the other way round. China has done its share so far. It is unfair to say China is the world polluter #1 or #2. You need to take out pollution due to the production of goods for export. Then, you calculate the pollution per capita. From this calculation, the U.S. is #1 and China is way, way down. Per capita basis and after deducting pollution due to export, China pollutes less than 1/4 of ours. Here are developments and facts about the environment in China:

- China is #1 or #2 in most renewable energy such as solar, hydro and wind energy. Actually China has turned itself from nothing to pioneer in many of these areas by heavy investment in research. In most areas, it is the lowest priced producer. It would have benefitted the world more if its products are allowed to compete freely with local products.

- China is blessed with coal, but lacks oil resource. Coal generates heat via burning the carbon. It can never be clean even with the best technology from the West/U.S., which can improve less carbon monoxide and acid-rain-causing SO_2.

- The better quality of coal is in the north east. Transporting coal from this area to urban cities adds pollution. It is more effective using barges in coastal regions and the cities on the banks of the main rivers such as Yangtze.

The current grid to distribute energy in China is primitive at best. It needs a lot of technology from the West/U.S. plus its own development to exploit and copy / enhance the technology. Grid technology 'Made in China' is idealistic, but it is a long way to catch up with the state-of-the-art technology.

- Hydro and nuclear generators when strategically located would cut down the grid dependency and transportation of coal to certain regions.

  A wind farm in Mongolia had been idle for a long while due to it was not connected to the grid. Hope it will not happen again with better planning.

- China's nuclear generation program is very aggressive, but it will still be a small percentage of the total output of energy. All use foreign technology. China copied and developed the pebble nuclear technology which is promising for safety / cost but its capacity is very limited. I do not hear much development today.

- The priority to highways (auto) and some air transportation should take a back seat to public transportation such as buses, trains and high-speed rails. The recent cut in gas subsidy is a good measure. China failed to start such a system and discourage citizens from owning cars.

- How ironic the U.S., the #1 polluter of the world (based on per capita), accuses China, who does not even make to the top 10 worst polluters?

- China has transformed some semi desert in a very small scale to livable land in the Northwestern China. The big impact will be from the diversion of water from south to north / west. This semi desert will turn to an oasis easier than the real desert. Will see the cost / benefit and its impact on its neighbors (India and SE Asia) who depend on the water from Tibet.

- My friend Irene provides the best way to fix the environment. First she lives in a small apartment even though she has millions. Secondly, she uses public transportation to go to work. Thirdly, her well-built car (a Prelude) is over 14 years old.

  All our products should be well-built at a reasonably higher price, so they will last longer and are worth the costs to repair them. Imagine half of the cars junked and the 'obsolete' computers and smart phones would not be in our landfills. However, if we are that frugal, we would drive some car companies and components makers in the auto business out-of-business. All remedies have some side effects, but the gains are better than the losses.

My in-law told me the tools passed from his father are still working fine and of top quality even his father paid a higher price. Do you prefer a tool lasting five times and costing double?

China should build the next generation of products based on quality, innovation and durability as it has passed that the cheap and copycat stage of moving to a developed country.

Afterthoughts.

- As of 8/2012, Fukushima's nuclear problem actually has helped China:

  Fortunately for China, it is on the east coast. Otherwise, there are more problems to China with the radioactivity damages.

  It is a wake-up call to China that safety enforcement is important: Better concrete enclosure and better storage of the used fuel.

  Less nuclear generators will be on-line in the future, so less competition will be on the nuclear fuels.

  Japan will buy a lot of farm products and energy products from China due to the Tsunami.

- Bill Gates, China and nuclear reactor.
  http://www.cbc.ca/news/technology/story/2011/12/07/technology-bill-gates-china-nuclear-reactor.html

Links

Renewable energy in China:
http://en.wikipedia.org/wiki/Renewable_energy_in_the_People%27s_Republic_of_China

Pebble reactor: http://en.wikipedia.org/wiki/Pebble_bed_reactor

10 Intelligence Property, the key to a developed country

The U.S. was once a major intelligent property (IP) violator. The Colonies copied / stole ideas from Europe without paying any royalty in the colonial days. Charles Dickens refused to visit the USA as he was angry that his work had been copied without paying him a penny. Even at the end of WW2, the U.S. did not pay royalties to Germany in using the atomic bomb technology; the U.S. must have learned how to improve their atomic technology after Germany was defeated) and jet engine technology from Germany.

In its history, the U.S. industrialized rapidly to a developed country as it became the top country after WW2 as all its competitors were reduced to crumbles.

There are phases of a country moving to a developed country. Their major characteristics are listed below. My theory. I am sure that this has been discovered before. If so, blame me for not reading extensively.

Phase 1. Low labor cost. Copy/steal. Low-quality consumer products.

Phase 2. Moving up the value chain. Good infrastructure. Higher quality.

Phase 3. High-end products. High quality. Innovative. Protect intelligent property rights.

As of 2012, China has long moved already from Phase 2 to Phase 3. Quality is still not up to par in many areas if not only perceptually. However, the space program is in Phase 3 though that is still decades behind the U.S. When you compare China to itself ten years ago, you will find their products have moved up in quality and value.

Around the 16th century, about half of the inventions and their derivatives were from China and no one paid royalties to China. This is the time when China was advanced in Phase 3 relative to the rest of the world. After the semi colonization about 220 years ago, China degraded to bankruptcy and slid back to Phase 1.

In the past 35 years they have overcome huddles and problems. Judging from the government and its educated and determined citizens, the road to a developed country is a question of when. Chinese have learned the bitter lessons from the Opium Wars and the bi-century humiliation that followed. It motivates them to work hard and save for the future.

I wish the Western / the U.S.'s media report both the problems and successes of China fairly. Same for the Chinese media on U.S. and the west.

China has intelligent citizens who are innovative and will be able to invent such intelligent products as Facebook and Google. However, as long as there are not enough laws in protecting intelligent properties, this will not be materialized. As of 2013, it may take about ten years (hopefully less) for China to fully enforce the laws that protect IP.

Afterthoughts

Should IP be protected in developing countries?
Most citizens in developing countries cannot afford to buy DVDs and software packages at the same prices we are paying, so there are no real heavy losses to Hollywood and software providers.

New drugs are copied by China and India illegally and they are distributed to poor countries. Haitians and most Africans cannot afford to buy the drugs even at half the asking prices. Should we let them die without the drugs? No, we should treat them as charities to developing countries or find ways so they can afford. Clinton Initiatives has some answers.

Is protectionism necessary?
Take Hong Kong movie industry as an example. If they did not protect the industry, Hollywood movies would capture the entire Hong Kong market due to its high production value and Hong Kong would not make movies to reflect local culture, society... However, Hong Kongers should not totally sham out competition otherwise they will not improve their own quality.

Today USA is reversing the role. It plays protectionism against many Chinese products. Even with heavy subsidies, the USA cannot compete with Chinese low-end tires (actually the USA does not make low-end tires), solar panels, wind turbines… They set up high tariffs against these products they cannot compete. Eventually it will start trade war and eventually China will say 'No' that Japan did not dare to say so.

Product dumping is different. Some steel products made in China are too low-priced. We cannot compete when we add up the costs of individual components without even firing the furnace. It has happened here too. Do you remember Word Perfect, some spreadsheets and several mail systems? Microsoft virtually gave their similar products free to drive out the competition. After they succeeded, they started raising prices.

.
#Filler: We're victims of our own success

A higher living standard means higher wages, more protections for our workers and more regulations for our environment. All these will make us less competitive.

#Filler: Art work by PowPaper

11 Chinese justice system

Chinese dominate about 16 of the last 20 centuries. The last three centuries was declining (just before the Opium Wars). Before then the strong judicial system supported the strong governance.

Before the Opium Wars, Xi raised cash to build her palaces by allowing common citizens to buy official and justice jobs and these officials used their power to make money. A corrupt system led to the fall of Qing ignited by foreign invasions.

Chinese is still developing their justice system. It is very crude today and it does not meet today's basic requirements. However, when we compare to what they have 30 years ago, it has come a long way.

Their weakest points (from me) are human rights, security regulations, corruptions, pollutions and intelligent properties.

Human rights is #3 after the right for food (#1) and right for shelter (#2). From one who is raised in Hong Kong, it is slow in developing. However, when we compare human rights 30 years ago, 20 years ago or even 10 years ago, it has been progressing.

With so many financial frauds such as IPOing the empty shell companies, foreign investors do not want to invest.

In 2013, corruptions have been suppressed with many major cases led by Xi. It is a good start and I did not expect so early.

Without protecting intelligent properties, Chinese will not innovate as the USA and the West. Why we spend all the time in inventing or making movies while they can be copied easily?

Chinese can learn a lot from the legal systems of the USA and the West. However, many are not applicable being a developing country. The following is an illustration.

You cannot practice the American justice system in most developing countries as it is too expensive. A bullet is cheaper than the millions a lawsuit would cost.

The trial of O.J. case would not exist in China as we all know he was 99.99% guilty. From the reactions from black colleges and white colleges on TV, it just turned out to be a racial issue instead of looking for justice.

It used to (and may still is but more underground) that execute prisoners were executed for harvesting the organs. However, I believe some prisoners cannot be rehab. It is more beneficial to the society dead than alive. I'm not 100% OK on this.

It is a Chinese saying "Kill one and warn hundred (a million in today's internet)".

A good trial may not bring good justice depending on how smart is the lawyer (my experience with lawyers in small business is not very good).

To conclude, justice system is good if properly executed. China is developing their justice system and we have a legal system. Our legal system and Chinese system are just extremes.

We're over-developed and spend too much. Most lawyers to me are Robin Hoods in reverse.

Links

Chinese judicial system:
http://en.wikipedia.org/wiki/Judicial_system_of_China

Filler:
On travel.
http://tonyp4idea.blogspot.com/2016/04/on-travel.html

On Chinese music.
http://tonyp4idea.blogspot.com/2016/07/chinese-music.html

12   From "Made in China" to "Designed in China"

After Deng's reform, China has been the global factory but not been innovative compared to the US. There are only several recognized Chinese brands outside China. However, we have been seeing changes in front of our eyes.

Why Chinese have not been innovative

- As of 2018, China is moving up from a developing country to a developed country. It is not there yet, but it is getting closer. In many sectors China has been in the leading edge.
- Protection of intelligence properties is still in the infancy in China.
- During Mao's communism era, Chinese did not think outside the box.
- Traditionally Chinese education system encourages students to be good in exams by remembering formula, data, facts and how to take exams.
- The global US brands are partly due to the spreading of US culture via movies and music. China only have a handful of global brands. Today Chinese products compete with low prices and in developing countries. It has changed in several sectors.

Why is changing

- As product value is climbing, it requires innovation for better profit margins. Most large corporations in China have strong research departments. With a large local and foreign markets, the research would be paid off and some already did.
- With a lot of innovative products, China naturally has to protect her own intelligence properties.
- Many do think outside the box. Chinese have seen the successes and the generated wealth from innovative products.
- We have not yet seen the geniuses like Gates and Zuckerberg in China. However, China does have schools for geniuses in most Tier I cities. Even the traditional schools encourage innovation thinking.

  Many of my classmates become innovators after the Peking-duck education in high schools. The owner of DJI, the largest company in consumer drones, graduated from college and got a small grant from his college to start the company. It is a successful model to follow among many.
- Chinese students work harder than American counterpart. If you believe the students working 3 hours less (my estimate) every day will achieve the same in life, you believe in fairy tales.
- The government encourages education while our leaders cut research and school budgets. I know three Ph.D. in space engineering in US: one retired

and two are still looking for jobs. All those talks on improving science education are just garbage or our leaders are out-of-touch.
- You can hire 4 engineers in China for the price of 1 engineer in US. They are dedicated with no distortion of sports, coffee breaks, long vacations…
- Most large projects have a technology transfer clause. If you do not comply, China gives the projects to your competitor. Some are due to the short-term profits. It would mean bonuses to the officials and stock appreciation. Some are due to the promise of the huge China's market for their products.
- China is also buying many US and EU companies for the technology and/or the market share. Many bankrupting companies were bought by Chinese. Many purchases may be backed by Chinese government.
- Many espionages and cyber hackings are proven or suspected that Chinese are stealing our trade and military secrets.

"Made in China 2025" is an important milestone for China to improve the core components to 70%. With the threat of banning China from buying from US core components such as chips for Chinese mobile phone, I believe the strategy will be changed and accelerated. It is easily said than done as US leads the chip and the manufacturing equipment. Hence together with farm products, China cannot say no to us right now, but in more than 5 years, she can.

Links: 1 2 3 4 5 6 7 8

How far behind is China

US tech had about 50 years advantage over China. Some still argue US is 50 years ahead for the following arguments:

1. US sent men to the moon in 1968 and China sent man to space in 2003.
2. China had built the first carrier in recently while US had the first one in 1920.

China was broke in 1949, the year People's Republic of China was formed. In the last 68 years, China has reduced the gap from 10 to about 8 years (higher or lower according to whom you talk to). In some sectors such as supercomputer and cyber, China is among the leaders.

Comparing the research fund in China, we're not that much behind but somehow our researchers are feeling the pinch.

Asians countries commercialize our technologies and China build them cheaper than most. In 20 years and if we do not correct our decline, our tech would go to toilet but definitely not now.

13   Feeding 18% of world population with 7% farmland

It is not easy for sure. Today, China can feed her citizens without import except during natural disasters such as flooding and droughts. China's famines such as during 1950 are a past memory.

China does import food. Beef cannot be raised profitably in China due to the land resources. Some corn and soybean are imported and they are used for animal feed. Lobsters and some seafood are imported for wealthy citizens. The wealthier China can afford to import more food, but it would be bad for poor countries. Hope China will be self-sufficient in food with my summary:

- Hard working. It is similar to other industries.
- Making use of limited resources such as rice terraces in hills and turning deserts into farmland.
- Aqua farming. Many seafood including oysters are farmed.
- Using technologies such as farming machines. Drones are used for fertilizing / insecticides which is efficient and saving fertilizers and water. Chinese can grow modified specimens of rice in salty water.
- Improving transportation to bring food from farms to cities.
- Encourages research and experiments in farming.
- Chinese farming has benefited from many scientific advances such as GPS, weather forecasts and genetics.
- Management. China bans fishing for months to prevent overfishing.
- "One-child policy" has limited population growth in spite of many drawbacks.
- Water redirection projects. Hopefully and eventually, the semi-desert in many areas in West China would be turned into farmland from the water redirected from the south.

Links Google "China agriculture".
General. 1
Farming technology: 1, 2, 3 4 5 6 7

14 The rise of China

Almost every rise of a nation has harms and benefits to the world and the rise of China is no exception. I bet China's rise has more benefits to the world than harms. China's rise is natural considering its huge population of 1.38 billion. Around 1800, it produced a third of the global GDP. The Great Wall had done a good job to keep the northern barbarians away so was the ocean from Japan until the last three dynasties. Today and even in the near future, China will not be a leader in politics, military, technology and culture compared to the US. She will be a leader in trading due to China's needs to import energy, other natural resources and agricultural products and export higher-tech products at prices far lower than the West/US.

Harms

From recent history, the rise of Germany led to World War II. Britain's Industrial Revolution and the advances of weaponry led to the semi colonization of China about 180 years ago.

In another 50 years, I suspect China's military might be strongest in its territory but not as strong as the US. At most, China will use her might to reunite with Taiwan. Taiwan, under Chiang Kai-shek, wanted to invade China to reunite and used to have meetings with the 'governors' of every Chinese province.

Hopefully, the islet disputes with its neighbors will be settled diplomatically. China's leaders have repeated they will not be "Ba" (roughly translated as #1 bully or #1 policeman). No one can predict that far away. However, currently China has a policy of non-interference and does not expect other countries to interfere with her internal affairs. She does not have much military alliance so far. With today's low price for oil, drilling is not economically feasible and the world is moving to green energy. Hopefully we allow all conflicted countries to fish in the disputed areas.

Economically, it will compete with the US and the west in all sectors. Many developed countries will lose their current financial strongholds if they do not adapt. Since its trade is already the largest, its currency could eventually be the reserve currency. When we concentrate our effort on the military, we pay less attention to economics.

Despite the younger population, India will not fare well with China's rise. Both have similar problems with a huge population to feed and shelter. India's protectionism does not allow the country to concentrate on innovation and quality to be competitive. China's friendship with Pakistan does not fare well with India.

With the growing wealth, the Chinese are eating better and using more of the earth's resources. China is solving the energy crisis. She has signed contracts on new natural gas with Russia that would not change the world's current supply initially. China is also exploring green energy sources.

Poor countries find it is hard to compete with China in farm products and energy products. China has about 10% of farmland but a 20% population. Many in these countries are supposed to starve as a lot of farm products are moved to China. I bet the high fertility rate is harmful for these countries and low wages will not fix their problems. With the severe climate, farming will be adversely affected. Hopefully, farming technologies and seed technologies would change the equation for the better.

Benefits

There are many and they should outweigh the possible harms. Here are some examples and some have happened already.

About 250 years ago, China was semi colonized by the US, the west and Japan and was bankrupted after paying all the unfair treaties. In the 1950s, China could not build a reliable bicycle. China started late but the progress especially in the last 30 years has been amazing. The Chinese learn the lessons: They have to be strong in all areas: economics, science, weapons...

China graduates more college students than any other country, especially in science and technology. In most cases, China has been run by engineers while our country has been run by lawyers. China invests in technologies such as space exploration. China invests in more infrastructure projects than any other countries such as owning more than 60% of the high-speed rail of the entire world. China invests more and consumes less, and that leads to a better future but also excess capacity. Here are some examples.

- Medicines will benefit the world. If you need a drug to save your life, do you care whether it is from the US or from China? With its fewer restrictions in drug development and the government subsidies, I bet China will be the front runner in this field. It is a question of when and not why.

- Public health. Hong Kong is the frontier in many medical procedures and inventions. It is one of the top cities, if not the only one that has experienced conquest of the bird flu. A city of 7 million citizens can contribute that much - imagine what a country of 1.35 billion can contribute.

- Shenzhen is the Silicon Valley of the East or the Silicon Valley will be the Shenzhen of the West in 20 years. To illustrate this, the drone was arguably invented by a Hong Kong student and assembled in Shenzhen. It has most of the components available within an area of about 30 miles. Besides the innovation, these high-tech products can be assembled fast and cheap.

- Cheap consumer products. They benefit even the poor in the US.

- Many corporations such as Walmart take advantage of China's low-cost products. Many high-tech companies such as Apple become wealthier to take China's advantage.

- Many poor countries copy China's model successfully while some fail.

- "One Belt, One Road" Initiative. It would make a lot of neighboring countries wealthier than before.

- The world, especially the poorer countries, will benefit from China's advancements. China benefits by learning from the US and the West's technical advancements. Now, China has some pioneer

- technologies including mobile, infrastructure... One example is the earthquake warning system.
- The world including China has enjoyed our culture via movies and music. We will enjoy Chinese culture more than today.

- China did not ask for foreign aid from the recent natural disasters. Imagine 20% (a little less today) of the world population begging for money.

- China has aided many poorer countries such as Pakistan and many African countries to build their infrastructure.

Neutral

- Weapons. From centuries of humiliation, I do not blame China investing in weapons. It helps China to defend herself from foreign invaders. China also exports to many developing countries who can only afford the second-hand weapons. If they are used to defend themselves, it would be a benefit to the world but not for invasions.
- Most of us do not recognize that **hard work is the primary reason for China's success**. Stealing IP and forcing IP are only a small part of it. If not, many other countries would rise too. The Chinese have had a hard time in recent history, and that is why they are hard working. In the U.S., we depend on the immigrants from China and India to help our high-tech companies to implement the ideas such as Facebook, Google and Microsoft.

Summary

China has to adapt to its rise, so are other countries, particularly the US. The balance of power will be changed and the eventual excess of capacity should be used for peace. We have to learn from the fall of China about 250 years ago and the rise of Germany during WW2.

It is dangerous for us to isolate China. We should understand Chinese culture as they understand ours. We should not use our standards to judge China or any other country as China should not use their standards to judge us. Our politicians should not use China to buy votes.

If China and the West do not adjust to each other, we will have economical conflicts that would lead to wars that the entire world cannot afford.

Links

Technology dominance (First of Part 3, Computer; great but a little pro-China to me). China still lags behind the US in many sectors. US has the benefit of immigration of many top scientists/engineers. Search for "China Technology" under YouTube such as this one and this one, and you should find many. Military link. Space link, 2. Quantum computing. GPS. Drone. Economy 1 2 3 4. General 1 2 3. Diplomat magazine (many articles), BBC. High Speed Rail 1 2, and train to Tibet.

China should develop public transportation more than cars. Local brands in China can only compete at low prices that have thin profit margins. EVs can only be popular in China when they have enough fast charger stations and/or better batteries. Most Chinese live in apartments.

"From follower to leader" (recommended).
https://www.youtube.com/watch?v=Psyy4KqEKtA

China is rising. 2
https://www.youtube.com/watch?v=eQjWtkdnhkg
https://www.youtube.com/watch?v=GiDTPSbVzhk
A second tier city better than many cities in the world.
https://www.youtube.com/watch?v=wYAoyakwHUk
China's new airport.
https://www.youtube.com/watch?v=YJODUxPrEs4&list=WL&index=2&t=131s
Misc. 1 2 Open up
https://www.youtube.com/watch?v=sg-bjX122u4
https://www.youtube.com/watch?v=5u4HoSbu07c
https://www.youtube.com/watch?v=-XgKOSrCkUg

Recommended article on China and the U.S. from Harvard Kennedy School.
https://www.belfercenter.org/publication/great-rivalry-china-vs-us-21st-century

15 Shenzhen

Let's start with a video from Professor X. Click here or type the following in your browser:
https://www.YouTube.com/watch?v=SGJ5cZnoodY&t=923s

Shenzhen has transformed from a small fishing village to a modern city with 12 million citizens. Shenzhen has become the **Silicon Valley of the East**, or in the next decade we would say the US's Silicon Valley is the Shenzhen of the West.

Shenzhen could be the first major city to have all buses running in electricity and so are most taxi cabs. If you bought all the stocks in the Shenzhen Exchange, you could be very wealthy and there is no need to read my books on investing.

For example, it would take 9 months to assemble a new product but only 3 months in Shenzhen as most of the components are readily available next door or in the next street. Shenzhen's advantages are no longer tax credit and cheap labor (but highly-trained Chinese technicians, engineers and researchers). Many tech companies from over the world come to Shenzhen to set up shops in order to be successful.

There are many high-tech products from Shenzhen and they're sold all over the world. Unless you've been living in a cave for the last 10 years or you are blinded by your dumb nationalism, you should know China is catching up with technology, science and infrastructure, and the gaps are narrowing.

Under Deng's vision, Shenzhen has become one of the (if not the) wealthiest cities in China. Your homework is to study the many articles on Shenzhen starting with Wikipedia or enter the following in your browser.
https://en.wikipedia.org/wiki/Shenzhen

Extra credits. There are several other YouTube videos on this amazing city. Why copying the current technology to make it better or using it for a new product is creative and profitable? Will any other countries copy Shenzhen's model and will they be successful? Do you agree from the video that open source encourages copying technology without compensation? What does our 9-year-old most likely do with no homework? Is it too early for a Chinese 9-year-old to study electronics and programming? Have a good day, class and no video game today.

More recent links: 1 (recommended).

My experience in Shenzhen. I visited this incredible city in 2017 for three days, a stopover on my way to Hong Kong. It was my first time in my life taking so many taxi rides in order to see many attractions on my first day. Actually, the subway was very convenient and was supposed to be free to seniors.

We took the taxi from the bus station from Canton to the hotel. It was a fancy hotel but it only cost us $140 U.S. during the off season. We took another taxi ride to Shenzhen Museum. I enjoyed it a lot, and from my memory it was free. From the museum, we walked to a beautiful park. Due to it getting dark, we skipped walking to the hill top to see Uncle Deng's statue.

We took another taxi ride to East Gate. The taxi driver took us to the old one, so we missed the new place with all kinds of street food. Of course, another taxi ride took us back to the hotel.

Next day we took the subway to "Splendid of China". Someone helped us buy subway tickets. So far we used cash (may not be that easy today as everything is e-pay). The admission was free to seniors over 70 and half price for seniors over 65 even for foreigners with passports. We had some problems with the ticket machine. A lady helped us with her e-pay and we paid her cash.

A lot of school children lined up there already before us. A child offered us some candies and crackers. The shows were spectacular and we could have spent two full days. The food in the park was quite good for the price.

The next morning, we saved money by having dim sum in another restaurant. It was a mistake as it could be one of the best dim sum places in China. Our hotel is just across the street. The traffic leaving China was heavy, but the train going to Hong Kong was fast and comfortable.

My general impression: Shenzhen is clean and modern. Living standards could be higher than most other cities in China, but there are a lot of freebies for seniors. The streets are clean and safe. I failed to find a beggar, and it was rumored that they could take e-pay. There are many famous corporations in one street in Shenzhen. Our entire government is fighting these companies in this street.

16   Necessity is the mother of invention

Our actions cause China to react, and I can say the same in the opposite way. Here is a brief summary. For further reading, read the included links to articles and Wikipedia if available, which also provides updates. You can also search the updated YouTube videos on these topics.

Quantum computing / transmission
We present computer information with 1 bit either on or off. Quantum theory suggests there is a third state. For simple illustration, a coin can be either head or tail, and the third state (superposition) is when it is standing.

China can transmit information between Beijing and Shanghai via a 1,300-mile fiber link and one Chinese city to Vienna via a satellite using quantum technology. The transmitted data is virtually impossible to hack.

IBM, Google and China are working on quantum computers that are supposed to be many times faster than today's top computers. As of 2020, China is ahead, but it may still take many years for practical uses.

Actions and reactions. China found out that the NSA was spying on them from the transmission network via Edward Snowden. They knew they had to find a better way. Most Chinese scientists learned this technology from the west. Trump wanted to ban the scholars from China on technology even though they have contributed a lot to the research and finance in U.S. universities. China's huge investment forces us to fund more on our research in science (about time!).

Article: 1 (recommended)
Wikipedia
YouTube: 1
https://www.washingtonpost.com/business/2019/08/18/quantum-revolution-is-coming-chinese-scientists-are-forefront/
https://en.wikipedia.org/wiki/Quantum_computing
https://www.youtube.com/watch?v=pD48IIcJQf4

China's GPS (BeiDou)
China has a decent system similar to our GPS. The EU and Russia have their own, but most cannot be compared to GPS and BeiDou. BeiDou is

better than the U.S.'s, but I bet they will leapfrog each other. Most missile products depend on GPS.

Actions. The U.S. had several incidents to stop GPS coverage on China. China would be a big disadvantage without their own GPS during a military war between the two countries.

Article: 1
Wikipedia

https://www.cnn.com/2020/06/24/tech/china-beidou-satellite-gps-intl-hnk/index.html
https://en.wikipedia.org/wiki/BeiDou

Carrier killer missiles, swarm drones and undetected submarines
They are supposed to be effective to down a carrier, but they have not been proven in actual wars. If the missile cannot be detected in the firing stage, it is hard to detect on its way towards the target as it changes its projectile. We may not feel the threat now, but who knows in their fast development?

In theory, it is hard to protect (and not economically feasible) from a swarm of drones with some carrying bombs. It may be a long way to be deployed in downing a carrier.

The technology of silent (harder to detect) submarines was most likely from the U.S. or Russia.

Actions and reactions. We have sent fleets to the South China Sea and Obama declared 'return to the Pacific'. We are developing solutions to China's new weapons. Supersonic weapons are a similar topic.

Article: 1, 2, 3
Wikipedia: Missile, Swarm drones,

https://www.militarytimes.com/news/your-military/2020/08/27/report-china-fires-carrier-killer-missile-in-disputed-sea/

https://www.businessinsider.com/china-test-launched-swarm-of-suicide-drones-from-a-truck-2020-10

https://asiatimes.com/2020/04/run-silent-run-deep-shang-class-subs-set-new-standard/

https://en.wikipedia.org/wiki/DF-21
https://en.wikipedia.org/wiki/China_Electronics_Technology_Group

China's carriers
The first one is for training and was refitted from a Ukraine's carrier. The second one is an improvement from the first one, but it is still old technology. The third one is a big improvement and should be ready in 2020 - 2021. The fourth one is nuclear-powered and it is in the design phase as of 2020.

Actions and reactions. China needs to protect the sea route supplying oil and materials. China is decades behind us in carriers, but the gap has been reduced.

Article: 1
Wikipedia

https://www.defenseworld.net/news/27842/China_to_Launch_Third_Aircraft_Carrier_in_2020#.X7fmllB7mM8

https://en.wikipedia.org/wiki/Chinese_aircraft_carrier_programme

Chip making
The Chinese can design many products using chips, but they do not have advanced chip makers and depend on many chips from us.

Actions and reactions. Trump banned Huawei and a few Chinese companies from buying U.S. chips and the chip makers if they have a specific percent of U.S. technology.

Banning ASML's most advanced chip makers is a blow to China. China now concentrates their effort and resources on building chip makers. You cannot build a house without a strong foundation.

The U.S. is losing big sales and profits from China. When China is ready to build their own advanced chip makers, the U.S. chip companies will be in permanent loss. This is why most if not all chip companies oppose Trump's decision.

Article: 1
Wikipedia

https://www.theedgemarkets.com/article/tech-why-uschina-chip-war-heating

https://en.wikipedia.org/wiki/Semiconductor_fabrication_plant

China's space program
The moon exploration could find rare ores (titanium and helium-3) that may supply almost endless energy for the entire world. China was rejected to participate with our space station program. China could be the only nation that has a space station after ours retires. I hope they learn from our shuttle program that has many problems including the costs (the 11 launches costs about the same as 11 carriers). We abandoned rockets then which was considered extra to the shuttles, which can also collect space junks. Journey to the Mars is not cost effective.

Wikipedia: space program, moon exploration, and space station

Misc.
Mao wanted atomic bomb as the other nations had them. China accelerated the hydrogen bomb development as they saw the no actual nuclear testing (as opposed to computer simulations) would be signed soon. It took China only 2 years and 2 months to explode the first hydrogen bomb compared to more than 4 years by other nations. It turns out to be the right decision otherwise China would be bullied by us.

When we weaponize the USD and/or exclude China using SWIFT, China will find a way. China can use Yuan for trading oil / gas with the Middle East and Russia. With the reckless printing of USD, the status of USD as a reserve currency has been shaken.

Summary. Newton is right that there is a reaction to every action even in politics; also, there is an action to every reaction.

#Filler: Advantages of high-speed rail for China:
- Reduce the wealth gap.
- Open some inaccessible rural areas.
- Support local government in riots and natural disasters
- Reduce the railroad burden.
- Reduce the air travel burden.
- Increase the land price along the high-speed stations; most lands are owned by the government.
- Provide jobs.
- Reduce carbon emission.
- Earn foreign contracts.

17   One belt, one road

The Chinese are building two modern silk roads, one by land (one belt) and one by sea (one road). It has been participated in by more than 60 countries. It is a $3 trillion infrastructure campaign funded mostly by China. It would take about five years to complete. The idea is from President Xi and was initiated in 2013.

It is natural for China: use of excessive infrastructure industry, higher wages in China, rising internal demands of foreign products, converting the U.S. treasuries into other assets, and most importantly creating alternate routes for energy / ores as described below in more detail.

- Obama announced "return to Asia" or "refocus on Asia" by sending about two thirds of our naval power to Asia. China realized that it was aimed at them. By blocking the sea route, China's oil supply would be cut. It is a strategic action to find another land route to these resources.

  China and Myanmar have opened a cross-border pipeline into south-east China. It would save a lot of transportation expenses and avoid the blocking in the Malacca Strait.

- China has built up a lot of USD reserves from the trade surpluses with most of her trading partners. It would be less risky by converting this reserve (especially from our U.S. Treasuries) to other investments such as the loans in building infrastructures in foreign countries. In case of a war, their U.S. Treasuries held by China could be frozen.

- Improve transportation of products between China and Europe and resources / energy from the Middle East to China.
- China exploits the excess capacity in building infrastructure. China leads the world in building high-speed rail, bridges and tunnels. Japan (with no experience in building rail in hot climates), India (with few successful projects by foreigners) and Vietnam have been experiencing many problems in building high-speed rail that are not built by the Chinese.
- Enrich the wealth and living standards of the countries that are in OBOR projects. Even the U.S. and the West would benefit by reducing their foreign aid to these countries.

China's objective is to make the poor countries richer as a responsibility to the world. Most affected regions should increase the GDP by 5% on average from my rough estimate.

- Eventually most of China's higher-value products will catch up with the West and the U.S. When the developing countries are richer, they are the target markets for China.
- China's Yuan has been used as the reserve/trading currency instead of USD though it is a long way to replace USD as a reserve currency. China has set up an exchange for trading energy in Chinese currency. Other commodities will follow if not already done.
- It could reduce some conflicts. The Philippines received billions on the loan and has downplayed the islet conflict with China. Hence the chance of Chinese military interference would be reduced.
- It would strengthen the economics, politics and cultural ties of China and the affected countries. Western China has not been developed due to the remote and less habitable conditions.
- It would make the U.S. very unhappy and the U.S. would take counter actions to protect her interests.

Many developing countries and provinces in west China will benefit. Many projects will be financed via Asian Infrastructure Investment Bank (AIIB), which is mainly funded by China. Today most of these projects are financed by the IMF and World Bank, which are controlled by the U.S.

China may supply most of their services such as building factories or improving ports. However, China will not see their profits from the investments in the short term. Some loans will be partly donated to friendly allies. Many countries may not be able to pay back the loans in cash.

China should continue to concentrate on soft power by promoting mutual respect, understanding local cultures and reducing military conflicts such as the islet dispute with Vietnam. All the signed contracts could be overturned when a new governor comes into power. The participating countries should be careful about the ability to pay back the huge debts.

The US is not participating in this campaign. We will not benefit from these agreements and we will lose our influence to the developing countries. However, some big projects require advanced technologies and they will be supplied by US corporations such as turbines from GE. Honeywell and Caterpillar will likely benefit. India may not participate due to the road through a territory claimed by Pakistan.

As in most projects, China will face problems and challenges. Thailand and Indonesia are modifying their original railroad projects. The project is easily accepted in developing countries but not in developed countries such as the EU. China is having its own economic problems. Some projects may not pay back and China would end up losing money. China needs to analyze projects carefully.

It is better to invest in profitable infrastructure projects than selling destructive weapons. Many finished projects such as the major railway in Africa and an empty airport do not benefit China and even the host so far. They need to select those projects that are beneficial otherwise it would be a waste of resources. A train started from a Chinese city to arrive in London and another one to Madrid. In general, it is faster than sea routes and less expensive than air freight. Or, it is more expensive than sea routes and more time consuming than air freight. Many products such as red wine are suitable to ship by train. It also depends on how far the products are from the closest seaport or railway station. In general, western China and their neighbors will benefit more.

China has or will face challenges and problems. The finance would drain China's reserve funds. Many top officers in the countries receive maximum benefits while their citizens do not. Need to resolve them by making more jobs available to common citizens. Some current highways would be abandoned. India will object due to her animosity with Pakistan. Russia may have their own ideas and/or not investing enough in their infrastructure. The southern route would weaken the importance of their northern route. The rails among countries are not uniform, and that's why they have dry docks to transfer goods from one rail system to another.

There will be reactions from the U.S. and Japan who would lose their influence esp. in Africa and S.E. Asia. China has made the ports in Germany and Greece busy and brought in a lot of wealth. China invested in Greece's port when Greece was in a deep financial crisis. For a successful project, China would get about 1.8 times the return while the receiving country would get 3 time the return.

Many countries in South East Asia have already been benefited by Chinese investment and infrastructure. There are many conflicts such as corruption by local governments, cultural differences and traditional military conflicts with countries such as Vietnam. China does not force any country to join this initiative. Most projects are opened for bids from China and many other countries. Ensure your country should not be in a debt trap. Some countries give part or full usage of a port to China when they cannot pay the loans. Under YouTube, search "Cambodia China Anthony". Here is <u>one</u> of the series.

Iran
The Middle East could cause WW3 and Iran could be a strong factor. Iran is rich in oil and gas. In recent history, the oil right was controlled by the U.K. and partially by Russia. The U.S. and her allies embargo Iran on their terrorist actions (some claim the U.S. army is terrorist), and nuclear development. To me, trading oil without using the USD is one of the major reasons. The recent murder of the number two leader did not get the approval of our allies. Iran bombed the U.S. bases to save face. The reason for not a full-fledged war could be due to Russia and China who may not want to do so now. China, a country without sufficient oil and gas, is eager to develop the land route to Iran's energy.

Links

Ethiopia Rail, Pakistan, SCMP, review, Central Asia
Trade: China's export
One Belt, One Road: Episode 2, 3, 4, 5, 6, 1 (poor screen quality)

YouTube: 1 (recommended), Iran (Recommended)
https://www.youtube.com/watch?v=nLrUdFURtqo

There are many articles on this One Belt, One Road Initiative (OBOR): 1 2.0 (very good from Germany), 3 and 4. Recommended.
Google it for recent articles. Here are some: Wikipedia, US & Heritage. Challenges

Poor product quality?

Do you find poor product quality in Apple's products that were assembled in China? Most poor products are due to the negotiation of the buyers for lowest prices. If a country can send men to the moon, it has to be supported by high-tech companies with quality products. It is the same for China's high rises, bridges, high-speed trains, etc. Ten years ago, it may have been true, but not anymore.

18 TPP and RCEP

Obama wanted TPP, a trade agreement (with less or eliminating tariffs and less regulations) with Asian countries excluding China. Besides eliminating tariffs, TPP includes human rights, protecting intelligent properties, environment and other ideas. The countries in Southeast Asia have a hard time excluding trades with China. On average, they have 20% of the trade with China. Most if not all of these countries do not want to upset the U.S.

China is the #1 trade partner with Australia. Australia's prime minister is the stupidest (not a typo) politician. What do you gain by upsetting your #1 trader (China)? You lose important trade by being a running dog of the U.S.

Trump did not want TPP, as it is better to deal with individual countries to maximize our profits. We did this with Mexico and Canada. These two countries depend on us, and hence the deals are better to us. It is time-consuming to do a deal one by one with about 22 countries in Asia. China should thank Trump for withdrawing from TPP.

RCEP includes the ten S.E. countries plus China, Australia, New Zealand, Japan and Korea excluding the U.S.A., which may join later on. India withdrew, as they would lose a lot. India's protectionism makes most of their products not competitive in the world market.

RCEP is as important as the EU in trade. TPP is dead now and the new TPP if there is one will not be effective due to the RCEP and it may be forced to include China.

In any case, China gains a lot in the free trade with these countries. The trade blockage on China is not working, especially with RCEP. Most likely, China will lead RCEP. So far, the U.S. is the loser. We have lost our concentration and effort with the new TPP due to spending too much time in reelection and fighting the pandemic. As usual, the media do not report RCEP and its importance.

RCEP is a new major free-trade zone after the EU and NAFTA (U.S., Canada and Mexico) and it represents about 1/3 of global GEP. China also signed a very important trade deal with the EU before the end of 2020.

Links
YouTube: 1 2 3

19   Can China say No to us?

In the last decades, Japan and some oil-rich countries could not say "No" to the USA, but China can to some extent and definitely can in 10 years.

China needs our farm products, jets together with Airbus, core technologies such as memory in the mobile phones, etc. We need China for their low-cost consumer products, rare earth elements, market for our global companies and buying our debts.

Being the major players in the global economy, a full-fledged trade war with China would mean global recession and actually we would lose more than China. A military war would likely cause market crashes starting in the US and Asia.

Today's China is not your Daddy's China

China is not as strong as the US, but the gap has been reduced in the last 30 years, and at that time China could not build a reliable bicycle.

China lacks natural resources that she can obtain from many countries. China can get many high-tech products from the EU and Russia such as jet planes and agricultural products from many countries including SE Asia and Australia. At the same time, the Chinese are advancing their products. China no longer is export-oriented. Basically, it is moving to a developed country with higher-value products. With its huge internal market, Chinese can manufacture products cheaply due to the economy of scale.

China's rise is primarily due to the USA playing China card against Russia and now the US plays India (and possibly Taiwan) card(s) against China.

Let's examine some critical factors in this book starting with a little history. About 250 years ago, the alliance of 8 nations forced China to trade. When China refused, they enforced it with battleships and cannons. When the Brits had nothing to trade, they pushed opium obtained from India and killed millions of Chinese. The alliance asked for 'damages' that bankrupted China and led to national humiliation for China. The US was generous to use the money to fund Chinese foreign students to the US. They returned and modernized China.

What if China withdraws all the debts we owe?

It would lead to the global depression starting in the US. It is too obvious and I go no further. China is one link in the global economy. It will survive without our trades. A full-fledged trade war would hurt us more than China. Our trading competitors are the EU countries, not China as we produce similar products such as airplanes. China would be more cautious in lending us money and/or buying US properties/companies. As of 1/2017, China was demoted to #2 by US debt holders. Unlike businesses, creditors have no weight in our political decisions.

The Chinese is still buying our Treasuries for their interest. If they stop, the interest rates would rise and it would cause a housing recession. As of Jan., 2016, our debt to China is just over 1.05 trillion, or about 28% of all debts held by foreign countries.

How about the deficit with China?

We had about $347B in trade deficit with China in 2016. A lot of products such as Apple's iPhones are counted as imports. We're a victim of our own success: A higher living standard means higher wages, more protections to our workers and more regulations for our environment. Our strong USD reduces the competitive edge of our export. However, we need China to take out the obstacles to our products. To illustrate this, most of our consumer products cost a lot more in China than similar local products.

Modern warfare

Modern warfare is different from the 60s. We need better cyber security for both the government and the corporations. We need to fight against terrorists in our own soil.

We have enough nuclear weapons to destroy the entire world. N. Korea is not a nuclear threat unless the guy is really crazy and we drive him to the cliff. We do have to replace the 5" floppy disk though – it could be a security protection.

Aircraft carriers are a drain of the budget. It will not be as useful as in the old days. They are sitting ducks for the carrier missiles. In addition, China's missiles can destroy GPS satellites which our guided missiles depend on.

China has modernized its arm forces via development, acquisition and espionage. China produces cheaper military drones, which have been tested in the Middle East. China has mastered stealth technology in their jets and submarines; the technology could be stolen from us. China becomes the largest export of the military drones due to low prices and no questions asked.

To conclude, China's military might be not that primitive and not that advanced as proposed by our defense vendors who want to sell their weapons. By quality and quantity, today China cannot compete with the US in military, but she is improving enough to defend her territory.

We cannot afford another war

The two wars in the Middle East have been draining our resources. We've been broke. We will become a real paper tiger when the wars continue for another ten years.

Obama's administration saved the market at the expense of our national debt which is at its recent height. Our competitive edge will be reduced by servicing the debt instead of investing on profitable projects such as infrastructure. The debts will be paid by our children and grandchildren who do not have a voice today. Are we following the footstep of Greece? We complain about Chinese military buildup without mentioning our military budget is more than the total of the next five countries not including China due to unconfirmed data.

China, the victim

China has not been an aggressor to foreign countries in her entire history. The last conflict was a brief war with Vietnam in 1979 to teach her former ally a 'lesson' and lessen the Russia influence in the region. China had no choice in the Korean War and she benefited by getting rid of the former Chiang's soldiers. The war with India was a joke as China could win it by redirecting the water flow from Tibet. China's involvement in wars is relatively less compared to our endless participation in wars.

In Roman times, China was as strong as Rome, but they very seldom colonized any country as opposed to the Roman. In around 1420, Zheng He's fleet was far larger in size and number than Columbus's and they just wanted the foreign countries to pay annual tributes and for that they received compensations in return. It contrasts significantly with Columbus. During the Tang dynasty (about 674), China was a world power. They have not conquered and colonized any country.

For the last three centuries starting from the Opium Wars, China was the victim of aggressors. Actually, the two dynasties of the last three were ruled by foreigners before Mao included these 'barbarians' as part of the Chinese minorities.

The late Deng X. P. said that China would recover most of its lost territories in 100 years: many islets in the South/East islets, Outer Mongolia (a buffer zone created by Russia) and many farmlands from Russia... The boundary line between India and China was drawn by a British general favorable to India.

Why do we identify China as an aggressor? Even if they steal our intelligence properties due to our lack of protection - it is not the reason to start a war that would hurt us more. Today they have some intelligence properties more advanced than ours such as 5G.

Triggers

They could be China invading (or 'reuniting') Taiwan and the islet disputes in the South/East China Sea. When China is richer and stronger in 50 more years or so, national pride will drive China to reunite with China. Hopefully it will be achieved economically rather than militarily. Without the US's full support of Taiwan, it would not be a tough job.

When the economy tanks, the US government would have to redirect our attention to other areas such as blaming China. Today we cannot as more jobs are replaced by lower-wage countries, not China. The job loss is also due to robots and less demands from the consumers since 2008.

China does not say "No" to us as the priority of political stability is more important than a trade war; but it will change.

Will the Chinese wake up and fight against the government?

It is the common thought of the China bashers. Most Chinese will not as most are busy making money. After they taste the fruit of capitalism, no one is stupid enough to fight against the government and they learn the bitter lesson from the Tiananmen Square incident.

Our investment in China
Currently, GM has about 25% profit from China and Ford has 16%. They will be replaced by cars produced in Europe and Asia. The first victim could be Boeing when China can buy jets from the EU; it is worth more

than $1 trillion in the coming 20 years. Walmart's products will skyrocket in prices reducing the buying power of the low-income citizens.

Apple is a good example among many high-tech companies. Can Apple move their manufacturing back to the US to eliminate the 35% to 45% proposed tariff?

How can they find enough rare earth elements for their phones? They are available but most cannot be mined without damaging the environment. Many of these mines outside China were bankrupted. How can they motivate an army of educated workers for a new model with slavery wages and unions? It is easier to collect generous welfare than working in these monotonous jobs. How can we get 40,000 technicians? How can Apple move all the component manufacturers from China? What is the impact on Apple in losing the China market (131 million iPhones vs. 110 million in the US in 2015)?

One solution is to manufacture the individual parts in China and have the final assembly here in the USA with a label of "Made in USA" even if the label is made in China.

Counting friends and enemies
The US used to have a lot of friends and formed powerful allies with them. When the allies embargo a country, they're successful. However, our relationships with many of our allies are changing. Russia is not our enemy now and we have avoided some of the conflicts by not participating in actual wars. Russia is an important trade partner of China. Israel, our important ally, has been arguing with our political decisions more frequently than before. China is building two modern silk routes: one by sea and one by land to connect Asia, Africa and Europe better. The US has little use for these routes.

Strange relationships
The chess masters are the US, Russia and China. Japan, N. Korea, Taiwan, the Philippines, India, the SE Asia countries, Israel and the EU are the chess pieces. The US and Japan are friends and both want to 'contain' China. Russia and China are trade partners with advanced weapons. Trump seems to be friendly with Russia to build a partnership. However, if we have any war, Russia will be sided with China, but we cannot count on the EU now. Many EU countries are busy fixing their economies and

some do not want us to be our puppets. They just want our contributions to their defense. We should be reminded we have a hard time to end a war. When we do not learn history from Vietnam and the Middle East wars, we will repeat history. Why should we always find an enemy and/or a war?

The US used to play the China card against Russia and attributed to China's rise by taking out the embargo. Now, it tries to play the Russia card against China. This is another example of "my enemy's enemy is my friend".

Being a US citizen and born in Hong Kong, it will be my saddest day if there is a war which is predictable as unavoidable by many. I hope it will not happen in my lifetime.

Investors have to watch the development of the possible conflict. The only winners are the offense sector and precious metal miners. The recent news of the capture of a submarine drone drove the market lower. What will the market react to when there is a military war between the two countries?

I have different feedbacks from readers with different backgrounds. Being born in Hong Kong, I'm naturally biased.

Afterthoughts
- Taiwan bought a lot of weapons from us including the state-of-the-art fighter jets such as the $1.83 billion of military arms in Dec., 2015. We did not allow Russia to install missiles in Cuba and we clearly know the purpose of these fighter jets. I do not think China is over-sensitive. It provokes them to spend more in defense.
- The US has been spending too much in defending other countries such as Japan, the EU... We have too many problems to fix at home.
- Trade wars between the countries have been started many times and both sides lose.
- Most Taiwanese are those who retreated with Chiang after losing the civil war and their children / grandchildren.
- Taiwan's economy did not catch up with S. Korea primarily due to spending too much on defense, corruption as in most Democratic countries in Asia (have you heard of T.V. Sung?), mal governance...
- China is Taiwan's top trade partner (40% of its export).

- Taiwanese are educated together with Cuba and the Philippines. The difference is Taiwan has a better living standard. I can attribute this as the other two do not have enough natural resources as explained in my Coconut Theory.
- China has never expressed itself to be #1, but the US always does. That's why we have endless wars.
- The recent Trans-Pacific Partnership tries to exclude China while China has its own partnership open to all. The hidden agenda is using the country's currency as the reserve currency.
- The Chinese maritime power is effective to defend its own shore, but not enough to secure the oil route; I estimate about 8% of current foreign oil from this route. With the aircraft carrier, China can invade (or reunite) Taiwan and the 'lost' territories in South / East China Sea easier.
- I believe in "love over war" and also in free trade if both sides play it fairly.
- Chinese accomplishments.
- PBS's China. https://www.youtube.com/watch?v=JovtmKFxi3c
- Here are nice articles on Trump and trade balance.
  http://www.vox.com/latest-news/2017/1/19/14176896/china-facts-trump
  https://www.thebalance.com/china-s-currency-the-yuan-or-renmimbi-3305906

#Filler: Lazy but not stupid

If you take out all the benefits taking a job, do you work?

#Filler: Four generations of teenage mothers

Our generous welfare system forces them to be teenage mothers.

China and Africa
https://www.youtube.com/watch?v=ObefKNUEtKg

20 Defending China on pollution

Trump in his presidential debate, he claimed China was filthy. Let's look at some 2020 figures on most polluted cities and most polluted countries and compare them to India.

The top 100 most polluted cities are: Beijing #28, Shanghai #54, Guangzhou #69, Chengdu #72 and Suzhou #80. India has the most polluted cities. China is #11 as the most polluted country. In addition, there are 'excuses' or 'facts' why China is polluted as follows. However, they are trying to fix pollution.

Fact #1. As per capita, we pollute more than double (some estimate we're using 5 times more energy than Chinese per capita) that of China even including the pollution due to producing products for global consumption. A surprise to you? To start with, our average house is many times larger than the average Chinese apartment. We have more cars than Chinese per capita.

Fact #2. China is #1 or #2 in most if not all green energies. China also exports the green technologies and products. Better technology has been used to generate less carbon dioxide with newer plants.

Fact #3. China is blessed with polluting coal, not the non-polluting oil. New technologies are being used to cut down carbon dioxide and older, inefficient plants have been demolished.

Fact #4. China spends more than 3 times the U.S. spends in green energy.

From my rough estimate, electricity is generated by the following percentage in China: coal (70%), green sources including hydro, solar and wind (20%) and others including nuclear (10%). Compared to previous years, coal has been cut down significantly. China's ambitious program to promote electric cars could see fruit as early as 2020. In Shenzhen, 99% of buses are electric and many taxi cabs are electric too. China produces the best electric buses at the same price range.

Water pollution is another problem China is working on. China is using technologies from US/West to tackle the pollution problems. At the same time China is exporting her technologies and green products. Today China has the largest wind power and solar power generators in the world.

Links

China's pollution facts (recommended). Others: 1
Transform a desert to farm land
Green China. Ambitious green projects. DW magazine. Misc. 1

21 China's advances in 2020-2021

If you do not want to click the links here or want to see in bigger screens, click here or type the following on your laptop:
https://tonyp4idea.blogspot.com/2020/12/china-science-advances-in-2020.html

China has accomplished a lot in science in 2020, technology and applications. This article could be the shortest in this book, but could take the longest time to read. It consists a lot of links to YouTube videos and web articles. Search for new material yourself as this article could be outdated fast from the pace of China's advancements.

The general young age of the Chinese scientists is just amazing. They will contribute a lot in the near future for a long time to China and to the world.

Science / Technology
Will China dominate science?
https://www.youtube.com/watch?v=pGO26c5G90w

China High-Tech Fair 2020.
https://www.youtube.com/watch?v=Twjx5pRQV3E

Most Chinese live in a flat consisting of 600 square feet (my estimate). Hence, how would most of these advancements benefit an average Chinese at home? Driverless cars need 5G; the problem of U.S. is lack of enough 5G coverage.

Quantum computer
https://www.youtube.com/watch?v=E5MBAJJU9Hk

We need to subsidize our research and welcome top scientists to come and work in the U.S. We will not see benefits within 4 years (election cycle), so they will not be approved by our politicians. When we work together, the world will benefit. The race is to use the computer to find drugs and vaccines.

Hypersonic aircraft engine.
https://www.youtube.com/watch?v=YgRBsEOhjhc

Artificial sun.
https://www.youtube.com/watch?v=3CKd4SybOak

Space exploration
China space program.
https://en.wikipedia.org/wiki/Chinese_space_program

The rise of the China space program.
https://www.youtube.com/watch?v=OMAmTpflL-E

We had put all eggs in the shuttle project and failed miserably. Without decent rockets, we had to ask Russia to transport our astronauts to our International space station. The high maintenance and safety issues killed the shuttle project. Almost all projects such as Boston's Big Dig start out rosy without 'unpredictable' problems, then they are over-budgeted and do not meet schedule. Lastly we find culprits and blame everyone instead ourselves.

China's space station.
https://www.youtube.com/watch?v=pextBkh5seI

With the retirement of our international space station, China could be the only one out there. How far is China behind us?

China is very close to our status in exploration of Mars. It is amazing that they have completed it so fast.

Application
China's latest super technology innovation (as of 6/2020).
https://www.youtube.com/watch?v=9lak2nMH_2I

Almost every month, China has a new important innovation. China speed!

Farming technology.
https://www.youtube.com/watch?v=czsBryVnS80

Seawater rice.
https://www.youtube.com/watch?v=rHJ86oW2TB4

22 China is not war hungry

In recent history, China tries everything to avoid wars and has been a war victim more than as an invader. China has a policy of no interference clause. China has no ambition to be a global leader and does not force any country to adopt her rules of order, governance, culture, etc. If your country does not join their "One belt, one road" projects, it is fine with them. So is trade. Let's look at recent history.

- China built the Great Wall to defend the invaders from the north.
- Two of the last three dynasties were ruled by 'foreigners'. Mao declared them to be minorities, and hence China was ruled by 'foreigners'.
- With a flagship eight times the size of Columbus' flagship, China's Zheng Ho could easily colonize all the countries they sailed to, but he just asked them to call China 'big brother' with goods exchanged.

   It is quite opposite to what Europeans did to S.E. Asia. In 1511, the Portuguese came. In 1642, the Dutch came. In the 18th century the British came. Malaysia and most neighbors were colonized by each, one after another.
- China in the coastal areas was robbed by the Japanese many times.
- Europe had been fighting against each other for a prolonged period in the 1800s. As a result, weapons had been enhanced. China ignored this and the industrial revolution in England. It led to the invasion from the west and pushing opium to China.
- China had been semi-colonized by foreigners since the Opium Wars. The Summer Palace was looted and burned for 3 days and 3 nights.
- Japan killed millions of Chinese during WW2 including the Nanjing Massacre. One estimate was killing 300,000 citizens in 40 days. These war criminals raped all women. If you believe in Karma, the Tsunami is it. We can forgive them, but not forget. https://www.youtube.com/watch?v=DMWQ32vwMxI&feature=youtu.be
- China was forced to participate in the Korean War and the Vietnam War.

- The war with Vietnam after the Vietnam-U.S. war caused China about the same number of deaths as the U.S. in this the struggle between the U.S. and Russia. It was rumored that the U.S. backed China in this war.
- China has her own values and rules of order, but she does not enforce others to follow hers – quite different from the west.

We are war-hungry, judging from our endless wars
- We need to find an enemy. 911 helped China as we found our enemy in the Middle East.
- The breakup of the U.S.S.R. required us to find a new enemy as Russia was no longer a worthy enemy.
- Our offense sector does not allow us to slow down wars.
- Our military does not allow us too, otherwise they do not have jobs.
- The hawk 'experts' will not get good consulting jobs than being 'dove'.
- The politicians can conveniently blame all our ills on our enemy (China this time), as they cannot fix our problems. Our high national debt is virtually unfixable.
- If you do not have nuclear weapons or if you trade without our USD, you'll see the US soldiers on your doorstep.
- If you do not agree with our law and order (that can extend to your country whether you like it or not), our sanctions with our allies would destroy your economy.
- We like to help your protesters financially (via NED for example) if the protests are side with us such as Hong Kong and Thailand as recent examples.
- Overseas military bases: USA 58 and China 1.

Section V: Other countries

1   Japan

Japan is not the Japan 25 years ago. As of 2016, I do not want to invest in Japan.

The policy has failed and the new policy is basically the same as the old one. Their problems are:

1. Agitate their major partner China on the disputed islets, which should belong to Taiwan by proximity. They're losing trade from China while China can buy the equipment and technology from many other sources.

2. The virtually zero interest rate (now negative rate) does not work before and it will not work in the future.

3. The higher tax and higher inflation in Japan will lower the living standard in Japan.

4. Any surge in export is just a mirage and cannot be sustained in the long run.

5. The recent Tsunami and earthquake will hurt Japan for another decade. I do not want to visit the affected area or eat any food products produced from the Tsunami area.

6. The impact of Japan's aging population is the worst among nations and is worsened by not welcoming immigrants. The smart and hard-working citizens are their major resource.

7. The baggage from the war crimes in WW2 to its Asian neighbors is still a burden. Japanese never compensate the comfort women who are disappearing fast due to aging. Japanese leaders pay respect to the war criminals in the 'shrines' every year, similar to paying homage to Hitler. I have moved on as the current generation are educated and will not commit the same war crimes.

Afterthoughts
- The point of this blog is not on the dispute itself but on: Why does the dispute re-surfaces after 50 or so years? I suspect it is the U.S.'s hidden agenda. My guesses are: Helped Obama reelected, the U.S. returning to S.E. Asia, selling weapons in the region (the U.S. is already #1 in weapon export), containing China...

- In Asia, Japan, India and China are all building carriers. It is not a good hint for peace.

- My Sentimental Journey: Nanjing Massacre.
  http://ebmyth.blogspot.com/2014/01/nanjing-massacre.html

- Does war benefit the economy? Yes, to some extent. No, for the long term to me.
  Norman: War got us out of the Great Depression in 1941. The inflation is a future problem, ducking the missiles is the current concern. War is a powerful business model and the countries over produce.

- China and Japan (a country with very few natural resources) will fight for natural resources. Most resources are stable but the global population is increasing. The rule of Supply and Demand will push the prices of most commodities (including farm products and water) higher.

- As of 5/2014, Vietnam riots destroyed several Chinese corporations over the disputed islets. Investing in S.E. Asia is risky now. Vietnam will suffer from foreign investment and tourism for 3 or more years.

  http://en.wikipedia.org/wiki/Senkaku_Islands

2   EU's mess

We follow the similar procedure in finding the reentry points and use VGK, an ETF for European countries.

There are two sectors that bring down the financial crisis in 2007 (or 2008 for some). We should reenter the European market via technical analysis (TA) and via fundamental analysis.

Technical Analysis

There are two ways to find the reenter points after 2007.

1. Use the same chart in described in TA chapter as follows. Bring up Yahoo! And then Finance from the browser. Enter VGK, an ETF for Europe. Select Chart, then SMA (single moving average), and enter 350 days for reenter points (different from our usual 30, 60, 90 or 120 days).

   Loosely we have two major reenter/exit sets: 08/31/09 to 08/01/11 and 08/20/2012 to 01/13/14. Without considering compounding, we calculate the averages of these two sets of data.

2. From the Market Timing chapter, reenter the market 2 years after the initial plunge for offending sectors. They are not the offending sector but the sovereign debt is partly the culprit. Hence we use 18 months instead of 1 year for the general market or 2 years for the offending sector.

   Assuming 01/14/2008 the market starting plunging, the reenter date is 07/14/2009.

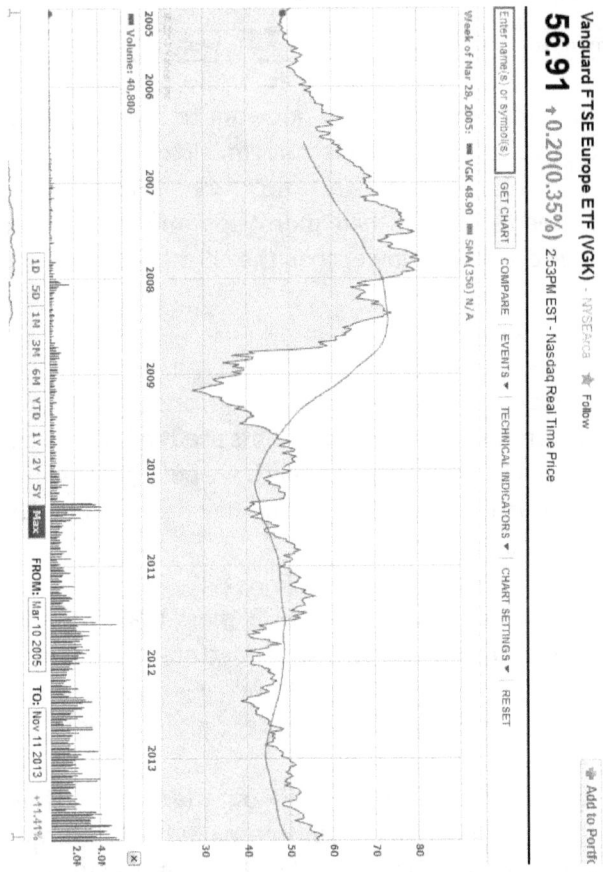

Source: Yahoo!Finance (http://ebmyth.blogspot.com/2013/11/screen-vgk-350-day-sma.html)

The 350-day Single Moving Average could be a good guide to trade VGK, an ETF for European countries. Buy when it is above the moving average line and sell when it is below.

The following table summarizes the returns based on reenter points to 01/13/2014.

	Reenter Date	Return	Annualized Return	Beat SPY
Chart	08/10/09	-9%	-5%	-185%
	08/20/12	29%	21%	0%
Average		10%	8%	-93%

18 months	07/14/09	59%	13%	-42%

If you have a time machine, you may not want to invest in VGK at all as SPY beats both strategies by a wide margin. However, the annualized return is 8% and 13%, not too far away from XHB's 21% and 21% respectively. It seems Europe had more ups and downs during the recovery and the recovery is slower than the US market.

Fundamental analysis

Here are my personal thoughts as of 2009. I prefer to stick with the technical analysis and fundamental analysis is used to further analyze the housing market such as the cities that may have better recoveries. By the time you read this article, the information may be obsolete. Use it as a reference for future guidance.

As of 1/1/2012, my predication about EU's mess that we talked about more than two years ago (my blog mentioned it long before most media). Even today (9/2013), there are not a lot of changes and EU is still on its early stage to recovery. Here are my random remarks.

- EU will be dissolved or will at least kick out the cheaters, free loaders and parasites such as Greece. In any case, Euro will depreciate a lot compared to gold [Update as of 2013: It has]. Germany wants to keep Greece in the union despite of all the problems and little to gain. Germany have to compromise to the opposition from her own citizens in not giving up their own money.

- After that, a default is not a bad option.

- There will be conflicts in the citizens in Greece between those who have (still a lot collecting over $40,000 USD pension) and those (especially the young generation) who have to suffer due to passing the debts / miseries to them.

- Greece will recover faster if it has its own currency and it can default its debts. At that time, it would be profitable to invest in Greece.

Their government will be halved and the salaries / pension obligations will also be halved. To conclude, it will run the country about ¼ of the original cost. Tax revenues will come back with tourists looking for bargains. When the other industries such as shipping (when global trade improves) and processing olive return, the investment will have a good chance to gain 100% in a year. Timing is everything.

- The days living off from the treasures / commodities they stole from their colonies have been long, long gone. Most European countries need to live within their means.

- The lesson of having a good life without working hard (short work week and long vacation) is learned again and again. First it is Ireland, Iceland, then Greece, then Spain/Italy and now the USA.

- When they learn so many bitter lessons, they will not repeat them for a long while. The USA should learn the same lessons as we seem to be heading to the same direction unless the shale energy rescues us.

- EU will be a problem for years to come. When the country has that high debt with regard to GDP, they will not be competitive especially the drain of their best citizens to other countries.

- Decoupling is the solution. The U.S. and China will not be stupid or big enough to rescue a sinking ship.

Afterthoughts

- Update on Greece as of 1/2013.

Greece should be bottom out in a year. Investing in Greek stocks at that time would double your investment for the following reasons.

1. Greece is small, so it may not be a big deal to recover as Iceland did. It is better than Iceland with its nice climate and many attractions for tourists.

2. Besides attractions for tourists, Greece has beautiful beaches. They need to cut down protests before the tourists would return.

3. The government could be mean and small with about 1/4 of the previous expenses to run it.

4. The olive industry and the shipping industry will return big time after the global recession.

However, there are no cures for laziness and stupidity; another living proof on my Coconut Theory. The major hurdle is that there is a brain drain of able citizens and the retirees suck up the resources of the country.

- Roots of the problem.

1. Euro is initially a good idea especially for tourists. However, it forces the rich countries to pay for the free loaders.
2. Laziness is a human nature. When you work 30 hours (even less if you consider the long vacation) a week, you cannot compete with folks who work 50 hours a week.
3. The loots from the days being colonial masters were long gone except the displays in museums.
4. Socialism encourages folks to be parasites until the host dies.

3 Africa

Europeans colonized many African countries and stole their resources. The U.S. enslaved them. The Chinese have been building roads, railroads, hospitals, stadiums, convention centers, etc. Some of the debts have been forgiven. Chinese shift many factory jobs to Africa to take advantage of the cheap labor. Many Africans have still to get accustomed to working in closed buildings. Africans have to limit the explosive population growth.

African countries should control their destinies and learn how to deal with all foreigners. I believe China's economic model is better suited to Africa than the Western model as China was at a similar stage before. The west/USA imports the same U.S. agricultural model to Africa which will not be useful when the U.S. advisors and technicians leave someday. We need to let them be independent for a longer term as Warren Buffet's son Howard mentioned. So are the foreign aid that make some African farms bankrupt as they cannot compete with free farm products from charities.

China helps them to build roads in order to extract their mines and oil. Without that, the natural resources will remain unexplored forever. That is strategic and it also benefits the majority of Africans. China "teaches them how to fish rather than giving them fishes" for the rest of their lives. Contrast to colonization from the West, China helps them to build infrastructure, opera houses, stadiums, hospitals and universities.

As in most of the previous investments from all foreign countries, Chinese make mistakes and hopefully they will learn from them and will not repeat the same mistakes. China and Africa should be good trade partners. When there is money available, corruption follows. That happens in most developing countries. Human rights typically improve with a better economy in most cases. Therefore in theory, China's economic improvement of the African economies ought to improve human rights.

Being a developing country herself, it is not China's responsibility to fight for the human rights / freedom of its trade partners. In many ways, China is close to a developed country. Africa is facing a lot of problems: debt, explosive population growth, competing with China's cheap products and bribery. Africans should start projects that can be paid back financially. Africa should force China to move some factories to Africa, especially those labor-intensive products. Following China's 'one child' policy is not a bad start.

The following is from an African. There was no new modern building, as they were expensive to buy from Europe. Now, there is almost a new one started every day with Chinese investment. China also helps us to have street lights even in villages among many improvements. The French had taken advantage of us in many ways as a colonial master, but not the Chinese.

Afterthoughts
Here is a great debate (http://www.YouTube.com/watch?v=FXck9BS3Hfw&feature=youtu.be) on China's aid to Africa. It has 7 parts and full of updated info. The two

panelists against China did not debate with facts but had their own agenda (one selling a book). Be your own judge.

Hillary Clinton talked about importing value to Africa. Value cannot feed Africans but Chinese investment does. Most of her arguments about civil human rights have overlooked the most basic human rights: food and shelters. The West dictates what African governments do with their own hidden agenda.

Her biased speech on China during the commencement was quite shocking as it was filled with unsubstantiated facts. The fact is China has improved miraculously in the last 30 years. As it has been slowing down recently, its economy has not crashed.

Obviously Secretary Clinton is more interested in selling her books and giving expensive speeches after leaving Obama's administration. She is impractical and irrational. She addresses China through controversies as controversies sell.

Links
Is China colonizing Africa? (Recommended)
https://www.youtube.com/watch?v=RENmQ2MBgZ0
From an African: https://www.youtube.com/watch?v=P5uzxV8ub9k
Filling the void
https://www.youtube.com/watch?v=wMCF2eu1D0E
Becoming China's China
https://www.youtube.com/watch?v=zQV_DKQkT8o

Section VI: Trade war with China

1   Trade war between US and China

I predict the trade war would not end soon, when China published their paper of no compromise. Trump-made problems would be fixed and Trump would declare victory. As of 2019, Trump cares about his election in less than 2 years and Xi's 10-year term has plenty of years left. A full-fledged trade war could not be good for both countries and the rest of the global economies.

I expect the forced transfer of technologies will be eliminated. It is an unfair bait for gaining the Chinese market. We have to blame the U.S. CEOs signing these agreements for their bonus consideration. So far, both sides have lost a combined total of 6 billion. Many long-term harms have been done to the U.S. Here is a summary of the actions and interactions from China.

	U.S.	China
Tariff	Will not gain a lot of jobs as other countries and robots would fill the gap.	Will pass tariffs to the consumers. Will have less profits. Will lose the market to some countries.
Barriers	Would open the market to more US products.	Patriotism would discourage citizens from buying our products.
Unfair rules	This is a bright spot for the US.	Could have had more impact 5 years ago. China depends less on foreign technologies than before.
Internal market	Will be reduced.	Will be expanded.
Treasury	Interest rates will be higher.	Reduce owning the US Treasury.
Depreciation of the Yuan	Harmful for export goods to China.	Make Chinese products more competitive.
Core technologies	Will lose these sectors to China eventually.	China will concentrate research on CPU and memory.

	Intel, Micron… have suffered already.	China may limit rare earth exports to US.
US allies	Eventually they will be sided with China due to economic reasons.	Eventually they will gain more.
US Corporation	Many will suffer such as Apple.	Less FDI.
Soy	A direct blow.	Will switch to other countries at higher prices. Soy will be reduced in the mix for feed.
Education & tourism	Will be decreased from China.	More universities and more tourists to Europe.

The U.S. wants China not to subsidize their industries. It is not valid as we subsidize ourselves such as in agriculture. Many new companies are formed by former MIT students and professors in the Boston area. Without the U.S. subsidies, there will be few of these companies. The above are my opinions on the outcomes. However, it is good for China in the long run as the huge deficit will not be sustainable. I expect there are winners with the settlement.

- Farmers will gain; the losers are the replaced countries such as Brazil.
- Boeing hopefully will gain despite the recent problem of the 737 Max planes. Should our government take out the ban on Huawei with China buying Boeing planes?
- Some selected drug companies will gain. I am looking for life-saving drugs that the Chinese do not have.
- Energy will gain such as LNG; the losers are countries being replaced such as Australia' LNG.
- S.E. Asia countries will be benefited as many Chinese factories will move there.
- The recent summit in Alaska reflected some of our problems and it was the first time China was so aggressive. Our negotiators were inexperienced facing the experienced top-notch counterparts from China. It is due to our two-party system. Our negotiators bashed China and could not prevent the media from leaving the room before Chinese counter attacks on our human rights records. BTW, this is the

year China signed the unfair treaty after the Boxer Rebellion 120 years ago, or 100 using the Chinese calendar (using 12 instead of 10).

2 Causes of the trade war

Besides the obvious huge trade deficit with China, the U.S. wants the world leading position not to be shaken by China. About 67% of our total deficit is from China from our estimate which is different from China's estimate. We need China to open their market to us and we also need why we are no longer competitive. Understand that the labor-intensive jobs will go to low-wage countries and China's labor cost is rising.

It is the response to China's "Made in 2025" and "One Belt, One Road" Initiatives. The first one challenges our technical leadership and the second one kicks us out of Africa and Southeast Asia. The U.S. does not want to lose the #1 position in world power and world influence.

It is right to slow down China from copying our technology. However, we need to do our own part such as stopping our companies from giving up their secrets for gaining access to the Chinese market. We have to have better safeguards on our secrets. China has violated a lot of trade agreements, and so has the U.S.

Trump believes we will be successful in the trade war with China with our upper hand in technologies if our allies compile with us. It could isolate us eventually. Even an iPhone can be used to spy as evidenced by the U.S. spying our allies. National security to me is more of an excuse.

Trump is a business man and the decision to reduce the deficit is correct. However, it is too fast and too full-fledged. There are many companies including HTC and Japanese chip companies that were destroyed by U.S. banning. This time it may not work with China. He cannot change the situation and globalization over-night. He is correct that we have a problem with China even though the market is at its height (as of 5/2019) and a good economy with almost full employment. With our national debt, the U.S. may have bankrupted already.

The trade war was started without considering the impact from both countries. Trump and his advisors did not understand the globalization and the economies that the world and especially the U.S. global companies are benefiting. In 6/2019, the U.S. economy is heading south in many economic indexes and Trump is in a hurry to settle the trade war during G20. Xi may not meet Trump to give him more pressure.

3 The root causes of a trade war

The trade war is supposedly used to fix the huge trade deficit with China.

The root cause is capitalism. The only objective of our corporations is making money. They take advantage of the cheap Chinese labor when China opened up.

The result of cheap Chinese labor means less jobs for the U.S. workers. The average family does not survive with one job in the U.S. The mother has to work and it floods the job market with more job seekers to make the conditions even worse. With the supply and demand, corporations reduce the wages and increase their profits.

As of the beginning of 2020, the unemployment rate is very low. But, is it a trick for the election year? In addition, the average salary is still lower than 2007 after inflation.

The government cut corporation tax rate. It is good for the stock market. The improved employment does not compensate for the revenue loss from the corporation taxes. In addition, the higher welfare expenses (due to the promises by our politicians in order to buy votes), our Federal deficit has increased to a record level.

We print money excessively and ask foreign countries to buy our debts; China and Japan are the top two lenders. When we cannot pay out the interests, the status of our USD as the reserve currency will be shaken. We know what happened to United Kingdom when the USD replaced the pound as the reserve currency.

The **second root cause** is that China is threatening the reserve status of USD. China, the biggest importer of oil, is replacing the USD to trade energy (mainly oil) with Yuan. China has purchased a lot of gold to back up her Yuan. Russia and Iran are the chief energy exporter to China. The petrodollar (all oil from Middle East countries are sold in USD) era may be over. The embargo to Huawei has backfire. I expect within 2021, Huawei will not need a single chip import from U.S., and that will be total financial losses from affected companies forever.

China had imported G1, G2 and G3 technologies from the U.S. and the West. Most likely most countries have been spied by U.S. There is not a single incidence of spying by Huawei so far. Huawei is the center of this trade war as it will threaten the U.S.'s own spying and the leadership in technology.

The **third root cause** is nothing to do with the trade war but the world leadership. China has been spending a lot on infrastructure, education and industries that would challenge the U.S. in the future. We have been spending too much on our endless wars.

The following are related topics:

Money talks

In order to capture the huge Chinese market, corporations gave out our secrets to Chinese. The CEOs care about their bonuses / options, which depend on the corporate profits.

Walmart becomes one of the largest companies by selling cheap Chinese products to meet the high demands of the poorer U.S. citizens.

Are we better off?

With low unemployment, you think we're better off. The additional tariffs will pass to us the consumers. It hurts the poor more.

Many states in the U.S. have the average income of $30,000. You would live like a king in many countries but you cannot survive in U.S. without all kinds of subsidies.

The rich gap is widening. The rich own stocks in the corporations and they become richer. The poor is getting poorer.

California is the 5th economy after Germany and before United Kingdom if it were a country. It has Hollywood and the Silicon Valley. It has about 1/5 of the total homeless folks in the U.S. Many homeless folks are not unemployed. Most have low-wage (relatively) jobs that they cannot afford to rent an apartment. It is an example of the worst of capitalism.

Can the politicians fix these problems with all the money? The priority is to satisfying the rich and in this case the corporations. They cannot tax the rich to the maximum as they can just give up the U.S. citizenship. All the projects such as infrastructure will not pay off for them in the next election (a four-year cycle). Seattle with corporation Microsoft, Boeing and Starbucks is another state with the same problem as California.

4   Potential impact of our trade war with China

As of 7/15/2018, Trump may ask for a forest and settle for a tree. Hopefully it would end the trade war. This article describes what China would react to the full-fledged trade war. Even if there is no trade war, China would prepare herself better for the future.

- China will not meet the demands of the US and cannot counter react effectively.

    The gap of trade deficit is huge. Part of the trade deficit is due to including the component costs (such as the iPhone), not counting the service deficit (Chinese tourism and Chinese attending colleges here) and profits of our companies in China. China's estimate of trade deficit is 60% less than ours.

- China would fall into a recession. I guess it would be brief and mild. Her GDP growth would fall to 5% (partly also due to high inflation), which is still good for most developed countries. The major problems are high debt, high inflation and low employment especially to the new college graduates.

    China's economy depends on her export to the US. It will turn to other partners such as the participants in the "One Belt, One Road" projects, outsource the manufacturing to other countries that have little tariff impact and concentrate more on her huge internal market.

- It would be a blow to China's scheme in cutting internal debt, which has been high and risky.

- China will speed up research and investment on core technologies such as manufacturing of chips. The middle class will suffer except those who involve in core technologies.

- From the ZTE experience, China should weigh more on US supply on core technologies such as chips than tariffs.

Once China masters these technologies in 10 or so years, China can really stand up and say no to us. Today we have about 65% of our science Ph.D. graduates are foreigners with a good percent from China.

China recently ban Micron's memory chip. The world's second fastest computer (after three times number one) is made of CPU chips by China after US banning US CPU chips to China. The world may under estimate China's potential in core technologies. In addition, it is not impossible to buy many components from other suppliers.

- China will continue to attract Chinese who have technical skills to return to the motherland. China will also attract top scientists from all over the world. It is easier than before when research funds in US have been reduced.

- China would have closer partnership with many countries such as Canada while we would be more isolated.

- China will withdraw or at least will not buy more of our Treasuries. It would raise our interest rates and it would have adverse effect on our stock market. The Fed would be forced to buy more.

- China will devalue the yuan. When it has been down by 10% recently, the tariffs would be not as effective as before. It would make her products cheaper and tourists will flood to China. The payback of the loans in USD will be beneficial to China.

- Profits from many corporations will suffer such as Boeing, GM, Ford and companies that supply chips and/or components to China. The stock owners of these stocks will suffer.

- India and many countries will benefit from the trade war. To illustrate this, India will be more competitive in farm commodities replacing US export to China due to tariffs.

- US will gain some jobs, but not as much as expected. Many even predicted we will have net job loss. Some jobs will be replaced by robots and some will be lost due to the trade war. Most manufacturing jobs cannot compete with low-wage countries such as Mexico.

- Some of our products depending on imported commodities will cost more to make and hence less competitive. More corporations will move their manufacturing to other countries to minimize the effect of tariffs. Tesla announced opening a plant in China. A motor bike company is moving their production line to S.E. country to benefit for tariff-free among these countries and less tariffs for steel and aluminum. Many other companies will follow.

- Some Chinese imports will be replaced by other low-wage countries. In this case, we gain nothing but our consumers will pay more. It happened before when we banned Chinese tires that were replaced by lower-quality tires at higher costs from other countries.
- Even with the tariffs, some Chinese imports are still competitive to US and/or other low-wage countries. Hence the tariff is a kind of tax added to our consumers.
- China has not used her most powerful chip: rare earth elements. If we ban core technologies such as memory chip to import to China, China will take this ultimate weapon.
- The farmers especially the soybean farmers will voice their discontent against Trump. Trump would not last for another term with the opposition from farmers, Hispanic voters and Obamacare recipients.
- China is waiting for the next political leader replacing Trump and s/he may have different view that is more favorable to China.

Trade war is a loss-loss scenario. In the long run, it would be good for China but bad for the US. In the short run, the reverse would be true.

Even without a trade war, the damages have been done. China will focus on long-term solutions such as core technologies. China will reduce the holding (more than $1 trillion) US treasury bonds. The yuan has started to depreciate. We become more isolated from our best partners Mexico, Canada and EU.

I hope the trade war will not materialize and we settle down with cutting at least half of the deficit (2018 U.S. estimated about 67% of our total deficit is with China). But, from whose estimate?

Trade war articles: Google it and here are some: 1 2 3 4 (deficit) 5 6 7

5   From "Made in China" to "Designed in China"

After Deng's reform, China has been the global factory but not been innovative compared to the US. There are only several recognized Chinese brands outside China. However, we have been seeing changes in front of our eyes.

Why Chinese have not been innovative

- As of 2018, China is moving up from a developing country to a developed country. It is not there yet, but it is getting closer. In many sectors China has been in the leading edge.

- Protection of intelligence properties is still in the infancy in China.

- During Mao's communism era, Chinese did not think outside the box.

- Traditionally Chinese education system encourages students to be good in exams by remembering formula, data, facts and how to take exams.

- The global US brands are partly due to the spreading of US culture via movies and music. China only have a handful of global brands. Today Chinese products compete with low prices and in developing countries. It has changed in several sectors.

Why is changing

- As product value is climbing, it requires innovation for better profit margins. Most large corporations in China have strong research departments. With a large local and foreign markets, the research would be paid off and some already did.

- With a lot of innovative products, China naturally has to protect her own intelligence properties.

- Many do think outside the box. Chinese have seen the successes and the generated wealth from innovative products.

- We have not yet seen the geniuses like Gates and Zuckerberg in China. However, China does have schools for geniuses in most Tier I cities. Even the traditional schools encourage innovation thinking.

Many of my classmates become innovators after the Peking-duck education in high schools. The owner of DJI, the largest company in consumer drones, graduated from college and got a small grant from his college to start the company. It is a successful model to follow among many.

- Chinese students work harder than American counterpart. If you believe the students working 3 hours less (my estimate) every day will achieve the same in life, you believe in fairy tales.
- The government encourages education while our leaders cut research and school budgets. I know three Ph.D. in space engineering in US: one retired and two are still looking for jobs. All those talks on improving science education are just garbage or our leaders are out-of-touch.
- You can hire 4 engineers in China for the price of 1 engineer in US. They are dedicated with no distortion of sports, coffee breaks, long vacations...
- Most large projects have a technology transfer clause. If you do not comply, China gives the projects to your competitor. Some are due to the short-term profits. It would mean bonuses to the officials and stock appreciation. Some are due to the promise of the huge China's market for their products.
- China is also buying many US and EU companies for the technology and/or the market share. Many bankrupting companies were bought by Chinese. Many purchases may be backed by Chinese government.
- Many espionages and cyber hackings are proven or suspected that Chinese are stealing our trade and military secrets.
- China needs to establish brand names for better-quality products at higher prices.
- China needs to set and enforce regulations for product quality. To illustrate this, if the battery can cause a fire, no one in the right mind would buy the products with Chinese-made batteries inside. It is the same for safety of food products.
- China is #1 in applying science in many areas such as G5 and many infrastructure technology, but not in basic science. That's why they have to steal from the West. Without total freedom, it is hard to advance in basic science.

"Made in China 2025" is an important milestone for China to improve the core components to 70%. With the threat of banning China from buying from US core components such as chips for Chinese mobile phone, I believe the strategy will be changed and accelerated. It is easily said than done as US leads the chip and the manufacturing equipment. Hence together with farm products, China cannot say no to us right now, but in more than 5 years, she can.

Links: 1 2 3 4 5 6 7 8

6 Decoupling

Trump proposed decoupling with China. It has materialized to some extent as of 4/2020. The U.S. citizens and the two political parties blame China for all their ills. Many jobs will not move back to the U.S. but to Vietnam and India. There will not be a lot of jobs gained and they have to pay higher prices at worse quality as illustrated by banning tires from China. Our corporations will suffer too, losing China's educated labor and the huge market in China. It also motivates China to advance to higher-value products and China will not depend on U.S. such as the computer chips.

China did not want to decouple from the U.S. However, it may not be up to China's choice and China is more frustrated with us. In 2019, China shipped about 18% of their total exports to us. It is high but not much compared to Hong Kong (14%).

The decoupling may not be totally agreed upon by both countries and that could lead to first a cold war and then a military war. In any case, we will be more isolated except with Canada and Mexico. Iran and Russia already have a strong tie with China. The following summarizes briefly the consequences.

Affecting both countries
- Our trade deficits with each other will be zero from a total decoupling.
- Chinese stocks will be delisted in U.S. exchanges. It will hurt these Chinese stocks for a few months.
- Our firms such as MacDonald's and GM will be withdrawn from China. Their assets (not including the names and trademarks) will be sold to Chinese companies.
- Citizens of both countries would have a record, unfavorable attitude towards each other.
- As of 2021, we have stopped most Chinese science students admitted to our top universities, which are suffering financially.

Affecting us
- In a survey dated 5/2020, 96% of U.S. corporations do not want to leave China even though our government pays the moving expenses

due to increasing the costs of goods and losing China's huge market. They may not support Trump's election.

- China would sell our debts. It would shake the USD as a reserve currency.
- China would ban exporting rare earth elements to us. There are not too many substitutions and the prices for these elements would skyrocket.
- China would ban exporting active drug ingredients to us.
- There will be zero Chinese tourists. Chinese tourists have the highest spending among all foreign tourists. Coupled with the pandemic, many retail stores would close.
- There will be zero Chinese students. The 370,000 Chinese students in 2019 had been financing the U.S. colleges as most pay full tuition. Coupled with the pandemic, many colleges would be in tough times. It is happening in most of our English-speaking allies.
- Chinese foreign students.

https://www.youtube.com/watch?v=jDlEI_ugL7k

China should open more colleges and hence save a lot of foreign currencies. China should fund research and higher learning. Chinese students face a lot of competition to enter colleges, and they are very hard working. Before the pandemic, I estimate about 1/3 of all foreign students were from China, and most paid full tuition.

- The Chinese goods will be replaced by other countries. They will cost more and at worse quality. The previous example is replacing tires from other countries when Chinese tires were banned.
- We may not gain a lot of jobs as they will be moved to low-wage countries such as countries in S.E. Asia.
- Huawei will ask Verizon and other companies to pay royalties in using their technology and even worse banning using Huawei's patents in their 5G components. If they refuse, Chinese will freely use the U.S. patents without paying royalties.
- U.S. companies making chips will lose their needed export to China and eventually they would become competitors to Chinese chip makers in the global market.
- Apple would face losing the market and manufacturing capacity in China.

Affecting China
- China's economy will deteriorate for at least 3 years. However, China's government has a lot of cash reserves and Chinese are still happy to go back a decade or two when the country was poorer.
- Many small factories are out-of-business. Many factories are moving to Southeast Asia. It affects the lower class of workers in South China and many workers have been moving back to farms where they came from.
- Chinese will pay more for farm products that are replaced by other countries.
- China will concentrate more effort on agriculture and farmland. Today Chinese do not really need American farm products. China is close to feeding her citizens by her own agriculture, which would be enhanced.
- Chinese high-tech will suffer initially. However, if they can get them from foreign countries other than the U.S., they should be fine. The U.S. is trying to stop our allies from importing these products to China. If the U.S. does not or cannot stop TMSC (a Taiwanese company) from manufacturing chips for Chinese companies, China should be fine. Huawei's phones and 5G network do not use U.S. chips.
- For the first time in the last 30 years in my memory, there are no Chinese students entering M.I.T. this fall of 2020. The return of Chinese students has been helping China to advance in technologies.

Affecting the world
- The trade war between China and the U.S. is taking a break until the pandemic is controlled in the U.S.
- There will be a global recession for at least a year.
- World supply chain will be changed.
- De-globalization would make products more expensive.
- Low-wage jobs are being moved to low-wage countries. High-value products are being moved to Japan, Taiwan, South Korea and even the U.S.A. Mexico is benefiting from jobs in between.
- Japan, Taiwan, Saudi Arabia, Canada and Mexico would stay with us. The EU countries will take side initially and they will side with China for economic reasons. Finally, Australia will side with China due to

economic reasons; today about one third of their exports to China and Chinese accounts to 15% of the foreign tourists.

Summary

There will be no winner in decoupling. The worst is that it would lead to a military war. We no longer force China to accept our standards and our way of doing business. The global order is the same as the U.S. order that China does not abide by. As of 4/2021, the entities list of including the advanced computers is close to total decoupling. Pew's survey has over 80% of citizens are negative towards China. However, the high-tech companies and many corporations such as Boeing and auto companies have more than 50% wanting to be on better terms with China.

7 The hawks and the doves

I am one of the doves hoping China and the U.S. can co-exist peacefully. It would benefit my (and most likely your) wealth and living standard by doing so. For example, by decoupling, all the chicken feet will be dumped into the ocean instead of selling them to the Chinese, who treat them as delicacies.

There are many hawks including Esper and Pompeo. Many work for the military or are retired from it. Without wars, they do not have jobs. Yes, we need to have a small army to defend the country and I'm grateful for all the arm forces fighting for us. Many work for the defense sector. Without wars, these companies would go bankrupt, even if it is good for mankind. Most of our leaders want to flex our military muscle to ensure we are on top and boost their shameless ego. That's why we have had endless wars since WW2. Our huge war expenses should be redirected to improve our living standard and our deplorable infrastructure.

The media reports what you want to hear. They usually demonize China so they can sell more stuff. The following are my opinions. Take out nationalism for a moment, and determine for yourself which are right or wrong.

The following article outlined Defense Secretary Mark Esper's opinions and I will discuss his points.
https://www.defensenews.com/opinion/commentary/2020/03/19/espers-dark-vision-for-us-china-conflict-makes-war-more-likely/

Mark: It will take to complete the U.S. drawdown (in Afghanistan.).
Tony: Is this the reason we deploy our military to the South China Sea?

Mark: And the Air Force described a flight by a nuclear-capable B-52 bomber over Somalia in February as, in part, a warning to China of engagement to come.
Tony: What do you think if China does the same close to one of our coastal cities?

Mark: The United States is in a new 'era of great power competition'.
Tony: China has not expressed 'great power competition'. In addition, China has a non-interference clause in their foreign policy.

Mark: China that continues to grow its military strength, its economic power, its commercial activity...

Tony: What is wrong with being stronger? Did the U.S. at one time get stronger and stronger?

Mark: do the things that really undermine our [and our allies'] sovereignty, that undermine the rule of law, that really question [Beijing's] commitment to human rights.

Tony: That is our standard. China has lifted millions from starving to death in the last few decades. Is it the #1 in human rights? In addition, we use double standards. Do you believe Saudi Arabia and many countries have far worse human rights than China? We keep our mouths shut and our eyes closed, as they are supposed to be our 'friends'. Which nationalists did participate in the 911 attack? Is our constant gun shooting at each other a human rights violation?

The article: in illicit business practices, including hacking and theft of trade secrets

Tony: Most if not all countries spy on each other and steal trade secrets. If you believe the CIA is a friendly information gathering agency, you believe in fairy tales. Do you believe Microsoft, Google and any major companies do not steal secrets from each other? Should we blame someone for not protecting our secrets, especially those secrets on national security?

The article: But none of it remotely justifies twisting great power competition into a shooting war.

Tony: I agree whole-heartedly.

The article: a U.S.-China war would pose a real threat to the American homeland.

Tony: I agree whole-heartedly.

The article: Our goal with Beijing (and Moscow, for that matter) should be diplomacy, mutual economic benefit and peace — not war.

Tony: This is my goal too.

Do you agree with me more or our 'Offense' Secretary more?

8 Trade war to a military war

The failure of one or more of the following would lead to a military war with China: trade war, our economy (partly due to the Pandemic), resolving the conflict between China and Taiwan and our loss of USD as a reserve currency. From this pandemic, we know cooperation between countries works. If we sue China on this virus, China would take counter actions and it would spell military conflict.

This time is most likely started by us. China's objective is improving the living standard of her citizens and capturing her status in the world's stage. China has a non-interference clause in her foreign policy.

Why do our leaders want to start a war? It is for short-term gain in their political positions. We never care about the long-term consequences. In addition, WW2 had not occurred physically in the U.S. country.

We never learned from history

One of the reasons for the breakup of the U.S.S.R. was the huge expenses of the war in Afghanistan.

The French failed in Vietnam before us. Does Vietnam threaten the safety of our country today?

We have never found a mass-destruction weapon in Iraq.

All these wars cause us a lot of resources that should be used to improve our economy. We have wasted money in our military expenses, maintaining foreign military sites.

Chances of a war with China

It has been reduced due to the advances in Chinese weapons. It is decades behind. However, it is more than enough to defend herself. The fast missiles could make our carriers sitting ducks though it has not been tested.

If we send the children of our leaders to the front line, there will be no war. The youths should spend the best time of their lives in education and jobs instead of being sent back in body bags. The percentage of black soldiers is high and hence it is a kind of social injustice.

We have a lot of hawks in our government. Most are sponsored by our offense industry.

Link
Destined for war
https://www.youtube.com/watch?v=U0BlhVdQ1Wo

#Filler: A stupid act

Pompeo wanted to travel to Europe during his last week as the secretary of the State under Trump's administration. Obviously, it is for his ego, future books and /or his ambition in politics. European politicians have nothing to talk to him about, as he is not important any more. Finally, this puppet is not loyal to his master.

#Filler
The lame duck period should be further reduced to enough time for a peaceful transfer. We should reduce the time for no important actions by our government.

9 The end of mankind?

The possible military war between the U.S. and China could bring the end of mankind. Excuse me for treating this serious subject less serious. With an open mind, let's evaluate what could possibly happen with several scenarios. I will compare their military forces. If the military war starts, most of our wealth would lose about 80% from our recent peak in 2021. It will adversely affect to the next generations to come as they have to pay for our increased debts.

I hope the war will never happen. If they discover the first virus patient is not from China, the U.S. will not ask for damages from this pandemic and hence there is no military war. The conventional military war could be promoted to a nuclear one, which would destroy the coastal cities in both countries.

The root cause of the war
The conflict between the two countries started with the trade war. It is not just about trade but the U.S.'s protecting our #1 position in the world. Our leaders have to do it militarily today before China is gaining more strength especially in military – you decide whether it is right or wrong. China is passing us in several technologies such as 5G and mobile pay. China becomes #1 in building high-speed trains. Compared to U.S., it is a small leak that would get larger. Our GDP per capita is many times that of China.

Foreplay
As of 4/2020, decoupling has been exercised to some extent. Our leader has asked our citizens to return from China after the outbreak of the virus in Wuhan and our factories to be moved back.

Our leader wants to put the blame of this pandemic on China. Some of our allies have been convinced. We do not want to agitate China further now, as we need China's medical supplies to fight this pandemic.

After the pandemic, our leader would ask China for damages. Naturally China would not agree. The world has not asked for damages for many similar cases such as H1N1 (most likely started in Mexico), Ebola, AID, Mad Cow and the 2007 financial crisis caused by Lehman Brothers.

The U.S. may want to repeat the history of the Eight-Nation Alliance and this time it would be led by us. China today is not the China in the Eight-Nation Alliance era, during which China lost to the alliance's military might and went bankrupt. China has learned this bitter lesson.

It is similar to spreading the word of "mass-destruction weapons". It convinced our allies, and then gave us the reason to conquer Iraq. The media were crazy reporting this 'lie'. Shame on you, media! How many died from this lie? Now, no one finds any proof of such weapons. It is another example of "when a lie has been repeated 1,000 times, it becomes 'fact'. China is no Iraq, and it could lead to a cold war, a military war and even a nuclear war.

Looking back at recent history, the U.S. had not won a war when China was on the other side, such as the Korean War and the Vietnam War.

Most likely the participating allies would be the United Kingdom, Australia and Taiwan. Japan and S. Korea would weigh the consequences on the economic ties with China. With very close economic tie, Australia would be a loser if she joins the U.S. in this war. I expect most European countries would agree with us but not participate in the military war.

China's spokesperson on foreign affairs has been more aggressive to our accusations than before. It seems China has prepared to the decoupling. For example, Huawei's new phones can use non-U.S. chips; it could be a big loss for our chip companies.

Trump asked our Federal retirement program to sell all Chinese stocks; I warned on Chinese stocks in August, 2020. I predict many Chinese from China would move a lot of their U.S. assets somewhere else. China's counter-action chips are our Treasury bonds, rare earth elements, medical supplies and active ingredients of drugs to start.

From trade war to a military war
The following is what I expect to happen. I sincerely hope I am wrong.

China would refuse to pay for damages for this pandemic. A U.S. court would side with the U.S. Then the U.S. would freeze China's assets and ignore our debt (1.07 T as of Dec., 2019) owned by China. China would take counter actions such as freezing U.S. factories (3M and Tesla for example) and investments such as MacDonald's assets in China.

There are other catalysts. Trump would divert attention if he loses the reelection. Taiwan declares independence (not likely). The islet disputes in the China Sea; it is not likely due to today's very low cost of oil. N. Korea invades S. Korea; it is only likely unless the war between the U.S. and China materializes. China's water redirect project would cause India to ask the U.S. for help; it is not likely that we will help India. The constant showing military might could lead to accidents.

The next step is the military. The first strike would be important to weaken the other side by destroying the war capabilities. Both countries have nuclear submarines and mobile launchers that cannot be detected easily. The U.S.'s first strike would cost them a lot politically especially inside the U.S. China's first strike would be less damaging to them as the enemies are at the gates.

Comparison of military power
The U.S. is far **more powerful** in military strength. However, the U.S. is further away from the battlefield. The participating allies are not powerful enough to make a dent. Japan's air force is negligible and S. Korea has only helped us to fight against N. Korea. Taiwan has a lot of older fighter jets from the U.S. Russia would help China, but she would balance the consequences carefully. Most likely Russia would not send military force until China is winning.

The U.S. has full combat experience in wars as have been in wars most of the time since WW2. China has several brief, regional conflicts beside the Korean War and Vietnam War.

Today's war is decided by technology. China has their "carrier killer" missiles and supersonic missiles that have not been tested in the field against our super missile protection system. We have some hints on how good they are from China's older missiles purchased by Saudi Arabia. The superior fighter jets demonstrated effectiveness in the desert, but not against today's Chinese missiles, especially intermediate range (that U.S. is behind due to the treaty with Russia), and the superior Russia's AS400 defense system. Hence, China could shoot down jet fighters and also the airfields.

China has the capability to destroy our satellites that our smart missiles and missile defense systems depend on; we have the same capability. American drones are superior to their Chinese counterparts. However, China can deploy hundreds of drones each carrying a bomb simultaneously from their coast. The other tool is cyber weapons which have not been used in wars.

The U.S.'s superior technology could be a big factor. During the U.S. first strike, many Chinese military airfields and missile sites with the exception of the mobile missile launchers would be destroyed, if China had not destroyed the U.S. satellites. The low-flying jets cannot be detected easily by the Chinese radar systems. The U.S. outnumbers the number of jets with aerial refueling capability that makes the distance less important. In desperation, China may launch nuclear missiles to California via their nuclear submarines, which are hard to detect. We have about 4,000 nuclear heads versus China's 300. We have bombers that can carry nuclear weapons, while Chinese jets cannot fly long distance. Both countries have submarines that can go long distance and carry missiles.

When the war drags on, China would be more favorable to win. Our citizens would not agree with any lengthy war such as the Vietnam War. Regardless of the result of this war, China would be more united as a nation. Contrary to what our government expects, China's government would be strengthened. China can supply their warfare machines / missiles faster as they are the world's #1 factory. In the last few years, China also solves their energy supply bottleneck via the "One Belt, One Road" Initiative. In a sentence, China has been preparing for this war for a long while.

Scenarios
- The U.S. and China settle the disputes peacefully. I hope this is the trick of passing the blame to China for Trump's reelection purpose. Both would declare victory. This is what I wish for.
- The U.S. and China settle the disputes with a lot of treaties and the two countries will be decoupled partially or totally. Both countries would lose trades, but lives will go on. In a decade or two, China would by-pass us in many areas with the exceptions of the military and living standard.
- If there is a military war, it would last for a long time. The longer the war, the better China would fare. Hopefully it would be a brief war if it happens.

- Both countries destroy each other. The EU and Russia would be the winners. It is similar to why we became #1 after WW2 when Europe was destroyed. There is a good chance that the EU would become the reserve currency and our USD would lose a lot of value.

  China would prepare for the next war better. China would replace her legacy military weapons with up-to-date weapons and China would learn how to combat in a modern war. Our beaten economy (that is already in bad shape today) would take our military to the back seat.
- It would boost the arms race and hence make the defense (or offense) sector for both countries more profitable. During the war, gold prices would rise.
- Destroying the world using nuclear weapons. Although China said that they would not be the first country to use nuclear weapons, who knows when they are desperate? It is better for me to build an ark in Alaska. China declared that China will use nuclear weapon on Japan if Japan sent soldiers to Taiwan.

I hope the two countries will settle the conflicts peacefully. There is no winner in this military war and citizens of both countries would suffer for decades.

Links

Coming war with China (recommended)
https://www.youtube.com/watch?v=vAfeYMONj9E&t=1118s

From the expert
https://nationalinterest.org/blog/buzz/we-asked-military-expert-fight-us-china-war-we-wished-we-didnt-107826

China military
https://www.globalfirepower.com/country-military-strength-detail.asp?country_id=china

Filler: Our culture

Did you notice many received free groceries in the luxury cars? It is our "someone will bail us out" culture.

Filler: Trump said he was very rich

Most folks say the opposite. I am very dumb. See the logic.

10   Winners in a trade war with China

Winners are:
- Vietnam is obviously the largest beneficiary from this trade war. Many factories have been moved from China to Vietnam. Many are owned by Chinese. China has helped Vietnam to improve their infrastructure. It has already gained about 8% of its GDP from the new business and is experiencing an influx of foreign direct investments.
- India could be a beneficiary too. They have a lot of problems to be fixed internally. They should copy the model of China by opening a special economic zone.
- Malaysia is a winner too. China will eventually cut the rare earth elements to the U.S. Many countries including the U.S. and Australia produce these ores. They do not refine them due to the damage to the environment. Most will be refined in Malaysia instead of in China.
- Countries may replace the U.S. as the chip and product suppliers to China. Japan, S. Korea, Taiwan and many EU countries are obvious beneficiaries. Some of them do not want to do business with China at the fear of being punished by the U.S.
- Russia will replace the U.S. as the supplier of energy such as LNG to China. They will have a closer tie than their history has shown.
- The South East Asia countries and some South American countries such as Brazil and Argentina would benefit and replace American agricultural products for China.
- Ericsson and Nokia will be the primary supplier of a 5G network to countries that ban Huawei's products. However, Ericsson's initial implementation is very poor compared to Huawei's. Taiwan could be the biggest winner when many consumer electronic products will be switched here from China. Rural areas in the U.S. will suffer without Huawei's network.
- Many companies such as Samsung and Apple will capture Huawei's mobile phone market in Europe.
- More tourists and Chinese students will come to Europe, particularly the EU countries.

Some of the symbols of the affected companies and country ETF are: VNM, INDA, EWT, ARGT, ERIC and NOK. As of 6/2020, INDA, ERIC and NOK are not doing well.

11   Losers in a trade war with China

The following are based on my predictions on a full-fledged trade war with China. I would buy the winners and short the losers. When the trade war is settled, reverse the losers and winners. Losers are:

- American farmers and their suppliers such as fertilizers and farm equipment will be the chief losers. The government subsidies cannot last forever. Many have already lost their farms while their products have filled up storage spaces. Currently Brazil and Argentina are filling in the gaps to supply these products to China. It could change as China has to satisfy the trade talks plus their flood and pig flu problem.
- After the cutoff date, many chip suppliers to China will lose a lot of sales as China is the chief importer. It will take at least a year for countries to take up the slack. In 10 or so years, China will develop their own chip products. Hence, they will be back to normal in 2 years, and they will face China's competition in 10 or so years. I bet Huawei will have all chips made in China in 2030.
- Many U.S. companies are still profiting in China. These days are numbered with the trade war. Apple and many U.S. fast food joints will suffer.
- China in the future will reduce their number of buying new planes from Boeing and/or switch the orders to Airbus. Today China still needs a lot of new planes and hence the effect may not be immediate. China is the largest market for airplanes. If the U.S. bans selling GE's jet engines to China, China will buy them from the EU and/or Russia.
- Australia siding with the U.S. will be a serious loser. Australia supplies China with iron ores and agriculture products. Ironically, some of Australia's farm products were replaced by the U.S. It will be a big blow to Australia's economy. The losses of Chinese tourists and students add to the suffering. The current government may be reelected. Actually, national security would be better if they sided with China.
- Many Chinese companies, especially Huawei, will suffer a lot even with the help from the Chinese government. Huawei could lose their popular mobile phone sales outside China.
- The markets in both the U.S. and China will fail. It could lead to a global recession.
- China would withdraw the Treasuries they own. Together with trading energy without using USD, it could shake our current status of our USD as a reserve currency. In 2008, the U.S. asked China to buy our Treasuries, and China did but not this time.
- China would limit their export of rare earth elements and active ingredients to our drugs to us.

Phase one of the trade war as of 1/16/2020 is a win for Trump. However, it is not sustainable in the long run. For example, China cannot consume the amount of the farm imports. When China is ready to say No, they will not honor this unfair treaty and phase two will have more problems. At that time, Iran and Russia will side with China for oil / gas. The EU will too or they are losing a lot of orders such as Airbus from China. Our EU allies Germany, Italy and Spain most likely will side with China. It would force the EU countries to seek a side.

Link: China & US
https://www.youtube.com/watch?v=XepCi0l_g6I

12 What and who will replace Chinese products?

In early 2020, the U.S. government will not benefit from the tariffs. There are several scenarios:

1. Some Chinese products are still competitive after the tariffs. In this case, they are not replaced.
2. The Chinese products will be replaced by U.S. It is not likely as it is too expensive to manufacture here and some jobs would be done by robots. In reality we are losing jobs. Huawei moved the research in the U.S. to Italy and we're losing about 1,000 high-paid jobs.
3. Supply chain is not easily set up in the U.S. or other low-wage countries. We have to deal with the reduced import of Chinese rare earth elements. Australia ores and S.E. Asia countries to refine them could be a long-term solution. In the meantime, we will depend on limited reserves and recycling. China has provided political stability for decades.
4. Many factories have moved to South East Asia. Most if not all have problems such as skilled labor (Apple can get hundreds of engineers to work on a new design for example), unions, inadequate infrastructure, corruption (yes, worse than China)...
5. In some ways, China is solving some problems such as in S.E. Asia by building infrastructure and supplying educated labor. Many factories moved to this region are owned by Chinese.
6. There may be some low-wage countries who did not compete with China but now they can with the tariffs on China. Judging from banning Chinese tires, I bet these products cost the consumers more and at a worse quality.
7. The U.S. will be better in handling cross shipment as they did in the last decades. A shirt could be completely made in China, except two

buttons and the "Made in Vietnam" label. The buttons, the label and the thread are most likely made in China.
8. The world including the U.S. depend on China's ingredients in making drugs. Some ingredients are almost monopolized by China. It is evident from the current Wuhan's Pandemic with the reduced export.

Our trade deficit will be worse on the contrary. These low-wage countries do not buy our airplanes and computers as the Chinese do. China is biting the bullet and betting Trump will not be reelected.

Will India replace China?

The short answer is "No", at least not in the near future. Using Apple as an example, it is hard and risky to move the Apple factory away from China. It involves many factories that build components for Apple (i.e., the supply chain). It has been built up for many decades. The recent riot in Apple's India factory is a roadblock .Our politicians can understand one side of the equation.

Many factories for low-value products will be moved to Southeast Asia and Africa. Besides the tariffs, China's wages are increasing and the population is aging. China has to move to higher-value products such as 5G and concentrate on her huge internal consumers. China has moved 800 M from poverty to middle class in the last 4 decades. Here are the reasons why India will not replace China, even though India is democratic and has a relatively young population. Many Indians in the U.S. are doing very well. However, they are the upper class, and they do not represent the entire India. To summarize, India's problems are protectionism and bureaucracy. The strengths are her young population and fertile farmland. If they can copy China's economic model, they could be as strong as China in the next decade.

- Corruption. You need to apply for many permits to set up a business from securing land to applying for electricity. Every step you have to pay a bribe. If you think China is corrupt, India is far, far more.
- The government is not stable with a lot of unrest and protests compared to China. Wealth gap is huge compared to most other countries. The 2020 problems are the financial system, farm protests and Apple plant.
- Weak infrastructure. India lacks good roads, bridges, ports and airports. You need a stable electricity supply. It is primitive compared to China.

- Education. Yes, we see a lot of educated Indians in the U.S. and heading many corporations. They are the minority and the upper class in India. Those who can write the name cannot be classified as literate. Chinese have 9 years of free, compulsory education.
- High birth rate would consume all the limited resources. They need a 'one-child' policy.
- India is not safe. Tourists are being treated. Rapes even raping babies are common. The rich have a small army to protect themselves.
- India has the most of the top polluted cities in the world.
- There are too many languages, but most speak some English. So are cultures and religions. Social class is a big problem in India.
- India always takes advantage of foreigners such as the high-speed rail project by the Japanese. GM found the hard way and knew there was no internal market for their cars assembled there; they moved out.
- There are too many protests.
- Protectionism. India uses tariffs to protect local products. As a result, most of their products are poor quality. That is the reason India withdrew from RCEP.
- When they spend too much time on religions, the economy would be neglected. There are so many 'holy' cows roaming in cities.

Link: https://www.youtube.com/watch?v=mWQdZoq3iN4&t=1829s

#Filler: Simple measures to reduce net security.
Do not click any links from unknown sources. MalwareBytes, for checking viruses, is free for download (they do not pay me). Personally, I use a Chromebook for my financial transactions and a two-factor login for my stock trading.

#Filler: Silence is golden

I am glad I did not give advice to a friend who had to decide whether to take a lump sum payment or an annuity. The correction in March, 2020 would wipe out a lot of his portfolio if he took the lump sum payment. No one would share his profits when the predictions are correct, but the blame if it does not materialize.

It is the same in investing that nothing is certain. With educated guesses, we should have more rights than wrongs especially in the long run.

Section VII: 2020 disasters

Coronavirus could increase fire in our conflict with China. I have predicted China's disaster back in August, 2020 correctly as the article has been published in that time frame in several of my books.

1 Pandemic

II have to wear two hats, one for humanity and one for investing. I am very grateful to all the front-line workers such as doctors, nurses, drug researchers, ambulance workers and police. Many have died from this pandemic. The majority of our population have suffered from serious financial situations. Do not be depressed as there is always a better tomorrow.

As of 1/2021, more than 410,000 U.S. citizens have died of this disease. There will be an impact to the global economies. The U.S. pledged trillions of rescue money and it would affect her economy adversely in the long term. The root cause of this virus has not been found and there is a good chance it may never be found. So far, there is no concrete proof how this pandemic started. There are rumors and some are belonged to the conspiracy theories:

Causes
- Caused by Chinese eating game food. It is likely but there is no concrete proof so far. An Indian scientist said that it was almost impossible. I do not rule out that the disposed lab animals were sold in the wet market.
- A YouTube video indicates it was caused by two Chinese scientists who stole the virus and it escaped from the lab in Wuhan. Seems a rumor fabricated in the U.S. It is denied by several prestigious organizations and articles.

Several scientists argue that it is not possible this virus is created in the lab. The outbreak is in Wuhan, but we cannot conclude where the source is. The earliest patient could be a French who did not travel to China. I wonder whether some of the substantially increased deaths from flu this year are actually caused by this virus instead of e-cigarettes. So far and according to some unproven sources, China has 3G of this virus while the U.S. has 1G to 5G. The first patient so far is a female U.S. soldier attending the sports event in Wuhan.

China and many other countries will take preventive actions such as limiting eating games. China should also set up an organization such as CDC to speed up the warning without waiting for Beijing's decision to publicize.

The U.S. should have more preventive measures such as building up inventories for the masks, ventilation machines, covering hoods and the manufacturing capacities of them. When we have enough masks, the public should use them routinely, especially the sick ones, similar to many citizens in Asian countries after SARS. The drug / vaccine research has responded very fast from the virus genome provided by China. However, they normally take more than 6 months to be ready for the general public.

The good sides
The current generation of Japanese are educated, polite, generous and civilized. Translated the following broadcast from a Japanese TV:

The Japanese special plane will fly to Wuhan tomorrow to pick up the Japanese who are stranded in Hubei province, especially Wuhan city. The plane is not empty; it will fly to Wuhan with relief supplies to Wuhan. The medical team of 1,000 people will also be sent to Wuhan, compared to South Korean petition to stop Chinese tourists from entering, Taiwanese refusing to export the mouth masks to China, the Philippines deported Chinese tourists, and North Korea banned Chinese people from entering. The Japanese government quickly recruited factories, overtime making masks, etc.

Now the streets of Tokyo and Osaka are full of cheers for Wuhan. I hope that our **fellow compatriots will remember** this scene. No matter where disaster encounters, be considerate and helpful with actions. Love has no boundaries in race or country! I can forgive them for the terrible deeds to China during WW2. This generation of Japan has nothing to do with the war. China donated a lot of aid to Japan during the breakout in Japan.

The bad side
There are at least two 'famous internet posters' in Hong Kong posting YouTube videos against the Hong Kong government aggressively every

day. They must be financed and/or they are Chinese bashers. No matter what nationality you are, you should be proud of your country especially during a disaster.

China has gained points in building two hospitals in less than 12 days. For them the hospital is a death concentration camp. How ridiculous! They oppose everything the Hong Kong government and China do for no reason.

Some doctors and nurses in Hong Kong wanted a strike if their political points were not approved by the government. They forget why they wanted to go to this sacred professional. I saw many taking this opportunity to promote their political views. It is a disaster and these political views have OPPOSITE effects to me. What happens if they themselves or their family members have this virus? To me, they should go to the lowest level of hell.

Globalization and just-in-time inventory are popular in the last 20 years. With this virus, the destruction of global economies is huge. For example, Apple's iPhone could need parts from more than 10 countries and few have stored enough inventory to last for months. The U.S. has the highest rate of casualties for this disease. It could be due to initially not identifying the patients. Companies do not provide enough masks as they are not profitable when the virus is suppressed. It should be solved by the government such as maintaining factories and inventory.

We should learn lessons from this outbreak. In this case, China's authoritarian government works better than our system. We would face a lot of opposition to close a city to start. We should maintain some manufacturing such as producing masks and not depend on a sole country such as China for some medical ingredients and / or keep adequate inventory for real national security. We should depend on the opinions of the experts (CDC in this case). I knew this outbreak in China at least a week before the U.S. public but I did not act on it due to my emotion. I should wear two hats: one as a human being and one as an investor. China controls this virus better than most countries. We are lucky that China with the best manufacturing facilities recovered first. China is still a developing country judging by the low income per capita. China's sending medical supplies and medical folks to Italy improves her prestige a lot (as opposed to sending soldiers). Italy had helped China many times. Denmark made fun of China's virus and now asked China for aid. The world should have no border.

We do not want to follow China's model of fighting this virus and do not want to accept aid from China. Is our face more important than our citizens' lives? As of 3/29/2020, the first plane from China with a lot of medical supplies has landed in NYC to ease some shortages.

The U.S. demonizes China and calls it the Chinese virus while China did not do the same on U.S.'s H1N1 in 2009. A tale of two countries! Trump has been playing a political game on this virus. There is no president not reelected when unemployment is 4% or less. However, unemployment is rising very fast; as of 5/2020, it is 15% and some expect the real figure to be 20%. NY Governor Cuomo faces reality and has been doing a great job. Xi advises the world to be co-operative to fight this virus. We need to listen more to the experts and particularly those in WHO.

Afterthoughts

\# Bill Gates predicted this virus 5 years ago and his solutions to fix it.
https://www.mercurynews.com/2020/03/25/pandemic-bill-gates-predicted-pandemic-in-2015/

https://www.ted.com/talks/bill_gates_how_we_must_respond_to_the_pandemic_pandemic

\# Blaming China (recommended)?
https://www.youtube.com/watch?v=-jZXEa-XOVw
https://www.youtube.com/watch?v=46DfBFWxTuM

\# China and the U.S. should cooperate to fight this pandemic. Unfortunately they are not.

\# China recovered from this pandemic and the export has increased. It is good for the world as we all need the medicines, masks and PPE from China.

\# Some countries criticized China and at the same time asked China for vaccines. Illogical? The data on victims of this pandemic from India and Brazil could be far, far higher.

\#Build a hospital in 10 days.
https://www.youtube.com/watch?v=3Sh7hghljuQ&list=WL&index=6

\# CDC screwed up: 1. The initial test Kit is too expensive to test the general public and 2. Wearing masks is good as indicated by many in Asia.

\# Great leadership

https://www.youtube.com/watch?v=-vT8e7lkjl8&feature=youtu.be&fbclid=IwAR0rrV9yYhr6wGVROqxQSlTnyyVmrBo7crDTO1vo8L9GvgeLUMNfTinOBgI

China asks our leaders for answers.
http://en.people.cn/n3/2020/0501/c90000-9686382.html

Why WHO was blamed? According to Trump, a friend of my enemy is my enemy. WHO was blamed to side with China on several occasions.

China, Cov19 and 5G.
https://www.youtube.com/watch?v=n4yLfALGZKY

The spirit of China
https://www.youtube.com/watch?v=H9IkFdAA8_A

A simple life is the best life.

#"Turn back to land" is a Chinese saying from the monks, and is lost in translation here.

2   Disasters in 2020 and 2021?

2021 is not a good year according to Chinese astronomy. The curse of Tippecanoe has materialized from 1840 to 1960: The presidents who were elected in the years that are evenly divided by 20 died.

There are some predictions that the U.S. will suffer a lot in 2020. Some predictions are correct and some including the "world end in 2012" are not. Hence, this article should belong to the Conspiracy Theories. Even with some good arguments, I am **not totally convinced**. However, I would take actions, similar to buying insurance. I would like to invest in gold and foreign countries (but all countries will be on fire if the prediction is correct). I will limit my Chinese stock holdings in 2020 for sure.

Prediction #1 (materialized as of 2/2020). To some, China has a cycle of disasters every 60 years and 2020 is supposed to be the year for disasters. It happened in the last three: 1960 Great Famine (1959-1961 estimated 30 million died), 1900 Boxer Rebellion (1899 – 1901) and 1840 First Opium War (1839 – 1842). I cannot find any major disaster in 1780 and the Sino-Japan War was not in the cycle year. It has 3 rights and 2 wrongs – not a bad bet. If Trump lost the election, China's nightmare is over. I bet Biden most likely will continue but he is more reasonable.

Prediction #2. Some predictors believe the USD would lose the reserve currency status. It is quite possible as we have been printing too much USD and our national debt is ridiculously high compared to our GDP. The hint today is that some countries are without using the USD for trading. The "One Belt, One Road" is another example, where the participants are trading with Chinese and /or Russian currencies.

Secondly, they also believe there will be an overdue earthquake that would destroy California. Despite any predictions, it would happen but hopefully not in my lifetime. It could destroy Silicon Valley and Hollywood, the most important areas for our economy. The stock market could lose most of its value. The Federal government would not likely be able to rescue California on this scale and that could lead California to become independent. It is likely but I do not bet on it. Luckily, this prediction does not happen in 2020.

The two events if materialized would possibly cause a global depression and even civil wars. Election year is traditionally a good year for the market, but we should be cautious with our money this time.

Believe it or not? Another conspiracy theory? But, do not say you were not warned. Personally I do **not** believe it, but I will take some actions just like buying insurance. I hope the predictions are wrong. For more info, check out Billy Meier from the web. He did have some correct predictions but some of his photos were falsified.

It could be the most entertaining article in this book, or the most important one. Even if there is no disaster, it is always better to diversify with gold (about 10% I suggest) and to sell short when the market is risky.

https://www.thebalance.com/dollar-collapse-how-to-protect-yourself-and-survive-3306263
Written on 8/2019.

My wishes

To summarize, I wish the two countries would co-exist and be mutually prosperous by working together with less conflicts. Chinese would enjoy the farm products and energy resources from us, while the U.S. would profit from the cheap consumer products from China.

On the opposite end, the trade war could lead to a global depression, a military war and even the end of the world. China will most likely fight to the last citizen / missile, if the U.S. invades China. China has learned the bitter lessons from the Opium Wars, "the Eight-Nation Invasion" and WW2.

With the retreat of Afghanistan and the inconclusive results of the pandemic virus from a Chinese lab, I hope the chance of a nuclear war with China would decrease. The deployment of the soldiers to the Pacific would not be useful. It is my original thought that there is no biotech weapon of this virus in China; if there were one, it should be in a thinly-populated city.

Of course, there is no perfect policy including China's 'one-child policy' and the 'One belt, one road' Initiative. When the media from the west cherry picks a 'problem', they would not discuss the advantages, but amplify the shortcomings. The following are the few examples I encountered recently.

#1. 'Separation of children / grandparents for young migrants'.
It is the choice of the young migrants. No one forces them to leave their villages. It is similar to accepting a job offer as it is the best offer among many. They've weighed the advantages and disadvantages before they migrate. The migrants' children if they come with their parents have to return to the villages to get education and other benefits. It is similar to Mexican migrant farmers to the U.S. and our K-12 school system keeping out students from other towns. The children of India's migrants to urban cities do not even get any benefits.

#2. 'housing waste'.
It is a choice too. The investors always evaluate which is the best investment; as of Oct., 2020, housing is the best. They do not rent them out as that would depreciate the property value. Do you believe the developers are foolish to build houses that no one wants? It is a bubble to me. However, it would not have the same problem we had in 2008; most properties are not highly leveraged, and there are no derivatives to deepen the problem.

Of course, there are mistakes as in all investments we made such as the one in Inner Mongolia.

1   My wish on what U.S. would do

First, I have to say the U.S. is the most desirable country judging from the number of immigrants (including myself). I understand why we ban Chinese scholars from studying and researching here. However, most come here for education. Those who were born here should not be a threat to national security evidenced by statistics. Indians should be welcome. Most Indian immigrants are well educated and from the top class of their society. Most do not return to India as the living standard in India is poor. It is a brain drain for India but good for us. At the same time, we need to encourage **more students into STEM.**

We have a lot to do at home. We need to learn and work on how to reduce / prevent the miseries from natural disasters (such as floods, hurricanes and forest fires) and this pandemic. Climate change could be a major factor. China emits carbon monoxide about twice as large as the U.S. However, per capita wise, we are twice as large as China since China has about 4 times our population.

Excessively printing money will hurt our economy in the long run. We need to reduce the wealth gap. Currently printing money benefits the stock market (hence the wealthy citizens), but threatens the well-being of the working class and the long-term economy.

China would not help us to buy our national debts as they did in 2008. Actually China has been cashing out since a senator proposed to freeze the Treasuries owned by China to pay for the pandemic. If it happens, many countries would dump our Treasuries, and what would happen to our investment in China?

The U.S. is still leading the world in many sectors including entertainment. Our citizens are rated as the most educated and civilized after Japan and some Scandinavian countries. There are many good policies / systems in the U.S. We should improve our system as there are many holes such as wasting time in arguing which political party is on top.

We should avoid the conflict with China. Otherwise we would end up in a fierce military war with China, and that will not be good for the world.

We have to abandon some industries such as manufacturing, but we have to maintain a small portion by subsidizing some for national security such as making masks. Without our restrictions and environmental protection, some industries would never be profitable to manufacture in the U.S. We do not solve the trade deficit by moving some factories from China to S.E. Asia for example. Actually it could hurt us more by paying more for less quality. It also hurts the global warming as the new factories in S.E. Asia may produce more pollution than China. Today for the first time, the green energy that China is also promoting is cheaper than the polluting fossil fuels in many locations.

We need to re-join and **lead the world organizations** such as WHO and many treaties. Opposing our allies' connections to China and Russia would alienate our allies and eventually ask them to make them select us or them.

When Obama mentioned "returning to the Pacific" and "moving 2/3 of our naval might to South China Sea", we told China to start the arms race. Since then, China emphasizes more on military instead of their economy and that is not good for the world. We should **cut down our military expenses** and use them to rebuild / maintain our infrastructure.

The "One Belt, One Road" Initiative has a secondary purpose for wars. Chinese ensure the oil supply via the sea route would not be cut off during war and conflict. Their navy's carriers are employed for this purpose besides invading Taiwan. It is similar that we needed to protect the oil route from the Middle East.

I prefer to **cooperate with China** than to contain China. On the contrary, co-operation would boost America's value, prosperity, peace and interests. We can slow down China's growth via today's trade war and even decoupling. Today we force China to work on chips and basic science that we would lose a lot of sales in the long run. Decoupling with China would hurt us more than China. Our global companies will suffer financially as many get more than 20% of their total sales from China.

It also forces many countries, especially the EU, to choose sides. Initially more of them will stay with us, but for how long? With our allies especially the EU, embargo is a powerful tool, but many EU countries are not our running dogs any more. Germany is furious at our intervention on the second gas pipe to Russia. Spain and Italy pretty much side with China more than with us. Italy will benefit with China's "One Belt, One Road" projects.

Australia may side with China eventually as their economy depends on China. The leader of Australia is the STUPIDEST politician I can find past and present. What do you gain from asking China, their #1 trading partner, to find the source of the pandemic besides banning Huawei? Nothing but China could ruin your economy for decades by reducing exports and tourists. Banning Huawei would lead to billions of dollars lost. Is it his white supremacy covering his eyes? The banned exports to China except iron ore could be replaced by their master, the U.S.A. and many other countries. If you side with this leader, you are stupid too.

Japan and S. Korea do not want to pay for our defense as requested. So is NATO. The U.N. should be the global policeman and financed by all countries in the U.N.

Taiwan is the only country that needs us most. Although China's military's might have not been proven (compared to our experience gained from our endless wars) and not that advanced, she can defend herself. From their recent humiliation, I do not blame China donating a good percent of their GDP in weapon development.

Singapore with our military base would suffer if China opens a port in Malaysia.

We lost Africa long time ago. China has improved their infrastructures in addition to stadiums and hospitals. They want to copy China's economic system rather than the U.S.A.'s.

Most countries want globalization as they can see the benefits. The U.S. is the only country that opposes it today, even though we have been prosperous in the last decades due to globalization. With the pandemic, we depend on China on many sectors such as medicine and parts. The world should learn a lot from this pandemic. Our dumb ego / nationalism and our freedom do not allow us to learn from China, an enemy to many of us. They are successful in controlling this pandemic. Learn how they close a city, build hospitals in a hurry, use mobile technology to identify the source, etc. We are one of the few countries that can be self-contained to some extent. We need to keep some critical manufacturing. However, it is more beneficial to import some.

Confucius Institute bridges China and other countries via language and culture. Chinese understand more of us than the other way round. It is a good idea, but it has been banned with political influence. No country would include their controversial sides in the teaching for sure.

We have wasted a lot of time in impeaching the president. If we spent their energy in fighting the pandemic, we would have saved many lives and recovered the economy sooner. Our political system has many holes to fill. Presidential campaigns are too expensive and funded by special-interest groups that may not be beneficial to most citizens.

First, I should say China is no angel, but we have been **hypocrites** in many incidents:

- China lets our high-tech companies in such as 2G and 3G and we do not let their 4G and 5G in. We have been spying even on our allies for a long time.
- We ban China's TikTot and now bus and train cars on the grounds of national security, which is absurd.
- All companies / countries steal technologies / ideas from foreign countries. We stole Charles Dickens books in the colonial days, technologies from Germany at the end of WW2 and many other examples. We should protect ours via better security guards.
- We have naval exercises close to China's coast, but China has never had one close to our coast as of this writing.
- We support openly in Hong Kong's protests and China has never done the same, such as our mass shooting and police brutality. Most countries have similar laws to protect their countries from separatists / terrorists.
- We have interfered in the internal affairs of many foreign countries and sometimes toppled foreign governments. China has not done so.

- We have endless wars for the following reasons: 1. Our leaders are influenced by our defense industry and 2. We need to ensure the status of USD. China has four wars in recent history and two brief ones with India after the Vietnam War.
- We have demonstrated we can spy on any one including the leaders of our allies while there is no hint of spying by Huawei.
- We do not take any action on Saudi Arabia on 911 and human rights violations.

Filler: Another double standard?

The U.S. rampage in the capital is 'riot', but the ones in Hong Kong and many other countries are 'freedom protest'.

2 My wish on what China would do

How can I argue with success as proven in the last decades? China has been doing a lot of good deeds such as reducing the wealth gap, suppressing corruption, etc. When their economy is doing better, they have money to improve their living standard. Broadly speaking, China pursues a prosperous society and against the imperial aggressions by the west as experienced in her bitter, recent history. I do not say China is perfect; she has her own problems. I only outline what should be of higher priority in my humble opinion.

China still has a lot of problems, but many problems have been exaggerated by the media from the west. The major problem is high debt. Expanding the high-speed rail should consider the financial benefits. Some routes to the west may never be paid back. Ghost cities have existed, and many investors have lost their investment in new houses. The government has many measures to prevent them from happening.

Governance

- Continue to concentrate on public health (esp. from a lot of lessons learned from the pandemic), clean water and clean air. Wealth does not do us any good when we have to breathe in polluted air, drink polluted water, eat unsafe food and live in expensive and small apartments.

- Central government has set up good policies, laws and regulations. However, the local governments do not follow them. Need more inspectors to check and enforce the central policies. The important thing is corrupt officials pocket the money from the central government for aiding the poor or informing the factory owners that the inspectors are coming.

- Continue the poverty alleviation program. Unfortunately, some poor areas cannot be developed effectively and relocation is the only choice. Continue to reduce the wealth gap between the coastal regions and the western China.

- More regulations and rules in all sectors such as stock exchanges and building codes. Enforce them by the local government and inspect them by the central government.

- Evaluate new projects in economic return. I believe some HSR development has diminishing returns now especially in rural areas. It is the same for "One Belt, One Road" projects as some projects may never be paid back.

- Allow more freedom and transparency. Without freedom, scientific advancement is limited. The living standard has improved in the last 50 years and hence the riots / protests have been far less. China should be ready to allow U.S. social media such as Google and Facebook in.

- Fighting corruption is a continuous task as the problem is widespread. Xi has accomplished a lot. Deng allowed some to get rich, and today it is the time to ensure the wealth is obtained legally. "Relation" is not the primary reason to get ahead or secure a contract. Most policies in the last decades are great. However, when the implementation by the local governments are full of problems such as corruption.

Technology

- China should concentrate more on basic research.
- China should solve the bottlenecks such as the chip making today.
- Protect IP. Prosecute those researchers stealing research from foreign universities and patenting them in China. If not controlled, there will be backfire and have adverse long-term consequences.
- Today China does not need to steal foreign technologies even though it is common for companies around the world to steal technologies from each other.
- Continue applying technology into agriculture and green energy.
- China has woken up the U.S. to fight the technology war such as the law requiring corporations allowing the government access and the declaration of their future milestones.

Economy

- Move the country from a trade-oriented system to a consumer-oriented one. China has enough middle class to support the consumer market.
- Negotiate with the U.S. with better terms to them. China and many other countries have taken advantage of the U.S. for a long while. China still needs the U.S. for their farm products and many other products for decades to come. Same with Australia.
- Reduce all debts, both individual, business and national. Continue to reduce easy credit. It is a dangerous warning when the debts reach 300% of GDP.
- Further reduce ghost buildings by limiting heavy investing on real estates.
- Punish violators of counterfeits and stop low-quality products especially for exports. Set up a consumer regulation agent. The recent case is counterfeits

of N95 masks. If they are not enforced, it would hurt China's image and also the confidence of foreign buyers. Many foreign products have been reduced in quality after they have been imported into China, and in some cases cause lives.
- China should not buy and should reduce the U.S. Treasuries. The downside is appreciating the yield (and hence hurting exports), but it is better than holding the valueless Treasuries if all central banks are dumping. It is a Ponzi scheme as the dollar is a fiat currency.

Environment
- Use brand names to ensure quality, especially food quality. Bad quality gives our exports a bad name. Control it.

- A toaster lasting for 10 years is better than one lasting for 1 year even though it is 2 times more expensive. It helps the environment too.

- This pandemic shows that China can lower air pollution by reducing factory outputs. Carbon neutral is on target. However, China has recently built a huge electricity generator using coal.

International relation
- Continue to avoid the military conflict with the U.S.
- Settle island disputes with all neighbors without using military force. Explore the resources by both countries. With the low cost of oil (due to the rise of cheaper green energy), the disputes are not economically justified.
- Be patient with Taiwan. China will invade Taiwan only: (1) U.S. has a military base in Taiwan or (2) Taiwan declares independence. With the current economic growth, China can reunite (or invade) Taiwan without firing a bullet. They have been integrated in the business sector. After WW2, many countries have been reunited such as Vietnam and Germany. China may ban rare earth elements to the U.S. firms selling jets (with jacked up prices) to Taiwan.
- China should restrict herself in building islands in the South China Sea.
- I hope China's "Water redirection from the south" would leave about half of the water flowing south as a good neighbor would do.

3   My final thoughts

The following serves as a summary and it may repeat my opinions. I am making suggestions to both the U.S. and China so they would live happily after. I am not too optimistic and most likely we will have a global recession and the trade war would last for years. Please read this article with an open mind as there are so many gray areas.

Trump mentioned the trade war will be negotiated after the 2020 election. China is furious at the U.S.'s "Hong Kong Human Rights Democracy Act". It looks like the trade war will not be ended in at least a year. The chance of a decoupling between the two nations and the global recession are both increasing. Will it change to a cold war and then a military war? Will Biden be more flexible with China? Only time will tell.

Misconception
Even in 2021, I still heard of many naïve arguments on China such as poor quality, stealing our IPs and no innovation. It was true ten years ago but not any more in 2020. Should our government and our corporations keep their secrets secret in the first place?

We have been bombarded with news (both from the media and the government) demonizing the Chinese.

A while ago, a syndicated article (appearing in most major Sunday papers) said that colonization is good using Hong Kong as an example. The fact is Hong Kong's success is due to the proximity to China. When the Stanford 'professor' wrote this article, how can the common citizen understand the facts?

Now, we passed the "Hong Kong human rights democracy act". Should China pass a similar law on our citizens shooting each other? It is interference in the internal affairs of other countries that China has avoided. We have been interfering all the time using our embargo with our allies, financing local rioters / protestors, and even our mighty military. That's why many countries, even our allies such as the Saudi, and many other Middle East countries hate us. We accuse China of human rights violations, but we conveniently cover our eyes with Saudi Arabia's human rights hatred and the actual terrorist attacks. Actually we have had virtually endless wars in the last several decades.

We have been busy bombing other countries if they do not use USD as the reserve currency and / or do not want to adopt our system. Many wars such as the Vietnam War were not justified; are we threatened by today's Vietnam? Russia was resolved due to the huge resources lost in Afghanistan. We were not smart enough to learn the lesson.

If we did not want to be the global policeman (a job for United Nations), we can solve a lot of our problems such as wealth gap, terrorism, homeless and drug/alcohol addictions.

Many complain about the poor quality of Chinese products. It may be true 20 years ago as most developing countries have gone through from cheap products to higher-value products. First, do you find poor quality in Apple's products and most of them are assembled in China? Quality control is the responsibility of the companies who outsource their manufacturing to China. China needs to establish brand names to boost consumers' confidence.

If they can send a spaceship to the moon, these projects have to be supported by industries with advanced capability and decent quality control. They have many innovations in building infrastructure. The new Beijing airport has been built in less than 5 years; we would spend 5 years arguing how to build such big projects. We cannot build such huge projects as they may be credited by the next political party, which may not be themselves.

Take 5G as an example. Huawei has nothing to steal from us as they have more advanced products such as their new phones and we do not even sell 4G networks. Verizon is using Huawei 5G patents and so far they have not paid royalties to Huawei. ATT's '5G' is not 5G.

Our government is trying to stop China from passing us (will discuss each item). It will stop China in a few years, but it will backfire and make China even more dominant in five or so years. The trade war is not about trade any more but who will be on top.

It is too late to control China today. Global trading is advantageous if all countries play it fairly. You do not want to grow sugar cane in Alaska. Let the best country produce the best products at the least costs. The trade war between the two largest economies would lead the world to a global depression. China's rise in military technologies would prevent WW3 contrary to popular belief.

- **5G.**
  Ericsson and Nokia are years behind Huawei. Some countries, such as Germany and the United Kingdom, have to choose sides. Verizon may have to pay Huawei royalties in using their 5G patents.

  Most countries cannot find any security backdoors on Huawei as claimed by our government.

  The U.S. consequences. There is a good chance that some African countries will use the 5G network earlier than us. We asked Vietnam to ban 5G from China. Now Vietnam has a lot of problems in implanting the 5G from Nokia.

  If the U.S. wants to give Huawei a hard time, Huawei would lose most of the mobile phone sales in Europe and China would have counter actions. Samsung would benefit and maintain the world's #1 mobile phone seller. In 2018, Huawei's smartphones almost passed Samsung.

  Is there a security leak in the rural networks that depend on Huawei's 4G equipment?

- **Trade and GDP**
  Both U.S. and China will suffer from the trade war. The U.S.'s GDP will fall below 2% and China's will fall below 5% (or even more with Wuhan's Pandemic) for the first time in the last 30 or so years. It would affect economies in most other countries. I bet China being poor for decades until recently would bite the bullet. Our wealth gap has widened considerably in the past decades. The tariffs would make the poor even poorer that would stir up social unrest in the U.S.

  We are moving a lot of manufacturing to low-wage countries such as Vietnam and very few jobs back to the U.S. These countries are not rich enough to buy our advanced products. Only a very few jobs come back to the U.S. and most jobs will be replaced by robots. The products depending on cheap materials from China will become more expensive. China would not be a total loss as many factories moved to these countries are Chinese. In addition, China is helping them to build roads and ports.

- **China would accept some of our negotiations.**
IP will be protected better by China. China has to accept the global trademarks and IP patents rather than those filed recently in China before the patents filed earlier elsewhere. China would not force the transfer of technologies in return of accessing China's huge market.

It is hard to define subsidies. We subsidize our research in colleges and farm products. For example, one bushel of soybean is sold to China for $8.50 and it actually costs $10 to produce including the government subsidies.

- **Chips (or core technologies).**
China has been investing heavily today in core technologies such as chips. It will take time to catch up. Huawei has announced a phone without any software and hardware from the U.S. It is harder to sell their phones outside China without Google's apps, but they can be easily loaded illegally to Huawei's phones. China can have the memory chips from other sources and/or using some chips made in China but not as good initially. Within 2022, there will be no U.S. components in Huawei's phones.

The U.S. consequences- Most chip companies will lose financially. Recently I sold my MU and QCOM. This would be a long-term loss for our chip companies and Google.

- **Decoupling.**
It is on many fronts such as foreign students from China and research cooperation. Chinese students will be diverted to many other countries, such as the United Kingdom and there will be more universities in China, some of which are formed by foreign institutions. We are #1 in many sectors and research in universities.

The U.S. Consequences- Our colleges will lose financially as most Chinese students pay full tuition. The research institutions will suffer due to lack of qualified students / researchers.

We also lose a lot of money from tourism as Chinese spend most per tourist (due to high import taxes from China) and the large size of tourists from China. The incomes from Chinese students and tourists have not been deducted from our trade deficit with China.

There are cases that Chinese scientists transferred their research legally or illegally to China. We should limit the specific research in the U.S. to Chinese researchers. It should not affect admitting undergraduate students from China as they finance our colleges. In addition, Chinese companies such as Huawei welcome foreign researchers from any country to work in China.

The U.S. also limits H1-B visas. If you go to any high-tech companies and technology institutions, you will find many Chinese and Indians. Without them, the U.S. would fall behind in a decade or two.

//www.scmp.com/news/china/politics/article/3038491/fbi-and-us-senate-raise-alarm-over-chinas-recruitment-us

Decoupling and our high debt will reduce the value of USD and eventually will shake the status of USD as a reserve currency.

- **Space station.**
  By 2025, China could be the only country that has a space station after ours retires. China welcomes all countries to participate in their space station program while the U.S. bans China from participating in ours. It would make the EU countries siding with China.

- **Hollywood** will suffer from the loss of the second largest (moving to #1) movie market. The incremental net profit is huge after a movie is made.

- **Delisting Chinese companies.**
  In 2018, the top 4 IPOs out of the top 10 in the U.S. were Chinese companies. It will hurt the Chinese in funding new companies. London, Hong Kong and eventually Shenzhen and Macau will benefit.

  The U.S. Consequences. The investment bankers managing IPOs will suffer. It will be a mess delisting so many Chinese companies. I do not know what China will retaliate against the U.S. companies doing business in China.

Apple's sales have been suffering in China. The U.S. is looking for a solution on the tariff on Apple's products imported from China to fend off Samsung's advantage whose majority of their products are assembled in South East Asia; most likely we will exempt or reduce tariffs on Apple's products manufactured in China. Apple cannot move the manufacturing from China due to the rare earth elements and skilled workers.

- **Chinese fight back.**
It may withdraw their debts; China is #1 or #2 foreign country in buying our debts. With our high debts, the reserve status of USD will be harmed. China has already used their currency in their oil exchange. I predict in 2025, USD would be down to 50% from the current 65% of global country reserves. The EU would gain from 20% to 25% and China's Yuan would gain from 1% to 5%. However, USD is still very strong and is backed up by a strong economy.

China may ban export of rare earth elements to the U.S. Since many weapons depend on these elements, China has a real argument on national security. However, China would most likely lose in a filing in WTO. Japan may already have decades of reserve of rare earth elements. Australia is another source for rare earths.

The losses in Chinese companies in the U.S. and the U.S. companies in China should be about the same. The U.S. companies make good profits in China, but many of them are jointly owned by the Chinese.

China continues to build / improve infrastructure. They just opened the second airport in Beijing (the other one was opened just before the Beijing Olympics) while most of our airports are outdated. Our subway system is a shame in most cities while China's has been improving fast. It is a fact that we can build better HSR and 5G if we use China's technologies.

- **World peace.**

With China's advances in military technology, the world is more peaceful than before. It is the balance of power as evidenced by the cold war between the U.S. and Russia.

With the low oil prices, the disputed islands in the South China Sea will not be a concern now. The only concern is the invasion of Taiwan. Taiwanese at one time wanted to invade China, so it would be a civil war then and now, and most likely China would win. I wish all countries would disarm nuclear weapons.

- **S.E. Asia, Africa, S. America, Iran and Russia.**
  Most countries, especially Russia, win big by supplying farm products and energy to China. There is a huge project of a building natural gas line from Russia to China. It will take 30 years to complete. At that time, it would satisfy about 14% of China's consumption of natural gas and it would lower China's air pollution. It is also a strategic win as the sea route supplying energy would be blocked in case of war. Russia will gain a lot of benefits and a good bargain chip in negotiating energy prices to Europe.

  Iran, Russia and China would be combined to form a powerful economic and military alliance.

  China helps S.E. Asia and Africa build infrastructure as part of their "One Belt, One Road" Initiative. Many Chinese factories have been moved to S.E. Asia due to the trade war between the two largest economies.

  China has built many infrastructure, hospitals and stadiums in Africa. Hence, China is looking for a long-term relationship. I bet most U.S. decision makers on S.E. Asia and African issues have not been to these regions lately.

- **Chinese neighbors.**
  They are benefiting from China's "One Belt, One Road" Initiative by trading with China. They have to watch out on the debt burdens. When they cannot pay back, they may cede some of their territories to China. Pakistan is a chief beneficiary. China can use the railroad to ship goods to a port in Pakistan that could be another gateway to Europe by-passing the sea route via S.E. Asia.

- **Europe.**
  The EU will spit in their decisions to support China or not. So far, Germany, Italy and many smaller countries side with China. Italy and Greece are enjoying the benefits of being ports for China trade. Today Spain can ship their products such as red wine to China via the railroad. The United Kingdom most likely will not implement 5G from China, but this decision does not make any economic sense.

- **Mexico, Canada, Australia, India and Japan.**
  They will side with the U.S. due to the financial ties. Australia is a surprise to me as they have been benefiting from the China trade; China is their #1 trade partner. It is more politically and financially insecure by not siding with China. Japan, South Korea and Taiwan are benefitting in exporting their chips to replace our chip export to China.

  Japan gained a project to build high-speed rail for India. It is not financially feasible for Japan with the generous loan and India does not have a good record to pay back debts. Vietnam may run into similar problems with their high-speed rail.

- **IP** will be enforced by both sides as China has more IPs to protect. The force of transfer technologies in accessing the Chinese market will be eliminated.
- Will the trade war lead to a **military war**? The chance is increased. Most likely it is caused by the conflict in shipping oil from Iran. China's marine power is limited compared to ours. The Burma-China pipeline would reduce the blockage problem.
- Eventually and hopefully, the trade war will end soon. With the prolonged conflict, most global economies would be in a recession and so would be the stock markets. I hope the two countries will settle down and save faces (for their own citizens). There is a chance the two countries could decouple and that way spells a global recession. The worst case is starting a military war. Hope both countries can escape the so-called Thucydides's Trap. It seems I am very negative on the U.S. It is just the opposite. I love the U.S. the same as I love China. Every citizen should love their own country. I hope they can work together to lead to a prosperous world.
- With the development of China's supersonic missiles and their GPS system, the chance of a nuclear war has been reduced. The politicians

are not stupid to risk such a war that would destroy us too. But, who knows?

Links
Trade War. Digital Iron Curtain, Trade war and the market, SCMP
https://www.YouTube.com/watch?v=d-8wXrF2ZeE
https://www.YouTube.com/watch?v=kQftC4Vcl-s
Google "SCMP (South China Morning Post) Trade War" for many articles.

Mega projects.
https://www.YouTube.com/watch?v=qzvTE6uOIWs

Food: Mega project, farming
https://www.YouTube.com/watch?v=AmVNwilQJvc
https://www.YouTube.com/watch?v=zri_Mm54Vvl

Manufacturing: Mega project
https://www.YouTube.com/watch?v=_bVaMUds5gw

Engineering: Innovation, 2, HSR
https://www.YouTube.com/watch?v=s3qma0pROi0
https://www.YouTube.com/watch?v=SiRs289rQ7s
https://www.YouTube.com/watch?v=P_Sa1YHmxog

Energy: Mega project
https://www.YouTube.com/watch?v=wfG0USvDTew

Transportation & infrastructure: Mega project, infrastructure
https://www.YouTube.com/watch?v=IYJ4-fTDy_E
https://www.YouTube.com/watch?v=wX0ky8PITPg

One Belt One Road: 1 2
https://www.YouTube.com/watch?v=JZGv78iN6Bk
https://www.YouTube.com/watch?v=fuslComNEvo

Technology: Mega project, Challenging, 5G Another 5G
https://www.YouTube.com/watch?v=veEMMi9BCUE
https://www.YouTube.com/watch?v=abA4NZdwba8
https://www.YouTube.com/watch?v=7VV0guR4bgg

Education: 1 Better than US?
https://www.YouTube.com/watch?v=FTndlELsh48

Military: Drone, Carrier killer, why war

https://www.YouTube.com/watch?v=r_3DmSQ-p50
https://www.YouTube.com/watch?v=BIxEawGbiH0
https://www.YouTube.com/watch?v=_ldVgrbzSuc

Trade war: Jim Rogers, Huawei
https://www.YouTube.com/watch?v=HnXFq7PvOmc

Market Crash: 1, 2
https://www.YouTube.com/watch?v=5C43i3yclec
https://www.YouTube.com/watch?v=Ca9uu36w_Vo

Misc.: 1, 2, BBC on Capitalism, PBS on China, USD
https://www.YouTube.com/watch?v=dt2W2uOyLGw
https://www.YouTube.com/watch?v=O0f4o7n5UdQ
https://tv.YouTube.com/welcome/?utm_medium=np&pid=dmea-acq-u-firetvb&utm_source=dmea&utm_campaign=dmea-np-firetv_nm_2
https://www.YouTube.com/watch?v=JovtmKFxi3c&t=152s
https://www.YouTube.com/watch?v=yGlPvsBnyHM

General thoughts

There are Chinese experts from U.S. looking at China in their own views, and there are American experts in China looking at U.S. in their own views. Many times, they are completely opposite according to what their bosses or readers want to hear. I hope I can present the conflicts between China and U.S. in an unbiased way.

Our government is convincing us and our allies that we should have a war with China. It has been a pattern similar to the Vietnam War and the invasion of Iraq. Does Vietnam threaten us today? Have we found the mass-destruction weapons in Iraq? With nuclear weapons, the war with China if materialized would lead to the end of the world. We have plenty of problems to fix at home. Why do we spend our money and efforts in wars that could hurt us? We did not win the Korea War against China's primitive military weapons. When we do not learn from history, most likely we will repeat history.

Are our media trustworthy?

Sometimes the news reported by the media needs to be further evaluated. The recent example is Bolivia's uprising. It has to be aided by our government to limit China's access to lithium, the important ore for batteries. The media did not tell us the truth. This is one of the many examples.

When you report ALL the problems in China, are you speaking the truth, or just following the order of your boss? What is your initial objective of being a reporter? Reporting news or **spreading lies**? You can cheat folks once a while, but not all the time. The entire profession has lost credential!

In the last 40 years, China has lifted millions from starving to death, and Chinese have been enjoying the highest living standard since the Opium Wars when the Brits pushed opium as a nation. The government has successfully alleviated poverty. China pretty much fixes their pandemic in less than 4 months. Nine-year compulsory education is free to all citizens. About 95 percent of the population has health care coverage.

Wuhan is dirty according to our leader and the media. Check out this video on Wuhan filmed on Oct. 2020 (no language barrier even it is in Cantonese) by a common Hong Kong citizen. It is quite a big contrast to most of our big cities. Notice that many U.S. companies are making money in China, and how clean the street is. How many fat folks and homeless folks you can find from this video? If you argue it is fake and staged, you are insulting our intelligence including yours.
https://www.youtube.com/watch?v=W34KvZyA_hQ&list=WL&index=96

China had no one-child policy to minorities. The minorities have extra score to apply to universities. Where are the human rights violations and genocides? There have been no riots / killings for over 3 years since the last one by separatists and extremists. China spends more money in Xinjiang and Tibet far more than the central government gets back. Living standards in these regions have been substantially improved in the last 40 years. At that time only monks in Tibet could get an education. Chinese minorities get extra scores to go to college. Can any politician tell us how we treat our own minorities and how many Indian nations have been killed to extinction such as the 'the last of Mohicans'? Go to any Indian reservation and most likely you can find no running water, no electricity, no basic health care but a lot of drunks. The black have been killed mercilessly. For proofs, look at the following videos.

https://www.youtube.com/watch?v=C0IRZW3V9oM&t=372s
https://www.youtube.com/watch?v=yIbmL17P3nc&list=WL&index=54
https://www.youtube.com/watch?v=LcK_h1aayY0&fbclid=IwAR2SOtUPu_bj1cqN69u5Ll_ARDm0FZJlj_a8td9twl2oGNt2_XY6WratYQs
https://www.youtube.com/watch?v=bhXZZ0iUqP8

Our two political parties are demonizing China every day. Obviously it is for votes, as they cannot fix our problems. If China is so bad, why the Chinese tourists are the largest, and they spent double the average tourist?

Why we and our allies criticize Hong Kong's laws on national security, while US and most developed countries have similar laws to enforce national security and suppress independence. Why we accuse of other countries on human rights while we still have Guantanamo Bay prison? Why we took no action on Saudi Arabia on human rights including the reporter disappeared in their consulate. Judge these incidents for yourself.

The U.S. and China

Let me tell you a story how U.S. has inspired many in the world. In Hong Kong, a very smart and hard-working girl living next door to my apartment was inspired to study in U.S., and her dream job was working for NASA. Most outside U.S. were inspired by the U.S.'s freedom and high living standard via Hollywood. From the recent speeches by Trump and Xi in U.N., the two countries seem switching roles in world leadership. Xi stressed again that China did not want to be the leader but would cooperate with foreign countries for mutual benefits.

Undoubtedly, U.S. is still leading the world especially in military. However, China is reducing the gap. Our military is more powerful than the next 5 military powers combined. However, China has enough power to defend her country with 'carrier killer' missiles and other advanced weapons.

Our government does not want to face reality, and blame everything on China using national security as a reason. The fact is that China will pass us eventually if we do not change the current policy. We together with our allies can give China a hard time by banning exporting chip makers. China will eventually fix this major obstacle, and at that time they will do the same to us, and our allies would turn to be their allies.

Furthermore we limit foreign scientists and IT folks to work here. It is a major mistake as we depend on them. It has a valid point to limit some folks from China. If India catches up with China, these folks from India would return home too with the technology learned from us. We need to encourage more STEM students, and enforce national security. If China can copy or steal our top-of-the-line weapons, should we blame ourselves first? All rising countries including U.S. had copied or stolen technologies from developed countries. There is NO exception.

The number of Chinese scientific papers is about half of ours in 2019. With the growth rates based on the last five years, China would pass us in 10 years or even less. It is partly due to our cutting of research funding. If you visit our high-tech companies and top colleges, you will find many

Chinese and Indians. Many Chinese scholars are returning home for better opportunities. Do you blame them? Many Indians are being banned to study and work here. Most U.S. citizens do not want to spend long years to scientific researches for risky monetary returns.

It is similar to limit workers from Mexico to work on the jobs our able welfare recipients do not want.

We have fewer problems than China. One proof of our freedom is that this book cannot be possibly published in China and China is not ready to accept this kind of freedom.

The U.S. wants to be the sole winner, while China does not want to lead the world. The "One Belt, One Road" Initiative, the rise of China's technologies such as 5G, mobile payment, drones and high-speed rail and her alliance with Russia and Iran challenge our global leadership and our USD as the reserve currency. We want China to follow our standards and orders, not the other way round.

Profits from many U.S. companies depend on China. Without them, many U.S. auto companies may have bankrupted and Apple would lose more than 25% of the stock value.

Trade war and the pandemic

Both countries are suffering in the trade war, the pandemic and natural disasters (flooding in China and fires in U.S.). Will the pandemic and the trade war lead to a military war? Historically the number 1 country would war with the upcoming country. In recent history, we ended the conflict peacefully with Japan and less peacefully with Russia. Japan was forced to lose economically and Russia was dismantled. China learns the lessons from them.

We have about 7 sources of vaccine to this pandemic. None is from China and China's vaccine is one of the most promising ones. China has set up a standard of preventing the spread of this virus. Judging from the results, sadly I admit we have lost it to China even we have the best public health system.

China strikes back

As of November, 2020, China has not reacted a lot to our trade war and restrictions. China would likely risk a war with us if Taiwan declares independence and/or we establish a military base there. It is reasonable to ban the sales of rare earths to our companies that sell weapons to Taiwan. We have a lot of rare earth ores, but we depend always 100% on China's processing of these ores due to environment concerns and technology.

In addition, we depend on antibiotics imported by China (about 97%). India is the largest generic drug manufacturer, but 80% of India's active ingredients are imported from China.

China has not bought a lot of our U.S. debts recently. In 2008, China had pretty much saved our economy by buying a lot of our U.S. debts. China could easily sell 20% of the holding or 100% even if there is a military war. It would trigger Japan and EU to dump the U.S. debts. Due to the recent depreciation of the U.S. currency, most of the foreign holdings suffer losses. When it happens in this large scale, all our assets that are based on U.S. currency would collapse.

Hopefully the relationship of the two countries would improve after the coming election (not too far away as of this writing).

Racial discrimination
I feel bad about the recent discrimination against the black by police brutality. First I have to thank the police and our military force to fight for us. However, there are many bad apples in the police force as in many other sectors of the society. Some shootings and killing are obviously caused by racial discrimination. However, some reactions are over-reacted to me. Looting cannot be forgiven.

Native Indians and the black are still being discriminated even today. We are ALL immigrants besides the native Indians, and hence do not ask. The native Indians had been reduced in alarming number in our first census. It has to trace back to the 15th century when the Spaniards colonized the 'discovered' land, stole their resources, enslaved and raped the natives. They claimed to be "good for the natives to make them civilized".

A long while ago, a professor from the top college in California had the same argument and used Hong Kong as an example. It was the wrong argument as Hong Kong's wealth was based on her proximity to China. When the top professor in the top college does not understand the truth, how can the average citizen?

Our politicians have the theme of arguing China on their minorities. It is more a joke to me by comparison. The U.S. constitution clearly stated that all men are equal. It means "white" men. We still had slaves for a long, long time since the constitution.

My biases
I was born in Hong Kong and U.S. is my adopted country, so technically I was a second-class citizen of UK. My yellow face 'betrayed' me, but I am proud to be a Chinese American. The trade war of U.S. and China bothers me a lot like my parents are fighting each other and asking for divorce (decoupling for countries).

First I have to thank U.S. for giving me the opportunity to study after high school when Hong Kong's higher education system was not ready. I admired U.S. for the freedom, scientific advancements and global leadership. It gave me an easy life. I contributed to the economy by paying more than my share of taxes and have not taken any social welfare.

I am naturally biased. Hence, do not be offended if I go too far to defend China. However, if I have to choose which country I should migrate to today, I still choose U.S. If there is an atomic bomb dropped, I do not wish it would drop in the U.S. as I and my family would be killed. It is possible to love your country and your race at the same time such as the Jews in U.S. Everyone should love their country, the race and the world no matter where they come from.

You may not agree with most of my opinions. Do challenge them. We need more thinkers than followers. Human nature is agreeing with the ideas to support their original thinking, and that's why we do not want to listen to the other side of the story.

There are pro-Chinese views and also views by Chinese bashers. I hope my book is in the middle. With the daily bombarding by our pro-U.S.

media, China has been demonized. I hope to present a balance view in this book. I hope you use an open mind with skeptic and contrarian to seek the truths and separate all the biases / fake news.

This book

So far, I have donated all my book profits to charities. My personal welfare is tied with U.S. I have no affiliation with Chinese government and I have not received any compensation from China. This book is dedicated to all the essential workers of this pandemic especially to the fallen angels.

It is hard for my American readers to read this book as they are not the facts we want to read (a human nature). However, if we do not know our arguable shortcomings, how can we fix them?

Many opinions in this book are from many sources. Most sources from the established U.S. and EU media such as SingtaoTV, BBC, DW and Economist are less biased. I find CGTN, an English-speaking, Chinese TV network is informative and not too propaganda. So is RT network from YouTube. It seems CGTN stays away more from the U.S. politics than RT. Both are financed (at least partially) by the Chinese government and the Russian government respectively. I also selected and translated from Cantonese on many YouTube videos. They do represent a lot of knowledge from Hong Kong that may not be available to the Western audience.

There are so many gray areas today that no one can claim s/he is always right. I have nothing against U.S. From the research of this book, I did find out several incidents that harm our image, reputation and our future. I am neutral in politics. I comment against current government as I want them to serve us better. China has her own problems. This book is addressing OUR problems, and hopefully we will fix most of them.

The above Highlights can be reproduced and distributed with the mention of this book.

Epilogue

I have never taken any class in economics, accounting, business and investing except those required in my Industrial Engineering degrees. Investing is extraordinarily multi-disciplined and all we need is common sense and a desire to learn.

After my early retirement, I have been spending most of my time in investing, running thousands of simulations and reading over one hundred books on investing. Starting with the year of 2000, I have been doing very well in my investing. I comment on financial blogs and save the good ones for my own blog, so I can refer to them later on. Then after several years, I had enough information to write a book.

It is far more financially rewarding working about my investments including finding new strategies. Writing books and articles takes time away from my investing and it actually costs me more money. However, it has been fun to write this book and to interact with my readers. Money cannot buy everything and the satisfaction of holding my printed book.

I do not believe that this book or any book can be the Holy Grail of investing. However, it has a lot of fresh ideas and good pointers that have brought me financial success (at least so far). I ask my readers to challenge my pointers and ensure they are applicable in today's market and meet their own objectives and requirements.

A good pointer can make you thousands of dollars, and a bad or misinterpreted one can do the opposite. Always do paper trading on any strategy and / or idea before you commit real money to it. Start your strategy with cash in small increments until you have more confidence.

Use the links in this book for reference and understand how we come to the conclusions. This book and similar books provide you ways on how to make decisions based on current events that can be obtained from TV, the internet and magazines.

Hopefully, this book's primary objective of enabling you to be a better investor is met. Actually, you should be a better investor than I am if you can integrate the knowledge you already have with mine – I called it adding wings to a roaring tiger. You also learn to avoid the mistakes I made.

This book should be read repeatedly to remind us (I am a reader too) of any error(s) we repeated. Some articles are not easy to read as this book is not intended to be so. You need to practice what this book suggests such as learning how to detect a market plunge.

There are many styles of investing. It is better to master one at a time than trying to master several. Personally I selected swing trading with 6 months to renew my investment. Sector Rotation and momentum trading are my other styles I practice.

I have made a lot of predictions. There have been more right than wrong compared to most other authors I have read. I never use after-the-fact predictions. Even when there are wrong predictions, I would show the logic behind.

Promoting books teaches me some human behavior, both good and bad. One oldie showed me his broker statement one day with over 8 million and asked me to show him mine with some racial remarks. Hope his racist attitude would not pass on his 'successful' children.

The major advantage of self-publishing e-books is the low cost to you. Without self-publishing, this book would never be done.

I will practice what I preach and what I've learned from writing this book. Jesse Livermore was probably one of our greatest traders ever. Yet he ended up losing most of his money and then killed himself. The major reason was he did not follow what he preached. We need to diversify our investments and it is better to be a turtle investor. Recently a 20-year-old, Robinhood trader killed himself after losing $730,000.

A link is provided for future updates and announcements.
https://ebmyth.blogspot.com/2020/01/updates.html
My blog:
https://tonyp4idea.blogspot.com/

Final notes

Thanks for reading this book and I hope it will be beneficial to your financial health. If so, comment on it on Amazon.com or the place you bought this book. I will be very grateful.

I believe the readers are getting a very good deal ibn reading this book. To benefit more, you have to try out the techniques described in this book and paper trade them thoroughly until you are successful.

I have put everything I know on investing in this lengthy book. The following book will have recommended stocks: "Best Stocks to buy in 2021" available after Dec. 15, 2020. This book is in the planning stage and there is no promise that it will be published. It may include the End-of-Year stock selection. For my political views, "China: Trade War and Pandemic." is recommended.

Appendix 1 – All my books

- Art of Investing (highly recommended combining most of my books on investing). It has over 500 pages (6*9), double the size of an average investing book. Similar books: Using Fidelity. Using Finviz.
- Sector Rotation: 21 Strategies and Shorting Stocks and ETFs have more specific chapters on the topic.
- Using Profitable Investing Sites. Investing Lessons.
- Best stocks for 2022.
- "Nuclear War with China?"
- Books for today's market: Profit from Coming Market Crash.
- The following books are in a series: Finding Profitable Stocks, Market Timing and Scoring Stocks.
- Books on strategies: Trading System, Swing (Rotation + Momentum), ETF Rotation for Couch Potatoes, Momentum, SuperStocks, Dividend, Penny & Micro Stock, and Retiree.
- Books for advance beginners: Be an expert (highly recommended), Introduce, Investing for Beginners, Beat Fund Managers, Profit via ETFs, Buffett, Ideas, Conservative and Top-Down.
- Miscellaneous: Investing Strategies. Buy Low and Sell High. Buy High and sell Higher. Buffettology. Technical Analysis. Trading Stocks.
- Concise Editions and Introduction Editions are available at very low prices and are competitive with books of similar sizes (50 pages) and prices ($3 range).

Most books have paperbacks. Links and offers are subject to change without notice.

Best stocks to buy for 2022

We care about performance only. Not considering dividends and fees, my last three books in this series have beaten the SPY (the market to most) by **110%, 71% and 25%** from the publish date to 07/01/2021. Next book could be on 12/15/2022.

Book	Stocks	Return	Ann.	Beat SPY by
Best Book for 2021 2nd Edition	10	20%	52%	110%
Best Book for 2021	4	29%	52%	71%
Best Book to Buy from Aug, 2020	14	42%	45%	25%
Avg.	9	31%	50%	69%

Sector Rotation: 21 Strategies

- On 5/26/2020, I searched for "Sector Rotation" under Amazon's Book. They are listed in the same order except my book Sector Rotation: 21 Strategies.

Book	Date	Size[1]	Kindle $[1]	Hard $
Sector Rotation: 21 Strategies	**05/2020**	**425**	**$9.95**	**$24.95**
Super Sectors	09/2010	289	$26.39	$49.95
Dual Momentum Investing	11/2014	240	$40.40	$42.20
Sector Investing	05/1996	260		$29.94
Sector Trading Strategies	08/2007	164	$26.39	$16.66
The Sector Strategist	03/2012	225	$26.39	$44.96
ETF Rotation	10/2012	125	**$9.95**	**$14.99**
Optimal… Sector Rotation	07/2015	80		$44.07

[1] From Amazon on size and prices as of 5/25/2020.

My book won in all categories except the price for hard copy in one. However, my book won as the lowest cost per page by a wide margin. In

addition, as of 5/2020 I bet that no author besides me made over 4 times using sector rotation starting the amount more than his yearly salary then.
- I have **21** strategies in sector rotation while most books have only one. It ranges from simple rotation of a stock ETF and cash for beginners to many advanced strategies for experts. Most other books have one or two strategies.
- Andrew, a contributor on Sector Rotation article at Seeking Alpha, said, "Great stuff, Tony. It's great to meet experienced traders such as yourself. I had a browse through the book and think your method is a little more refined than mine."
- "You have written the book in a way that makes good and logical sense." Bill.
- Do not be fooled by past performances. Just check the recent performance of the top 50 stocks selected by IBD in the last five years. The mediocre result (hopefully it will change) could be due to too many followers and/or there is no evergreen strategy. I seldom heard the fantastic results from the followers of O'Neil, our greatest chartist. The adaptive strategy of this book shows you how to select the most profitable strategy for the current market.
- I switched most (if not all) my sector funds in April, 2000 from technology sectors to traditional sectors (better to money market fund). We can reduce losses by spotting market plunges and the sector trend.

Shorting Stocks and ETFs

Recent performances.

Stocks	Short Date	Close date	Duration	Return	Annualized
ACVA	06/10/21	09/29/21	111	22%	72%
CCL	07/14/21	09/29/21	77	-8%	-36%
CENX	09/17/21	09/29/21	12	3%	105%
CLOV	09/16/21	09/29/21	13	10%	291%
CSPR	09/16/21	09/29/21	13	33%	917%
EOSE	09/15/21	09/29/21	14	10%	261%
MILE	07/22/21	09/29/21	69	53%	279%
NCLH	07/27/21	09/29/21	64	-5%	-27%
REAL	06/04/21	09/29/21	117	22%	68%
UAVS	06/04/21	09/29/21	117	41%	127%
Average	07/30/21	09/29/21	61	18%	206%
RSP	S&P 500			0%	

It is for education purposes and I am not responsible for any errors. As in most parts of this book, commissions, dividends and fees (interest for shorts) are not included, and hence the returns are less than specified. They are real and all trades for the period.

Stocks	Short Date	Close date	Duration	Return	Annualized
BBIG[1]	09/30/21	11/19/21[1]	50	35%	258%
BFLY	09/30/21	11/18/21	49	14%	107%
EOLS	11/10/21	11/17/21	7	10%	523%
FLDM	10/13/21	11/18/21	36	14%	147%
MKFG	10/27/21	11/18/21	22	-9%	-149%
PAVM[1]	10/20/21	11/19/21[1]	30	34%	413%
TSP	10/05/21	11/18/21	44	-11%	-91%
VRM	10/13/21	11/17/21	35	13%	135%
Average	10/14/21	11/18/21	34	13%	168%
RSP	S&P 500			4%	

Appendix 2 – Art of Investing

Art of Investing consisting of 15 books in 1. Besides saving money and your digital shelf space, it gives you quick reference and concentration on the topic you're currently interested in. It covers most investing topics in investing excluding speculative investing such as currency trading and day trading. It has over 500 pages (6*9), about the size of two investing books of average size.

The 15 books

Book No.	Amazon.com
1	Simple techniques
2	Finding Stocks
3	Evaluating Stocks
4	Scoring Stocks
5	Trading Stocks
6	Market Timing
7	Strategies
8	Sector Rotation
9	Insider Trading
10	Penny Stocks & Micro Cap
11	Momentum Investing
12	Dividend Investing
13	Technical Analysis
14	Investing Ideas
15	Buffettology

The book links are subject to change without notice.

"How to be a billionaire" is for beginners and couch potatoes, who can use the advanced features of this book in the simplest and less time-consuming techniques. Most advance users can skip this section unless they want to use some of the short cuts described.

We start with the basic books Finding Stocks, Evaluate Stocks, Trading Stocks and Market Timing. You can select and start with one of the many styles and strategies in investing such as swing trading and top-down strategy. Many tools are described in other books such as ETFs, technical analysis, covered calls and trading plan.

Many books start with "Why" to lure you to read more and are followed by "How" and then the theory behind the book.
If the book you're reading is beneficial to you, imagine how it would with 850 pages.

Most readers' comments are on "Debunk the Myths in Investing", which this book is originally based on. As of 2018, I did not know any of the commentators on my books.

"I skipped ahead to his chapter book 14 (of "Complete the Art of Investing"), Investment Advice just to get a feel of his writing style. His research is phenomenal and doesn't overwhelm with big words or catchy "sales-like" tactics.

I truly believe this ordinary man, Mr. Tony Pow, has a gift of explaining his experience as an investor without the bull crap of trying to make you buy his stuff. He seemingly just wants to share his knowledge, tips, and clarity of definitions for the kind of folks like me who want to understand something FIRST before jumping in with emotions of trying to make a boat load of money. I like the technical analysis side he brings.

Mr. Tony Pow talks about hidden gems in his book; well....quite frankly, he is a hidden gem. Thank you and I will also post my comments about this author to my Facebook page!" – JB on this book.

"Excellent book, recommend to all investors... great knowledge. It has fine-tuned my investing strategies... Your book is hard to set aside, as I read it all the time learning good techniques and analysis of stocks, ETF... Since I purchased your book in March, I have underlined, highlighted and placed tabs on top of pages for quick reference." – Aileron on this book.

"Tony, I just finished reading your 2nd edition. It's my pleasure to report that I found it most interesting. You're welcome to use this blurb if you like:

Debunk the Myths in Investing is an all-encompassing look at not only the most salient factors influencing markets and investors, but also a from-the-trenches look at many of the misconceptions and mistakes too many investors make. Reading this book may save not only time and aggravation but money as well!"

Joseph Shaefer, CEO, Stanford Wealth Management LLC.

"Tony, Great work!" from James and Chris, who are portfolio managers.

"'Debunk the Myths in Investing' is a comprehensive book on investing that deals with many aspects of this tense profession in which with a lot of knowledge and a bit of luck (or vice versa) one can greatly benefit…

Therefore 'Debunk the Myths in Investing' is an interesting book that on its 500 pages offer a lot of knowledge related to investing world and many practical advice, so I can recommend its reading if you're interested in this topic."
- Denis Vukosav, Top 500 Reviewers at Amazon.com.

"490 pages (Debunk) of a genius's ranting and hypothesis with various theories throughout, written light-heartedly with ample doses of humor…Yes, the myth of not being able to profitably time the market is BUSTED…

One might ask… Why is he giving away the results of his hard-earned research for only $20? He states that his children are not interested in investing and wants to share his efforts with the world." - Abe Agoda.

"Excellent book, recommend to all investors… great knowledge. It has fine-tuned my investing strategies… Your book is hard to set aside, as I read it all the time learning good techniques and analysis of stocks, ETF… Since I purchased your book in March, I have underlined, highlighted and placed tabs on top of pages for quick reference." - Aileron on this book.

"Great stuff, Tony. It's great to meet experienced traders such as yourself. I had a browse through the book and think your method is a little more refined than mine."
"Your strategy is very rules based and solid. I sometimes envy people who have developed something like this."

Making 50% in one month
I claim to have the best one-month performance ever for recommending 8 or more stocks without using options and leverage. My following return is 57% in a month or 621% annualized. They are slightly different as I

calculated the average from the averages of three different accounts. The average buy date is 12/26/18 and the "current date" is 01/28/19.

The performance may not be repeated. I will use the same screen for the coming years and even the expected 10% (or 120% annualized) is very good.

I used the same screen for searching stock candidates. I spent a total of about 20 hours from Dec. 15, 2018 to Jan. 5, 2019.

Stock	Buy Price	Sold or Current Price	Buy date	Sold or Current date	Profit %	Profit % Ann.	Status
CHK	2.13	2.99	01/03/09	01/18/19	40%	982%	Sold
MNK	16.41	21.45	01/03/19	01/25/19	31%	510%	Sold
MNK	16.43	21.45	01/03/19	01/25/19	31%	507%	Sold
NNBR	5.68	8.58	12/26/18	01/28/19	51%	565%	
NNBR	5.72	8.58	12/26/18	01/28/19	66%	727%	
ESTE	4.35	6.45	12/26/18	01/18/19	48%	766%	Sold
LCI	4.61	8.29	12/21/18	01/28/19	80%	767%	
MDR	8.01	9.13	01/08/19	01/28/19	14%	255%	
YRCW	3.29	5.78	12/21/18	01/28/19	76%	727%	
YRCW	3.26	5.78	12/21/18	01/28/19	77%	742%	
ASRT	3.56	4.18	12/26/18	01/28/19	17%	193%	
UTCC	7.13	11.00	12/26/18	01/28/19	54%	600%	
YRCW	2.92	5.78	12/26/18	01/28/19	98%	1083%	

Best one-year return

I claim to have the best-performed article in Seeking Alpha history, an investing site, for recommending 15 or more stocks in one year after the publish date without using options and leverage.

https://seekingalpha.com/article/1095671-amazing-returns-velti-alcatel-lucent-alpha-natural-resources

Your choice for your next book

"Art of investing 2nd Edition" should be your first choice. If you are short-term trading, I recommend "Sector Rotation: 21 Strategies" and "Shorting Stocks /ETFs 2nd Edition". These books together with "Using Fidelity" and "Using Finviz" share many articles.

Appendix 3 - Our window to the investing world

The paperback version of this chapter can be found in the following link.

http://ebmyth.blogspot.com/2013/11/web-sites.html

- **General**
  Wikipedia / Investopedia /Yahoo!Finance / MarketWatch / Cnnfn / Morningstar /CNBC / Bloomberg / WSJ / Barron's / Motley Fool / TheStreet

- **Evaluate stocks**
  Finviz / SeekingAlpha / MSN Money / Zacks / Daily Finance / ADR / Fidelity / Earnings Impact / OpenInsider / NYSE / NASDAQ / SEC / SEC for 10K and 10Q (quarterly) reports required to file for listed stocks in major exchanges.

- **Charts**
  BigCharts / FreeStockCharts / StockCharts /

- **Screens**
  Yahoo!Finance / Finviz / CNBC / Morningstar /

- **Besides stocks**
  123Jump / Hoover's Online / FINRA Bond Market Data / REIT / Commodity Futures / Option Industry

- **Vendors**
  AAII / Zacks / IBD / GuruFocus / VectorVest / Fidelity / Interactive Brokers / Merrill Lynch /

- **Economy.**
  Econday / EcoconStats / Federal Reserve / Economist /

- **Misc.**
  Dow Jones Indices / Russell / Wilshire / IRS / Wikinvest / ETF Database / ETF Trends / Nolo (estate planning) / AARP /

Appendix 4 -   ETFs / Mutual Funds

What is an ETF
ETFs have basic differences from mutual funds: 1. Lower management expenses, 2. Trade ETFs same as stocks, and 3. Usually more diversified

but not more selective than the related mutual funds such as NOBL vs FRDPX.

The major classifications of ETFs are 1. Simulating an index such as SPY, QQQ and DIA, 2. Simulating a sector such as XLE and SOXX, 3. Simulating an asset class such as GLD and SLV, 4. Simulating a country or a group of countries such as EWC and FXI, 5. Managed by a manager(s) such as ARKK, 6. Betting a market or sector to go down such as SH and PSQ, and 7. Leveraged (not recommended for beginners).

Fidelity: Index ETFs (https://www.fidelity.com/etfs/overview).
Wikipedia on ETF (http://en.wikipedia.org/wiki/Exchange-traded_fund).

List of ETFs
ETF database (Recommended): http://etfdb.com/
ETF Bloomberg: http://www.bloomberg.com/markets/etfs/
ETF Trends: http://www.etftrends.com/
A list of ETFs. Seeking Alpha.
http://etf.stock-encyclopedia.com/category/)
A list of contra ETFs (or bear ETFs)
http://www.tradermike.net/inverse-short-etfs-bearish-etf-funds/
Misc.: ETFGuide, ETFReplay
Fidelity low-cost index funds:
https://www.youtube.com/watch?v=zpKi4_IJvlY
Fidelity Annuity funds with performance data.
http://fundresearch.fidelity.com/annuities/category-performance-annual-total-returns-quarterly/FPRAI?refann=005

Other resources
Most subscription services offer research on ETFs. IBD has a strategy dedicated to ETFs and so does AAII to name a couple.

Seeking Alpha has extensive resources for ETF including an ETF screener and investing ideas. So is ETFdb.

Not all ETFs are created equal

Check their performances and their expenses.

When to use or not to use ETFs

I prefer sector mutual funds in some industries, as they have many bad stocks such as drug industry, banks, miners and insurers. Most mutual funds cannot time the market.

When you believe a sector is heading up (or contra ETF for heading down), but you do not have time to do research on specific stocks, buy an ETF for the sector; it is same for the market.

Half ETF

Taking out half of the stocks that score below the average in an index ETF could beat the same full ETF itself. I call it HETF (half the ETF). You heard it here first. To illustrate, sort the expected P/E (not including stocks with negative earnings) in ascending order and only include the stocks on the first half. Add more fundamental metrics. It will take a few minutes.

Disadvantages of ETFs

- When you have two stocks in a sector ETF one good one and one bad one, the ETF treats them the same. Stock pickers would buy the one that has a better appreciation potential.
- Sometimes the return could be misleading due to stock rotation. To illustrate this, on August 29, 2012, SHLD was replaced by LYB in a sector fund. SHLD was down by 4% and LYB was up by 4% primarily due to the switch. Unless you sell and buy at the right time (which is impossible), your return would not match the ETF's returns due to the replacement.
- Ensure the performance matches the corresponding index; it is hard due to excluding dividends.

Advantages of ETFs

- We have demonstrated that you can beat the market by using market timing. Between 2000 and Nov., 2013, you only exit and reenter the market 3 times and the result is astonishing.
- It is easy to rotate a sector vs. buying/selling all of the stocks in this sector. Rotating a sector is the same as trading a stock.

- The risk is spread out, and your portfolio is diversified especially for a market ETF or buying three or more ETFs in different sectors.
- Periodically the bad stocks in most funds are replaced by better stocks.
- Eliminate the time in researching stocks.

Leveraged ETFs

I do not recommend them. Some are 2x, 3x and even higher. They're too risky for beginners. However, when you are very sure or your tested strategy has very low drawdown, you may want to use them to improve performance. Most leveraged ETFs and contra ETFs have higher fees.

My basic ETF tables

I include some contra ETFs, mutual funds and Fidelity's annuity. Some of these may be interesting to you.

ETFs and funds come and go. Some ideas and classifications are my own interpretation. Refer to ETFdb for updated information. Not responsible for any error. Check out the ETF or fund before you take any action.

Table by market cap:

Category	ETF	Mutual Funds	Fidelity's Annuity	Contra ETF	Alternate
Size:					
Large Cap	DIA	See Blend		DOG	
	SPY			SH	FXAIX VOO
	QQQ			PSQ	FNCMX
	RYH				
Blend	IWD	BEQGX			
Growth	SPYG	FBGRX			FSPGX
Value	SPYV	DOGGX			FLCOX
Dividend	NOBL	FRDPX			
	VYM				
Mid Cap			FNBSC	MYY	
Blend	MDY	VSEQX			
Growth		STDIX			
		BPTRX			

	Value		FSMVX			
	Small Cap			FPRGC	SBB	FSSNX
	Blend	IWM	HDPSX			
	Growth		PRDSX			FECGX
	Value		SKSEX			FISVX
	Micro	IWC				
Multi						
	Blend		VDEOX			
	Growth		VHCOX			
	Value		TCLCX			
	Total					FSKAX
Bond						
	Long Term (20)	VLV	BTTTX		TBF	
	Mid Term (7 – 10)	VCIT	FSTGX			
	Short Term (1 – 3 yrs.)	VCSH	THOPX			
	Total	BOND	PONDX			
	Corp Invest Grade	VCIT	NTHEX			
	High Yield (junk)	PHB	SPHIX			
	Muni	MUB	Check state			
	Special situation					
	Buy back	PKW				

Table by sectors:

Sector	ETF	Mutual Funds	Fidelity's Annuity
Banking[1]		FSRBK	
Regional	IAT		
Bio Tech	IBB	FBIOX	
	XBI	Large	
Consumer Dis.	XLY	FSCPX	FVHAC
Consumer Staple	XLP	FDFAX	FCSAC

Finance	KIE	FIDSX	FONNC
	IYF		
Energy	XLE	FSENX	FJLLC
Energy Service		FSESX	
Gold	GLD	FSAGX	
Gold Miner	GDX	VGPMX	
Health Care	IYH	FSPHX	FPDRC
	VHT	VGHCX	
House Builder	ITB	FSHOX	
	ITB	Perform	
Industrial	IYJ	FCYIX	FBALC
Material	VAW	FSDPX	
	IYM		
Oil	USO		
Oil Service	OIH	FSESX	
Oil Exploration	XOP		
Real Estate	VNQ	FRIFX	FFWLC
REIT	VNQ		
Retail	RTH	FSRPX	
	XRT		
Regional bank	KRE	FSRBX	
Semi Conduct	SMH		
Software	XSW	FSCSX	
	IGV		
Technology	XLK	FSPTX	FYENC
	FDN	FBSOX	
		ROGSX	
Telecomm.	VOX	FSTCX	FVTAC
Transport	XTN		
	IYT		
Utilities	XLU	FSUTX	FKMSC
Wireless		FWRLX	

Footnote. [1] Also check Finance.

Table by countries outside the USA:

Country	ETF	Mutual	Fidelity's	Alternate

		Funds	Annuity	
Australia	EWA			
Brazil	EWZ			
Canada	EWC	FICDX		
China	FXI	FHKCX		
EAFE	EFA			
Emerging	VWO	FEMEX	FEMAC	FPADX
Europe	VGK	FIEUX		
Global	KXI	PGVFX		
Greece	GREK			
India	INDY	MINDX		
Indonesia	EIDO			
Latin America	ILF	FLATX		
Nordic		FNORX		
Hong Kong	EWH			
Japan	EWJ	FJPNX		
S. Africa	EZA			
S. Korea	EWY	MAKOX		
Singapore	EWS			
Taiwan	EWT			
	TUR			
United Kingdom	EWU			
Foreign:				
Combination				
Intern. Div.	IDV			FTIHX
Small Cap	SCZ			
Value	EFV			
Europe	VGK			

Appendix 5 – Better links to articles / YouTube

- **China global leadership**

The next superpowers.
https://www.youtube.com/watch?v=9dgpuzawqn8

"From follower to leader"
https://www.youtube.com/watch?v=Psyy4KqEKtA

China's rise (Recommended).
https://www.youtube.com/watch?v=IAYRd8IqAxg
https://www.youtube.com/watch?v=qw-FLc7Z01Q

- **Economy**

Our economy is doomed.
https://www.youtube.com/watch?v=nI_bxQHt73Y

One Belt, One Road Iran
https://www.youtube.com/watch?v=nLrUdFURtqo

Trade deals: EU, RCEP
https://www.youtube.com/watch?v=vDQY-R-9CBc
https://www.youtube.com/watch?v=TtwrjxBb6Ks

China and Africa. https://www.youtube.com/watch?v=ObefKNUEtKg

Chinese white paper on trade.
https://www.bloomberg.com/news/articles/2019-06-03/read-the-full-china-white-paper-on-u-s-economic-and-trade-talks

Winner and losers of the trade war:
https://www.youtube.com/watch?v=J_5u8guvAuI

- Socially speaking

Corruption at the top:
https://www.youtube.com/watch?v=2Lc5TQTAnrM
Life from an expat. 2
https://dailychinalife.com/reasons-why-i-love-china-4th-year-in-the-mainland/
https://www.youtube.com/watch?v=kB5AelJONnY

Blondie
She is the best Australian ambassador to China. Check out her YouTubes.
https://www.youtube.com/watch?v=BTCgMlXMxTQ&t=11s
https://www.youtube.com/watch?v=_XtIri6rlKI&t=3s

The spirit of China
https://www.youtube.com/watch?v=H9IkFdAA8_A
A second tier city better than many cities in the world.
https://www.youtube.com/watch?v=wYAoyakwHUk
Wikipedia: Targeted Poverty Alleviation - Wikipedia

- US and China

Coming war with China (recommended).
https://www.youtube.com/watch?v=vAfeYMONj9E&t=1118s
US / China war: https://www.youtube.com/watch?v=uj42_ymPsdA

Future of US-China Relations Part 1 (skip this one). Part 3.
https://www.youtube.com/watch?v=U1nCECSPURg

- China

The battle of China (Recommended). Do not know this before. Just incredible!
https://www.youtube.com/watch?v=DMWQ32vwMxI

China is rising. 2
https://www.youtube.com/watch?v=eQjWtkdnhkg
https://www.youtube.com/watch?v=GiDTPSbVzhk

China's new airport.
https://www.youtube.com/watch?v=YJ0DUxPrEs4&list=WL&index=2&t=131s
Shenzhen. https://www.YouTube.com/watch?v=SGJ5cZnoodY&t=923s

China military
https://www.globalfirepower.com/country-military-strength-detail.asp?country_id=china

Farming technology. https://www.youtube.com/watch?v=czsBryVnS80

Engineering: Innovation, 2, HSR
https://www.YouTube.com/watch?v=s3qma0pROi0
https://www.YouTube.com/watch?v=SiRs289rQ7s
https://www.YouTube.com/watch?v=P_Sa1YHmxog

#Filler: Honey, my book can play music.
https://www.youtube.com/watch?v=HxGT5z6d-GA&list=PLMZa6mP7jZ2b1otqG4tfbgZpLEdh6YiNF

It may cut down commercials by casting it to TV.
Chinese music.
https://www.youtube.com/playlist?list=PL93D367F5AC34BCDF\

www.ingramcontent.com/pod-product-compliance
Lightning Source LLC
Chambersburg PA
CBHW070742180526
45167CB00012B/1828